The Land of
Contrarieties

The Land of Contrarieties

BRITISH ATTITUDES
TO THE AUSTRALIAN COLONIES
1828–1855

F. G. Clarke

MELBOURNE UNIVERSITY PRESS

1977

First published 1977

Computer photocomposed by Computer Graphics
Corporation Pty Ltd, Adelaide,
and printed in Australia by
Wilke & Co. Ltd, Clayton, Victoria 3168, for
Melbourne University Press, Carlton, Victoria 3053
U.S.A. and Canada: International Scholarly Book Services, Inc.,
Box 555, Forest Grove, Oregon 97116
Great Britain, Europe, the Middle East, Africa and the Caribbean:
International Book Distributors Ltd (Prentice-Hall International),
66 Wood Lane End, Hemel Hempstead, Hertfordshire HP2 4RG, England

National Library of Australia Cataloguing in Publication data
Clarke, Francis Gordon, 1943– .
The land of contrarieties.

Index.
Bibliography.
ISBN 0 522 84112 0.

1. Australia—History—1828-1855. 2. Great Britain—History—19th
century. I. Title. II. Title: British attitudes to the Australian
Colonies, 1828-1855.

994

Contents

Acknowledgements

I wish to express my appreciation and gratitude to Professor Peter Burroughs under whose guidance this study was begun and to whom I owe an incalculable debt for his patience, understanding, and helpfulness.

Thanks are also due to the staffs of the Public Record Office, the British Museum, the Institute of Historical Research, London, Guildhall Library, London, Durham University Archives, Eire National Library, and the Mitchell Library, Sydney.

I am indebted to many of my colleagues and friends in the School of History, Philosophy and Politics at Macquarie University for their encouragement and advice, particularly Dr George Raudzens, Dr George Liik, Dr T.G. Parsons, and Mr John Ryan; and also to Mrs Betty Williams and Mrs Joan Elder for preparation of the final typescript.

Finally, I am deeply beholden to my wife who has been critic, typist of all the early drafts, proof-reader, and sustainer of morale in times of stress.

Conversion Factors
(*to 3 decimal places*)

£1	A$2
1 shilling	10c
1 penny	.833c
1 oz.	28·349 grams
1 pound (lb.)	·453 kilogram
1 acre	·404 hectare
1 cu. in.	16·387 cu. centimetres

Introduction

As a result of an understandable preoccupation with indigenous forces and tendencies, modern Australian historiography relating to the years between first settlement and responsible government has tended, until quite recently, to pay insufficient attention to the character of British colonial policy and the nature of British attitudes towards overseas possessions. Yet every facet of Australian economic, political and social development during these years was profoundly influenced by British opinion and policies. The ideas and preconceptions of politicians in Westminster or of bureaucrats at the Colonial Office represented a microcosm of the wider climate of contemporary opinion in which imperial policy took shape. Official decisions were not taken in an intellectually circumscribed atmosphere, and many statesmen and administrators responsible for guiding the destinies of the empire were active participants in the cultural, social, or political life of their times. This book therefore, is presented in the confident belief that Australian history in the years between 1828 and 1855 is not fully intelligible without some understanding of the variegated attitudes of Britons concerning the colonies, culture, and colonists of Australia.

Although considerable debate has taken place amongst historians concerning the character of British attitudes to empire during the first six or seven decades of the nineteenth century, little of this discussion has related specifically to Australia. Some contemporary Britons who were particularly interested in colonial affairs claimed that Englishmen in general were either indifferent or hostile to colonies, and until comparatively recent times historians have usually described this period as an age of anti-imperialism when most Englishmen regarded colonies as valueless sources of international friction and heavy financial burdens to boot.[1] Recent scholars have pointed out, however, that this view of British opinion is an oversimplification.[2] Undoubtedly during these years a vocal anti-imperial lobby did exist in Britain, but it would be misleading to obscure the variety of English opinion by labelling it collectively as anti-imperialist; and it would also distort our view of the course of imperial development during the first half of the nineteenth century. In fact, commercially and territorially, this was a period of rapid imperial expansion, and the forward movement at the antipodes was a minor part in the overall advance and enlargement of Britain's formal and informal empire.

With a few notable exceptions, modern historians of Australia have tended to confine their attention to indigenous achievements and evolution, and to detailing settler reaction to British policies rather than to describing the intellectual framework within which imperial policies were drafted.[3] In addition to the pioneer work of Brian Fitzpatrick, John M. Ward has written a short study of Australia and New Zealand between 1840 and 1860, in which he attempted to correct this propensity by stressing that the United Kingdom exercised a substantial degree of political control over her antipodean dependencies during these years and therefore that British attitudes towards them were always significant.[4] This line of approach has also been taken in the extremely idiosyncratic work of C. M. H. Clark and in Ken Inglis's book, *The Australian colonists*.[5] Most general narrative histories of Australia, however, concentrate almost exclusively on local affairs and even where mention is made of British opinions and policies the treatment is usually cursory.

This has not been the case with studies dealing with particular aspects of Australian history and development, and there have been quite a few recent monographs in which a detailed delineation of British attitudes is attempted.[6] The range of opinion, however, is circumscribed by the restrictions of the subject-matter, and one cannot expect to find a comprehensive study of British attitudes in books which limit themselves to a specific topic or a single aspect of Australia's past. Furthermore, English historians have tended to treat Britain's domestic and imperial history as separate, unassimilated areas of historical inquiry, and ignore the close relationship between imperial and domestic developments. Yet Australian wool and gold, for example, had more than a marginal effect on the British Isles, and contemporary observers believed that emigration to Australia was a social safety-valve which helped to keep Britain peaceful during the year of European proletarian revolutions in 1848.

The present work is an attempt to bridge the gap between imperial and domestic British studies by examining the changing attitudes of Englishmen towards Australia in the years between 1828 and 1855.

Ideas affected colonial policy and were instrumental in forming a climate of opinion, shaped by differing points of view and fluctuating public debate, which was influential even when the opinions of British participants were not especially well informed. The views of contemporary Britons therefore constitute an essential component of Australian history during these years and are an indispensable part of the historical context of Anglo-Australian relations in the first half of the nineteenth century. The book also represents a case study of British attitudes to the empire at large during this period and as such provides a useful corrective to the orthodox belief that these years fell within a period of widespread antipathy to empire.

It was originally intended that the study would cover the entire period from the first British settlement of Australia in 1788 to the concession of ministerial self-government to the four most advanced colonies in 1855. It quickly became apparent, however, that such an intention was over-ambitious. Such an abundance of material exists for the student of British opinion on Australia during the first half of the nineteenth century that some curtailment in the scope of the field of enquiry was plainly required. In the event, 1828 was selected as the starting point, although it is a date of convenience and is symbolic rather than specific. This was the year prior to the new Australian colonizing venture at Swan River, and the year before the publication of Edward Gibbon Wakefield's *Letter from Sydney* which first placed the theories of systematic colonization before the British public. In other words, to begin the study in 1828 was to take cognizance of British attitudes during the latter years of the 1820's, before a new decade of imperial development began in Australia, and preceding the emergence of an influential school of colonial propagandists in the mother country.

Attitudes are amorphous by nature, and an attitudinal study poses many difficulties of organization and arrangement. The research materials in this instance lend themselves to a thematic rather than a chronological treatment, though some overlapping of subject-matter has been unavoidable. Every facet of Australian affairs evoked some response in Britain, but material interest in the mother country fell broadly into four main categories which therefore form the basis of chapters: convictism, constitutional advance, emigration and native tribes, and land utilization.

British concern over various aspects of colonial expansion in Australia was not restricted to the governing classes but transcended traditional social divisions; consequently I have striven to avoid too heavy a reliance upon the range of comment to be found in official government records alone. Attitudes may be detected and their patterns traced in many sources including official, published, and private papers, government records, parliamentary debates, travel books, newspapers, periodicals, and a variety of contemporary ephemera. British attitudes were rarely synonymous with administrative opinions, and on many of the issues examined in this study there was an extensive sweep of opinion ranging from lower class street ballads and broadsides to the Entry Books of the Colonial Office and the reports of parliamentary debates.

Public opinion is notoriously difficult to assess, and although the writings and speeches of the day give some indication of the degree of information on colonial topics, they do not in themselves offer a reliable guide to the state of public interest. A.G.L. Shaw attempted to quantify parliamentary interest in empire between 1820 and 1850 by enumerating the number of printed columns of debate on colonies within this period;[7] but the quantity of references is no real measure of the level of apathy or concern. One can draw only tentative conclusions from scattered comments, and try, by taking as broad a canvas as possible, to arrive at some form of synthesis which gives a tolerably accurate indication of the outlines of contemporary opinion and debate. In such a study it must always be borne in mind that a lack of comment on colonies is not necessarily evidence of anti-imperialism, but may be an indication that colonies were taken for granted. Englishmen knew little about colonial conditions and many lacked the detailed information or the imagination that might have enabled them to make the mental leap to an appreciation that circumstances overseas were different from familiar ones at home.

Furthermore, opinion must not be analysed in isolation, quarantined from the actual course of events in Britain and the colonies. In many ways British attitudes towards the Australian colonies only become intelligible in the context of domestic developments in the United Kingdom, and historians of empire who ignore this relationship do so at their peril. The arcadian aspirations expressed by many British propagandists during the 1830s and 1840s and their effect on imperial land policies in Australia, for example, are not fully comprehensible without an understanding that for many people, during these years, emigration to the Australian colonies represented a means of escape from the dehumanizing forces unleashed in Britain by the industrial revolution. Similarly, domestic fears of democracy and the lower classes affected British attitudes to Australia, and some Englishmen were doubtful whether such egalitarian communities could be trusted with the management of their own affairs.

If conditions in the British Isles affected attitudes towards Australia, however, events in the colonies also played their part in shaping British opinion. The gold discoveries in the early 1850s provide one example of a rush of British emigration to the Australian colonies which was quite independent of domestic inspiration and entirely the result of what was happening overseas. The motivation for British emigration to Australia, therefore, must be sought both in England and in Australia, for the pendulum of causation swung back and forth between the two. The interrelationship between British attitudes and contemporary developments at home and in the colonies was both complex and crucial, and wherever possible an attempt has been made to set attitudes in Britain within this wider context.

British opinions did matter, and in many ways during these years the settlements in Australia were satellite communities. They were utterly dependent on the connection with Great Britain for economic livelihood and defence; and much of their cultural, political, and social life was similarly derivative. While it is a truism that dependence breeds resentment, what appalled Australian colonists even more than their inferior status was the apparent indifference of British administrators to colonial opinions or sensibilities. Rarely did imperial officials in the United Kingdom completely comprehend either the distant settlers or the vast country they were settling. To have done so would have required first-hand knowledge, or a degree of imagination and sympathy of which most were not capable. It was only after years of effort, for example, and with the utmost difficulty that colonists were able to convince the Colonial Office that control over Australia's waste lands should lie with them, and that land regulations designed to produce agricultural settlement were unsuited to a pastoral country.

If the Colonial Office was slow to reconcile itself to local realities and ambitions, however, this was the result of its unwieldy, bureaucratic nature and not because British attitudes were uniform or in any way homogeneous in opposing colonial demands. In reality there was considerable debate and wide divergence of opinion concerning Australia in the period under review, and this was by no means restricted to those sections of British society which controlled political power and the decision-making apparatus of the state. The lower classes had firm views of their own about the Australian colonies, and since the vast majority of British emigrants to the antipodes came from this portion of the populace, working class attitudes are relevant.

On occasion Britain's official policies towards Australia horrified contemporary Englishmen and caused considerable controversy. At other times, however, Australia's great distance from the mother country and the lack of real knowledge of colonial conditions meant that British notions and policies relied too heavily on abstract theories of the way things ought to have been and less on a concrete appreciation of the way things actually were. If British debate was, on occasion, enthusiastic, it was also on occasion rooted in whimsy and wishful thinking. Some Englishmen even believed that it was possible to shape the character of Australian society by exporting British social and cultural values, unaltered, to the colonies. To a certain extent British concepts were transportable, but it was a fantasy for Englishmen to imagine that the social levelling inherent in a pioneering environment could be halted or reversed by the importation of the cultural values of Britain's middle and upper classes. Imperial statesmen and British theorists alike found it difficult to realize that no matter how shrewdly conceived a British policy might be in terms of furthering national interests at home, the harsh realities of existence in the Australian colonies might render such a policy unworkable. It was inevitable that Australian realities modified and sometimes completely frustrated British policies, given the immense distances involved, the slowness of communication, the natural tendencies of Englishmen to think in terms of the advantage of their homeland and of the Australian colonists to be more interested in their own welfare. Britain had not founded the colonies for reasons of disinterested altruism, and when conflict between the wishes of colonists and the pursuit of British advantage occurred, imperial officials ruthlessly proclaimed that settlers must subordinate their demands to the overall welfare and stability of the empire.

Finally, as a thematic survey of British contemporary opinion this study has no pretensions towards providing a general or narrative history of Australia during these years. My aim is to delineate the climate of opinion in which imperial policy decisions and private judgements relating to such matters as emigration or investment were taken. The attitudes of Englishmen towards the Australian colonies between 1828 and 1855 form an essential part of the historical context within which Anglo-Australian relations in the first half of the nineteenth century must be studied.

1: *Convictism I 1828–40*

By the late 1820s Britain had been transporting shiploads of criminals to Australia for a period of forty years and the convict system had undergone little appreciable alteration throughout that time. In the following three decades, however, the British penal system was in a state of flux, and Englishmen vigorously debated the most efficient method of securing life and property, and whether Britain ought to persevere in exiling felons to the far antipodes. Transportation to the Australian colonies was one of the most common punishments for serious crime during these years, and much discussion revolved around the utility of this method of punishment, as well as the precise form that a system of compulsory banishment should take. Humanitarianism, theories of penology and colonization, the search for economy, and the need to encourage free emigration were but a few of the social and political concerns of the day which contributed to the general climate of opinion regarding convict transportation and convict colonies.

As a method of punishment, exile had obvious practical advantages to the mother country, and strong theoretical justifications could also be advanced in its vindication. Supporters of the system hoped that fear of banishment would deter potential criminals, whilst those who succumbed to temptation would be removed to a safe distance. Malefactors could be assisted by compulsory deportation to reform their characters. Transportation provided an opportunity to make a new start in a different environment, where employment would be readily available and self-sufficiency could be gained by hard work. At the same time, such an arrangement would provide the convict colonies with a labour force, thereby accelerating their economic progress.

Such was the theory. In practice, however, it did not work out quite

1

so smoothly. The penal colonies in Australia did not long retain their exclusively penitential nature, and even before the end of the eighteenth century free settlers had begun to occupy colonial lands in New South Wales. Moreover, most of the convicts remained in Australia upon completion of their sentences, and over the years the populace began to include an increasing number of locally born colonists. One result of this pattern of population growth was that the colonies of New South Wales and Van Diemen's Land developed a mixed society, and Britain's relations with and attitudes towards these dependencies became far more complicated than similar links with the isolated and specifically punitive establishments on Norfolk Island and at Port Macquarie. Such receptacles could be constituted and administered with the unique and restricted function of serving British advantage in penal concerns;[1] but heterogeneous populations like those in New South Wales and Van Diemen's Land were destined to pose many anxieties for imperial administrators both in the colonies and at home.

At what stage, if at all, should the metropolitan power begin·to administer composite settlements of free men and convicts in the interests of the free populace? Questions of economy and trusteeship were inextricably interwoven in such a dilemma, and British attitudes towards convict transportation and convict colonies in the years from 1828 to 1855 appear to have vacillated. Sometimes Englishmen felt that Britain's interests should always be paramount; at other times commentators argued that the mother country had a moral obligation to protect the long-term interests of colonists, even at the expense of her own immediate advantage. As the following discussion will indicate, it was possible, on occasion, for imperial administrators dealing with convict transportation to reconcile the two positions; but generally during the three decades before 1855 when Englishmen discussed penology, secondary punishment, and the social and moral effects of convictism on immature colonial societies, conflict between these two outlooks was unavoidable.

One of the primary functions of exiling convicts to Australia was to deter crime at home. Undesirables in Britain might be dissuaded from a life of crime if they realized what savage retribution would be wrought upon them once they were apprehended by the authorities. The vast majority of the criminals deported to Australia, however, came from the labouring classes,[2] and conditions under which they lived in Britain during the first half of the nineteenth century were extremely harsh. Consequently, a widespread feeling began to develop during the 1820s amongst the lower orders that transportation to Australia was a boon, not a punishment. This was particularly true of the growing ranks of Britain's industrial proletariat, and the high degree of social alienation caused by oppressive industrialism is reflected in the origins of convicts transported to Australia. The mainly urban areas of London and Lancashire, for example, provided between them more than one-third of all English felons deported to convict settlements.[3]

Letters from convicts in Australia to friends and relatives in Britain pointed out that in many ways they were better off than free labourers in the United Kingdom;[4] and Elie Halévy has commented that by 1820 the penalty of transportation to Australia had lost all its terrors. 'To be deported was simply to emigrate at the expense of the Government to a better climate, and emigration was becoming increasingly popular with the working class'.[5] In 1826 the Home Secretary, Sir Robert Peel, admitted that this point of view contained a grain of truth, but he claimed that no satisfactory alternative existed.[6] Both the *Times* and the *Courier* commented that transportation was desired by the criminal classes which, in the *Courier's* estimation, were identical with 'the lower orders of society'. Unlike Peel, who had the responsibility of disposing of Britain's miscreants, the newspapers took their argument one step further and maintained that penal banishment should be abolished because it did not act as an effective deterrent.[7]

Dissuasion from crime, however, was only one of the advantages Britain was supposed to gain from transportation, and other reasons could be advanced which stressed the desirability of continuing the system despite the failure of its intimidatory function. In 1828, for example, as part of a general discussion on emigration, the economist J. R. McCulloch suggested that Australia was not suited to receive the mainstream of British emigration because it was 'removed by distance beyond the *natural* sphere of European connexion'.[8] Nevertheless, such unfitness for normal colonization made New South Wales the ideal gaol, and McCulloch called for the abolition of the hulks and the speedy implementation of all sentences of transportation to New South Wales. He also proposed that exile should last for a longer period than the usual seven to fourteen years, and that facilities for remission on good conduct should be expanded in New South Wales and Van Diemen's Land to encourage convicts to behave themselves in the hope of earlier release.[9]

In the same year Australia's great distance from the mother country was mentioned by another critic as one of the main reasons for the continent's utility as a convict dump. This writer added an economic dimension to his discussion by pointing out that the expanding pastoral industry in New South Wales—upon which Britain was becoming increasingly dependent for supplies of raw wool—needed a larger labour force. With this consideration in mind he maintained that the existing rate of transportation should be augmented, and furthermore, that convicts should be sold to purchasers in the settlement for a fixed period of time to be conterminous with their sentences.[10] This suggestion, in effect, represented a return to the earlier system of involuntary expatriation of criminals which had operated in the former American colonies. Like later schemes of colonization propounded by Edward Gibbon Wakefield and others,[11] the sale of indentured criminal labour had the attraction of peopling a new settlement cheaply, since revenue from the purchase of convicts would reimburse the British government for the cost of their passage.

Edward Gibbon Wakefield's seminal pamphlet *A Letter from Sydney* appeared in 1829, and the *Gentleman's Magazine* was one of the few periodicals to recognize its importance. In its December issue, the magazine devoted a special supplement to the new publication and accepted Wakefield's premises that a shortage of labour existed in New South Wales, and that convict labour was both an inefficient and a numerically inadequate substitute for a free labour force. The article went on, however, to submit that non-convict labour in New South Wales could not fully satisfy the settlement's needs, and that both free and convict labour were required in Australia if the current rate of economic progress was to be maintained.[12]

As these views imply, commentators from the middle and upper classes tended to regard the convict in impersonal rather than in human terms, although the suffering and misery of individual exiles did excite a minor poet, named J. Bethel, to produce some cautionary verses for publication in *Fraser's Magazine for Town and Country* in 1830. The poem, entitled 'The Farewell of the Convicts', depicted the departing criminals as wretched and miserably unhappy individuals whose condition was so hopeless that they actually looked forward in a rather desperate way to 'a brighter day' in New South Wales. The following stanza from Bethel's poem illustrates the popular, contemporary, Tory view that convicts were bitter, vengeful social inferiors, and helps to explain the unfavourable opinions entertained by many Englishmen towards a colony which was almost totally composed of convicts, expirees, and their families.

> Farewell, juries,—jailers,—friends!
> (Traitors to the close,)
> Here the felon's danger ends:
> Farewell bloody foes!
> Farewell England we are quitting
> Now thy dungeon doors:
> Take our blessing, as we're flitting—
> '*Curse upon thy shores*'.[13]

Most transported convicts came from the lower levels of British society, and bourgeois doubts concerning the efficacy of transportation as a discouragement to lawlessness seem to have been well founded in fact. The grim struggle for existence resulted in the unskilled labouring population having an ambivalent attitude towards convict exile. Because such people were at best only semi-literate, they resorted to broadsheet ballads to express their resentment against an economic system which presented them with a choice between starvation and crime.

> The Transport's Lamentation (c. 1830).
>
> The rich have no temptation but all
> things at command
> It is for health or pleasure they leave
> their native land
> But great distress and want of work,
> Starvation and disease
> Makes inmates for the prison and
> transports for the seas.[14]

In such circumstances it is no surprise to find that the labouring classes viewed transportation in a very different light from their social superiors. On occasion working-class ballads, far from stressing the tribulations of exile, expressed optimism and a degree of envy of those banished to Australia; and convict transportation was favourably contrasted with domestic poor law relief.

> Penal Servitude (c. 1830).
>
> I have just arrived from Australia
> Where I have been for change of air;
> And, chaps, I have just come to tell you,
> That there is a lot of jolly living over there.
>
> *Chorus*
> Where they feed you, and they clothe you,
> Better than a working man or soldier—
> Penal servitude is the sort of life for me;
> Then we do a bit of work just a portion of the day,
> And then we go to church upon a Sunday, O.
> Man O, my yar, yar, yar!
> Give me penal servitude before the Union.
>
> But still I can't keep laughing,
> When I see your paupers look so pale;
> There's thousands in the work house starving,
> While we live like lords in the jail.[15]

Nonetheless, from the imperial government's point of view the convict system had one major advantage: it might not frighten potential criminals but it was a cheap means of punishing them when caught. In 1838 Sir George Arthur, the former lieutenant-governor of

Van Diemen's Land, estimated that assigned servants cost the government an average of £4 per head a year,[16] while a recent study has noted that the average cost of transportation to Australia in the middle thirties was approximately £16—17 for a man, and £21—22 for a woman.[17] On the other hand, imprisonment in a British penitentiary would cost the government £24 per head a year[18] in addition to the costs of a massive programme of gaol construction.

A system of transportation and assignment, therefore, was inexpensive because the imperial authorities discovered that they could relieve the Treasury of the burden of convict superintendence and support by making such costs and responsibilities part of the price colonists had to pay if they wished to employ convict labour. Since slightly more than half the total number of convicts in New South Wales and Van Dieman's Land became assigned servants while the system continued, assignment was a significant economy for Great Britain.[19]

While the nature of assignment underwent little substantial variation, opinions concerning its effectiveness as a punishment did differ widely, and this was partly caused by a lack of uniformity inherent in the system. In 1838 the Select Committee on Transportation explained in its report that there were actually three classes or degrees of assigned convicts in the penal colonies, and that conditions for each were subject to wide differential. Field labourers were the first and most numerous class of assigned servants, and the colonists considered them to be greatly inferior to the other two groups. Skilled mechanics formed the second class of assignees and a tradesman was generally valued by colonists as being worth two unskilled labourers. The third group of assigned convicts were the domestic servants who were in a quite prosperous condition, being 'well fed, well clothed, and receive wages from £10 to £15 a year, and are as well treated in respectable families, as similar descriptions of servants are in this country'.[20] Degrees of discipline within the assignment system fluctuated considerably, and some Englishmen felt that it was this very lack of uniformity in punishment which robbed a sentence of transportation to Australia of its potency as a deterrent.[21]

When it came to a reassessment of convict policy, imperial administrators found themselves in a dilemma. The Colonial Office had to choose between economy and increased retribution; to decide whether to sanction stricter confinement and greater severity in Australia with an unavoidable increase in costs, or to allow a relatively cheap form of transportation to continue unaltered. During 1831 a lively debate on secondary punishments took place in the Colonial Office between Lord Howick, the vigorous young parliamentary under-secretary, and the conservative Robert Hay, then permanent under-secretary. Howick viewed convict transportation as an ill-fitting portion of a wider mosaic of government policies relating to Australian development. He believed that colonists in Australia would find acceptable substitutes for convict servants amongst the swelling tide of free emigrants. As part of his overall attitude towards emigration and crown lands in Australia, Howick favoured the complete abolition of a system which in his opinion jeopardized the moral welfare of the empire.[22] Ironically, Howick's opinions on this question during 1831 differed radically from those he was to expound as colonial secretary in the 1840s. He may have changed his mind, but a partial explanation for this apparent contradiction may be that in 1831 Howick was an idealistic and inexperienced young man in his first political appointment, whereas by the 1840s there had been ample time and opportunity for him to have become politically cynical about the moral well-being of the Australian colonies. A thread of continuity does emerge, however, when it is remembered that on both occasions he attempted to impose his will upon dissenting colonial populations.

In 1831 Howick was primarily concerned over security: so many criminals had been deported to Australia that he feared a convict uprising. The likelihood of such an eventuality was strengthened in Howick's view by a rapid expansion of settlement into the interior of New South Wales which made centralized control over assigned labourers almost impossible. The under-secretary considered and rejected the obvious alternative to assignment—working all the convicts in gangs under military supervision. To Howick, this course of action was similarly fraught with peril. To group such desperate men together in large bodies would only increase the danger of a rebellion. Accordingly, Howick proposed that transportation to Australia cease forthwith, and that British criminals be exiled instead to the islands of Trinidad and Mauritius.[23]

On the other hand, Robert Hay was far more sanguine. He felt that assignment acted as a stimulus to good behaviour, and enabled the authorities in the penal colonies to effect *ad hoc* variations in the severity of punishment. Thus the harshness of convict discipline could be modified in direct proportion to the seriousness of a felon's crime and the rapidity of his progress towards reformation and good conduct. The core of Hay's argument lay in his belief that variation of treatment was endemic in a convict system, but that this inconsistency could be turned to advantage and used as a practical adjunct to the workings of justice. After all, British administrators should recognize that 'the prisoners confined there are not all equally desperate and incorrigible'.[24]

While justice might have been best served by leniency under the existing system, the practice of assignment greatly weakened the deterrent effect of banishment to Australia, particularly during periods of economic distress amongst the lower classes. E. G. Stanley, in 1833, made an attempt to restore an element of menace and instructive warning to a sentence of transportation, and government policy on convict discipline now placed considerable stress on a rigorous and relentless inflexibility. In August 1833, Stanley informed Governors Bourke and Arthur that assignment was considered by many in Britain to be a state of 'comparative ease and freedom from restraint', and that as a consequence some 'very erroneous notions' existed which held that 'Transportation is rather a Boon and a Benefit than a state of suffering and punishment'. To remove this impression, colonial governors were instructed that the most hardened recidivists were henceforth to be sent to the exclusively penal settlements at Norfolk Island or Macquarie Harbour. Other less serious offenders should also be treated severely and wherever possible placed in irons on public works' projects. Any convicts remaining, for whom the authorities could not find employment in chain gangs, were to be assigned as before, since free labour was still insufficient to meet colonial needs.[25]

During 1831 and 1832, a parliamentary committee on secondary punishment had also grappled with the problems of convict transportation to Australia, and the effectiveness of convict assignment as a method of discipline. This committee had reported in favour of a more detailed code of convict classification, which would enable distinctions to be drawn in the treatment meted out to those who seemed to become reformed, and to other more hardened recalcitrants who resisted discipline and showed little or no improvement. The committee also advised that convicts under assignment be excluded as far as possible from urban centres, and be forced to remove themselves from evil acquaintances by working in the pastoral industry or labouring in the rural districts. John Wontner, the Keeper of Newgate Prison, maintained in evidence before the committee that transportation to Australia could be rendered severe enough to become a real deterrent, if it was known in criminal circles that exiled criminals would be forced to work in public gangs for at least two years.[26]

Stanley's instructions, therefore, embodied sentiments expressed by an expert witness before the select committee; but greater severity was unpopular with imperial officials at home and with governors in the colonies. James Stephen, at this time a legal adviser to the Colonial Office, regarded transportation as a wicked, immoral practice. Interestingly enough, Stephen, who was a strong evangelical churchman and whose father had been associated with the Clapham Sect, objected to the dual system of transportation and assignment not so much because convicts were unjustly treated, but because as shepherds in the isolated rural areas where they could not be effectively supervised, they mistreated the aboriginal population. Stephen appeared to be opposed to the effects of the penal regulations rather than to the system itself.[27]

From the colonies both Bourke and Arthur protested against the new policy of severity, and contradicted official attitudes in Britain, though their representations were inconsistent. Bourke wrote from New South Wales claiming that the colony would develop better without convicts, and that convict assignment differed little from slavery. Furthermore, he maintained that sentences served in irons would be too long and counter-productive, because all hope of amelioration for good behaviour would be removed, and with it the chief motive for reform.[28] Arthur also complained, but unlike Bourke he was quite satisfied with the assignment system which he commended as effective and cheap. He did, however, agree with Bourke concerning the pernicious effect of long punishment without relief, and avowed that it would make discipline difficult and encourage escapes. In a series of dispatches this experienced colonial administrator submitted that British statesmen were unaware of the realities of convict transportation when they described assignment as a lax method of punishment. He stated his belief that under the regulations which he had drawn up in Van Diemen's Land, the great majority of convicts in the colony were already as miserable as any hard-hearted colonial secretary could desire.[29] Arthur's opinions were endorsed by the naturalist Charles Darwin who commented that assignment was for the convict a time of 'discontent and unhappiness'. Darwin believed that transportation and assignment failed to reform but did effectively punish; and 'as a means of making men outwardly honest,—of converting vagabonds most useless in one hemisphere, into active citizens of another, thus giving birth to a new and splendid country—a grand centre of civilization—it has succeeded to a degree perhaps unparalleled in history.'[30]

Despite reports from the colonies which indicated that transportation and assignment worked reasonably well, there was a groundswell of altruistic though uninformed British opinion led by Richard Whately, the Archbishop of Dublin, against the continuation of assignment. The early 1830s were a period when humanitarian sentiment enjoyed widespread popularity in Britain, and the campaign against the evils of West Indian slavery was at its height. The situation of assigned convicts in Australia was in many ways similar to a condition of slavery. In both circumstances a man's labour was compulsory and unpaid, and both convict and slave were subject to the pride and whim of a master. Many humanitarians, therefore, believed that following the suppression of negro slavery throughout the empire in 1833, convict assignment ought also to be abolished.[31] It was the principles underlying assignment which concerned such men: 'We do not dispute that improvements may be introduced into the system; but the only effectual one, we are convinced, will be to abandon it altogether.'[32]

Opposition to transportation was not the exclusive province of humanitarians, however, and objections also came from commentators who disapproved of the current practice of exiling Britain's criminals to settlements which were no longer exclusively penitential in character. Wakefield was one of the foremost British thinkers in this latter category. Following the publication of his pamphlet, *A Letter from Sydney* in 1829, Wakefield's theories on colonization received wide circulation and resulted in the development of a rather loose and informal combination of like-minded people. Known to contemporaries and later writers as colonial reformers they endorsed Wakefield's views on systematic colonization, wherein they claimed the hitherto undiscovered laws governing successful colonization could be found. Needless to say, colonization with criminals was not recommended as a method of establishing new settlements or of populating existing dependencies. On the contrary, Wakefield's speculations led him to propose that colonial populations should consist of a judicious blend of British middle-class entrepreneurs and a work force of free labourers.[33] One of the main tenets of systematic colonization was that convict labour brutalized colonial communities, and consequently that penal establishments should be restricted to isolated and unsettled regions.

In 1836 some of the proposals espoused by the colonial reformers received partial application in the new colony of South Australia. Convicts were specifically excluded from this region, and Wakefield and his followers argued that the continuation of convict transportation to New South Wales gave that colony a source of cheap labour, and therefore an unfair economic advantage over South Australia. In an effort to remove this differential, the colonial reformers had made common cause during the early 1830s with Archbishop Whately and other humanitarian opponents of transportation. The propaganda of the anti-transportation and anti-assignment forces stressed the horrific effects of convictism on colonial society, and the inconsistency of assignment in effecting either punishment or reform.

Thus by 1835 some leading periodicals began to question the contribution of transportation to the economic development of New South Wales and Van Diemen's Land, though what was to become of convicts if they were not sent to the antipodes remained an unresolved dilemma. One contributor to the conservative *Quarterly Review* suggested that it was a great injustice to the free population of New South Wales to continue transportation there, and asserted that the imperial government had a clear duty to ensure that the colony was afforded 'the best chance of entirely shaking off the lamentable taint of its original formation'.[34] The alleged moral inferiority of the colonial populations in New South Wales and Van Diemen's Land provided nineteenth-century Englishmen with a field of inquiry which they were to explore with an avidity which amounted almost to obsession. On this occasion, moreover, the *Quarterly Review's* contributor implied that an undeniable connection existed between the presence of convicts and the corruption of society, and he was adamant that the mother country should not risk its own moral welfare by suspending transportation. Criminals should not be kept at home, and ought no longer to be inflicted upon colonies of settlement; but they could be incarcerated in isolated and exclusively penal establishments in uninhabited areas of the empire. To this end the article proposed a remedy which was also to recommend itself to the British government ten years later, namely the establishment of a new penal colony in the wilderness of northern New South Wales.

Despite the economic importance of convict labour to New South Wales and Van Diemen's Land, the tide of British opinion in favour of discontinuing a system which many observers considered to be a form of modified slavery continued to gather momentum. The utilitarian *Westminster Review* appealed for the suspension of transportation in 1835 on the pragmatic grounds that convictism, in addition to being inconsistent with human dignity, was an ineffective form of punishment. When the Reverend John Dunmore Lang, the leading Presbyterian clergyman in New South Wales, published a book in which he admitted the use of convict labour on his own estates and supported the system of transportation and assignment,[35] the *London and Westminster Review* exploded: 'Neither the interested appeals of the slaveholders of New South Wales nor the mawkish nonsense of the Presbyterian Divine, will produce the belief that terror depends upon the uncertainty of the punishment, and that reformation is best produced by herding criminals together.'[36]

The historian, Archibald Alison, also wrote in favour of calling an immediate halt to convict transportation, and argued that should this occur the problems caused by the shortage of labour would be temporary and soon settled. Alison believed that convict society in Australia had a detrimental effect on free emigration. There were many workers who wished to emigrate to New South Wales and Van Diemen's Land, but held back because they disapproved of transportation and did not wish to live in close proximity to British criminals. At the same time, however, he attempted to place the problem in what he regarded as its proper perspective by reminding his readers that New South Wales was probably 'the most remote and inconsiderable of our colonial possessions'.[37]

Nevertheless, the anti-transportation lobby did not have everything its own way, and powerful support for the existing system came from Sir George Arthur, who reacted with annoyance to what he considered to be the ignorance of ill-informed critics in England. Arthur was convinced that gaols, penitentiaries and hulks were schools of crime wherein young or minor offenders became depraved by the company of more experienced recidivists, so that they lapsed quickly into further crime upon release. He commented on the hopelessness of attempting to reform criminals 'who, by several punishments, had served as it were an Apprenticeship of Crime, as compared with those who had been only once tried and the sentence of Transportation promptly carried into effect'. Assigned service in the comparative isolation of the rural districts of Van Diemen's Land was one of the best and most economical systems of punishment ever devised.[38] During these years transportation, as distinct from assignment, also received the endorse-ment of the penologist Alexander Maconochie, though he vigorously denied Arthur's contention that assignment was conducive to refor-mation, and proposed in its place a system of discipline of his own devising, which embodied marks for good conduct, as well as gang labour.[39]

Supporters of transportation valued the penal colonies for their utility; but no matter how remote and inconsiderable Australia may have seemed to Englishmen like Alison, the settlements there enjoyed a growing revenue from sales of waste lands which attracted the avaricious attention of imperial bureaucrats at Downing Street. Stan-ley's regulations of 1833 had insisted that convicts were to labour in government gangs for two years before becoming eligible for assign-ment to settlers. This had greatly increased the expense of the penal establishments and in order to relieve itself from such a burden, the British Treasury decided in 1835 to offset the costs of the Police and Gaols Departments in New South Wales and Van Diemen's Land against the local revenues of the respective colonies.[40] While this exaction provoked an immediate outburst of indignation from colonists,[41] they were then experiencing a period of economic boom and the substantial nature of the burden was not adequately appre-ciated until the depression which ravaged the colonies in the first half of the 1840s. Britain consistently refused to remove this impost until it was faced with the imminent bankruptcy of the Van Diemen's Land administration. Imperial officials argued in extenuation that penal colonies still enjoyed the benefits of very cheap labour;[42] but this fiscal encumbrance made plain to the colonists in Van Diemen's Land that the mother country's search for economy took precedence over good relations with the colonies.

Meanwhile, agitation in Britain against convict assignment had become so strong that some adjustments were palpably needed. In

1837 opponents of transportation and assignment succeeded in securing the appointment of a parliamentary select committee under the
chairmanship of the colonial reformer, Sir William Molesworth, to
inquire into the convict system. Known antagonists to assignment and
transportation on the committee included the colonial reformers,
Charles Buller, H. G. Ward, and Francis Baring. Lord Howick was
also a member and condemnation of existing penal institutions and
practices was certain.[43] The committee took evidence during 1837 and
1838, and its report provides confirmation that Wakefield and his
supporters used it as a forum to publicize and promote their own
theories. They hoped, by securing the abolition of convict assignment,
to lessen the attractiveness of New South Wales vis-a-vis South Australia as a venue for British Investment and emigration. Testimony
given before the committee stressed the similarity between assignment
and slavery, thereby playing upon the humanitarian predilections of
many Britons at this time and underpinning the committee's recommendation that transportation to the settled districts of New South
Wales and Van Diemen's Land should be abandoned as soon as
possible. The committee had also learned of the dreadful debasement
of the human spirit which took place in the penal settlements and in
road gangs separated from the free community. Nevertheless, the
committee recommended that all convicts be isolated from the rest of
colonial society in unintegrated and secluded penal cantonments.[44]

On this latter question the committee appears to have been much
influenced by the penological speculations of Alexander Maconochie,
who had travelled to Van Diemen's Land in 1837 as personal secretary
to the colony's new lieutenant-governor, Sir John Franklin. After
several months in the colony Maconochie had submitted a report to the
Colonial Office[45] which in many ways anticipated his book, *Thoughts
on Convict Management* (1839). He echoed the popular British argument that the central deficiencies of assignment were the uncertainty
of punishment, accompanied by favouritism and lack of system in
awarding remissions of sentence for good conduct. Maconochie proposed to remove the convicts from normal society and to make
punishment certain by gang labour. Convicts were to be made partly
responsible for their own discipline, and remissions of sentence
according to a fixed and known scale of marks were to be readily
available for good behaviour.

Even before the select committee presented its report, however, the
imperial government had recognized the inevitability of change. In
May 1837 the Colonial Office had instructed both Bourke and Franklin
that they should conduct convict administration in the knowledge that
it was Britain's intention to effect 'the discontinuance at the earliest
practicable period, of the Assignment of Convicts to individual

Settlers'. Both governors were enjoined to make strenuous efforts to induce settlers 'to look for the future to immigration rather than to assignment' as the source from which they might obtain the requisite labour for the cultivation of their lands and for other purposes.[46]

The metropolitan power had understood that no matter how enthusiastic colonial support for transportation and assignment might be, the British public would no longer accept the continuance of a system which many considered to be synonymous with slavery. This point of view had already appeared in a popular fictional account of antipodean exploration,[47] and it received widespread publicity from the transactions of the Molesworth Committee. It was an attitude which temporarily reflected the opinions of the strong-willed and influential Lord Howick.

In May 1838, Howick submitted a position paper to the select committee. He was clearly influenced by the prevailing climate of public opinion and by the evidence taken by the committee, and his paper referred to 'the extreme uncertainty of the punishment, and its general inadequacy, of which the most convincing proof is afforded by almost every page of the Evidence taken before the Committee, clearly establishing, as I think, the conclusion, that the practice of assignment should be done away with'. Howick went on to reject the idea of gathering the convicts together in gangs, since past experience had shown that this only served to increase mutual corruption. In Howick's view the ideal solution was to undertake a programme of building prisons according to the Benthamite Panopticon model, and in these new penitentiaries to follow the 'American System' of discipline by keeping criminals apart from one another and in continued solitary confinement. The expense of such a proposal rendered its implementation unlikely, and Howick came by a process of elimination to support Maconochie's scheme as the only practical alternative to the existing unsatisfactory system.[48] John M. Ward has stated that Howick's views remained substantially unaltered, and that he continued to support the principal conclusions of the select committee on transportation even when his official duties during the 1840s led him into attempts to renew transportation to the settled districts of New South Wales.[49] But Howick's private correspondence shows that he had changed his mind within six months of writing his monograph for the committee. By November 1838 Howick's long-standing interest in economy had outweighed his lukewarm enthusiasm for Maconochie's scheme—it may have been the prospect of increasing the costs of convict maintenance by nearly two hundred per cent—and he appeared to be no longer concerned over the deleterious moral effects of assignment either on the convict servants or on their masters. He now firmly maintained that any other alternative system of punishment or reformation 'would be attended with a very large expense', which would not contribute in any way to improving convicts or colonial society.[50]

The lure of economy also appealed to the home secretary, Lord John Russell. Like Howick, Russell favoured the continuation of convict transportation to Australia because it would involve a prohibitive expenditure if Britain were to erect sufficient penitentiaries at home to cope adequately with her domestic criminals. He put forward a proposal to remedy the noxious effect of criminals on the Australian populations, and in 1840 when he had succeeded to the Colonial Office he attempted unsuccessfully to implement it. Briefly, Russell suggested that the territory of New South Wales be divided, and that a new colony be established in the northern districts to give Maconochie's theories a fair trial. Convicts sent there would labour on public works for a fixed period of time before becoming eligible for tickets of leave which carried with them permission to join the local labour pool. Russell's draft memorandum contained a curious example of prescience. He predicted that if his plan was not put into effect and transportation was restricted solely to Tasman's Peninsular and Norfolk Island, economic circumstances would force ex-convicts to flock to the other Australian colonies upon completion of their sentences. There would be insufficient work available to employ them all in Van Diemen's Land.[51] This was in fact what happened, and at various times in the years which followed, the mainland colonies expressed concern over irruptions of such newly released ex-convicts from the island colony.[52]

Critics of transportation were sufficiently influential to secure its discontinuance in 1840 to New South Wales but their view was by no means unchallenged. British businessmen had undoubtedly found convict labour an attractive incentive for investment in New South Wales, and the expected termination of transportation and assignment was viewed as a brake on the colony's progress. 'It is generally thought', wrote the newly-arrived businessman, George Crawley, to his cousins in London, 'that the cessation of the assignment system will benefit Port Phillip, South Australia and other parts to the injury of this colony, inasmuch as new settlers will now have no convict labour which was the great inducement to settle here, tho' there was better soil and climate elsewhere'.[53] Similarly, economic considerations prompted a thoughtful reassessment by Sir John Barrow, the secretary to the Admiralty, of the government's decision to discontinue transportation to New South Wales. He claimed that the relative stagnation of the Swan River colony in Western Australia, when contrasted with the progress of New South Wales, provided ample proof of the continuing need for convict labour and convict assignment. A staunch conservative, Barrow mocked the 'priggish sentimentalities' of Archbishop Whately, and accused Howick and the government of 'hot-headed rashness' in abolishing convict assignment. As a final thrust, he compared—favourably to the convicts—the relative conditions enjoyed by convicts in New South Wales and children working in English factories.[54]

Implicit in such economic reappraisals of the convict system was a change in the outlook of an important segment of British society. In earlier years a transported felon was considered an aberrant personality, who by wilfully violating society's mores had brought retaliatory punishment upon his own head. Reformation always came a poor second to retribution in the popular conception of the convict system. Nevertheless, within the limitations of such a philosophy, the convict—although hideously debased—retained his essential humanity. The role of convictism in the imperial economy changed all that. By 1840 Britain had become heavily dependent on Australian wool, but Englishmen were only coming to a belated realization that they might dislocate the Australian source of supply by restructuring the pool of colonial labour. Some observers felt that the presence of convicts in Australia restricted the flow of free emigration and that cessation of transportation would cause an increase in free emigration from Britain sufficient to solve the labour difficulty.[55] But even if this were so, substantial movements of population took time to gather momentum and in the interim British industry could not help but feel the ill effects. Barrow typified the conservative reaction to such a possibility by calling for a return to the system of convict assignment and justifying this by an appeal to economic advantage. Convict deportation which had begun as a social corrective had become just another dehumanized entry on the balance-sheet of commercial imperialism.

Other conservative publicists, however, did attempt to obfuscate the economic basis of an opinion which favoured the retention of a system of secondary punishment so resoundingly condemned by the parliamentary select committee. In 1839, for example, *Blackwood's Magazine* reversed the stand it had taken three years earlier when Alison had claimed that transportation and assignment were inherently evil. A revaluation was suggested by the essayist, George Groly, who maintained that the good behaviour of convicts co-opted by exploring expeditions proved that moral renewal and character reform were taking place in Australia, and this being so, convict transportation should be permitted to continue to New South Wales. Moreover, New South Wales stimulated convicts to reform by offering them an opportunity to begin life anew in 'a country abounding with every advantage for mankind, singularly healthy, unlimited in its extent, offering the hope of competence and even of wealth'. Nor would the moral welfare of future generations of the free community be endangered, because Groly advocated channelling all free British emigration to the non-convict colonies of South and Western Australia. Both settlements were extensive enough in themselves to accommodate 'all the superflous population not only to England but of Europe'.[56]

Such reservations, however, did not alter the resolution of the Whig government and other parliamentary opponents of the convict system, that modifications were essential. Although there was scattered opposition to transportation in Australia it was either half-hearted like James Macarthur's,[57] or originated from the ranks of the politically powerless free emigrant proletariat in the urban centres of New South Wales and Van Diemen's Land.[58] In short, it was weak, divided and ineffective. The impetus for terminating convict transportation and assignment came almost entirely from Britain, and events during the following twelve years were to show that the metropolitan power had acted prematurely. In 1840 a two-pronged decision was taken by the government to abolish assignment but to continue transportation to Van Diemen's Land on a new probationary system which was designed to assure equality of punishment for all. The essential characteristic of the probation system and the aspect in which it differed most from assignment was that convicts were no longer dispersed as labourers for the settlers, but were gathered together at a number of probation stations throughout the island. The convicts worked in gangs and could advance through different stages of probation according to their behaviour. Good behaviour led to a steadily increasing degree of freedom and a state in which a convict was allowed to work for wages if he could find a settler willing to employ him; but he was subject to convict discipline at all times prior to the grant of a ticket of leave.[59] The government's measure won general acclaim, and the newspapers applauded the Molesworth Committee for stimulating parliamentarians to do their duty. Probation might restore a degree of salutary terror to a sentence of penal servitude in Australia.[60]

Nevertheless, humanitarian opponents to transportation found little to commend in the select committee's report, or in the subsequent actions taken by the imperial government to put the report's recommendations into effect. The committee had indeed condemned assignment; but it had then advised that assignment be replaced by gang labour under resident overseers. Humanitarians like Archbishop Whately felt that to replace assignment by such a system of discipline was the height of madness. Although the committee had taken a great deal of evidence concerning abuses which existed under convict assignment, it had also heard ample testimony which established beyond doubt that the iniquity of convicts working in gangs or gathered together in penal settlements isolated from the free colonists was infinitely worse than that of those under assignment. Molesworth himself described gang labour under overseers as productive of great misery and vice, and maintained that such convicts ended up as 'the most profligate and desperate portion of the criminal population of the penal colonies'.[61] At first glance, therefore, there appears to be some substance to complaints from New South Wales that Molesworth was seeking the abolition of assignment merely to disadvantage that colony in the interests of South Australia.[62] In all fairness to Molesworth, however, he dissociated himself from that portion of the transportation committee's report which had advocated continuing transportation and gang labour in Van Diemen's Land. On this question, Molesworth sided with the humanitarians and consequently lost control over the committee which voted against his view.[63]

Archbishop Whately outlined the humanitarians' dissatisfaction with the committee's recommendations for the continuance of a modified system of transportation. He described such proposals to the House of Lords as being 'at variance with the whole weight of the evidence', and looking like 'a graft brought from another plant, and displaying very different foliage'.[64] Molesworth himself was not so much actuated by humanitarian sympathy as by a profound conviction that government policies on transportation and free emigration were contradictory, and that the decision taken in 1831 to encourage and subsidize free emigration to Australia made it impossible for transportation to remain a deterrent to domestic crime. In the attempt to pursue both objectives the imperial government foisted two mutually exclusive lines of propaganda on the lower classes. In such circumstances Molesworth was concerned that the administration's conduct only weakened respect for authority and made the government look ridiculous. 'It not unfrequently happens', he informed the House of Commons, 'that whilst a judge is expatiating on the miseries of exile, at the same time, and perhaps in the same place, some active agent of emigration may be found magnifying the advantages of the new country, lauding the fertility of its soil and the beauties of its climate; telling of the high wages to be obtained, the enormous fortunes that have been made, and offering to eager and willing listeners, as a boon and especial favour, the means of conveyance to that very place to which the convict in the dock has been sentenced by the judge for his crimes.'[65]

Dissatisfaction with the recommendations of the select committee was not restricted to those members of the anti-transportation lobby who felt that the committee's report had not been sufficiently far-reaching. Viscount Mahon, the conservative Irish politician and historian, made an impassioned appeal to an unreceptive House of Commons in favour of retaining the existing system of secondary punishment. This was the only full-scale parliamentary attempt to meet and refute the assertions of the anti-transportationists, and he began with an unequivocal affirmation of his belief, 'that as a system, transportation is a better mode of punishment than any other system,—better for the penal colony, and better for the improvement of the convicts themselves'.[66] Mahon subjected the select committee's report to a searching examination, and rejected the abolitionists' claim that the torrent of vice poured into the penal colonies via transportation had endangered the lives and property of respectable colonists. He pointed out that in July 1838 the New South Wales' legislative council, 'which states the opinions of the most practical and eminent men of all parties in the colony', had condemned British attempts to abolish transportation—hardly evidence that they felt threatened by convicts.[67] Mahon also maintained that James McArthur's evidence before the select committee was contradictory and tended to prove that convict transportation stimulated emigration from the lower classes; for McArthur had testified that such people were confident that if convicts did well in Australia, they would do even better.[68] Finally Mahon reminded the House that the impact of any penalty for crime was entirely subjective and that assignment's alleged inequalities were not peculiar to that form of punishment. On the contrary, every method of penal discipline would produce a different reaction in each individual convict, and therefore it was as impossible to ensure equality of punishment in a penitentiary as it was under the far cheaper and more reformative system of assignment.[69]

Mahon's speech was a *tour de force* of cool critical reasoning, and he had the moral support of the experienced colonial administrator, Sir George Arthur, who had shown that transportation and assignment could be a quite effective combination of carrot and stick.[70] Yet Mahon was arguing on a different intellectual level from that on which Whately and Molesworth were operating. They saw the similarities between assignment and slavery, they saw crime apparently unpunished under the existing system, and they became convinced that transportation was immoral. Emotional prejudices of this sort expressed deeply felt convictions which were shared by a majority of their contemporaries both in and outside parliament,[71] and were not susceptible to change by appeals to logic or the voice of experience. Mahon and other supporters of the *status quo* failed to carry the day because intuitive opinions can rarely be shaken by deductive argumentation.

2: Convictism II 1840-55

The decision to terminate transportation and assignment to New South Wales in 1840 was only a partial victory for the humanitarian and colonial reformer alliance. Viscount Mahon had certainly failed to secure the retention of convict assignment in the Australian colonies, but transportation to Van Diemen's Land did continue throughout the 1840s, and successive colonial secretaries, Stanley, Gladstone and Grey administered the system against a background of deteriorating colonial economic conditions and a growing crisis in Ireland. The main effect of Britain's resolution to abolish all convict transportation to New South Wales and the system of assignment in both penal colonies was the imposition of an intolerable burden upon the island colony. Van Diemen's Land, with its appendage Norfolk Island, became Britain's only convict repository, and assignment was replaced by a system of probation which kept all convicts in labour gangs under the care and control of the local government. The costs of administration soared and these were defrayed from a declining land fund in the colony.[1] In these circumstances the metropolitan power was quick to recognize that in terms of British advantage and *realpolitik* the abolition of transportation to New South Wales in 1840 had been a serious error of judgement. The imperial authorities were to make repeated attempts throughout the ensuing decade to rectify this mistake, particularly by trying to persuade New South Wales to accept a renewal of convict transportation.[2]

These efforts were pursued against a contemporaneous deterioration of conditions in Ireland culminating in the failure of the potato crops in 1845 and 1847 which caused an outbreak of famine in that unhappy land. The growing desperation of the Irish lower classes was reflected in an enormous rise in the numbers sentenced to transportation. This unforeseen upsurge in convictions for transportable offences greatly increased the pressure on British gaols and made it doubly urgent that the government speedily discover some segment of the empire both willing and able to absorb the mother country's deported criminals.

In 1846 Gladstone proposed a solution which was disarmingly simple and direct. If New South Wales remained adamant in its rejection of convicts, then the colony would be subdivided and a new penal settlement established in the northern regions. In the event, the proposed new northern colony enjoyed only the most transitory existence. Founded in May 1846, it was abolished by Gladstone's successor, the third Earl Grey (formerly Lord Howick), in November of the same year.[3] Expense, the willingness of the Port Phillip district to accept exiles—convicts who had served significant portions of their sentences before being expatriated to Australia—and Grey's reluctance to found a colony which in the light of past experience might be expected to promote the spread of homosexuality—all these considerations militated against the establishment of a northern colony.[4] What is noteworthy in this episode is that colonial antipathy to a division of central and northern New South Wales—which had been forcibly brought to the attention of the Colonial Office in 1840—did not contribute in any way to Britain's decision to abandon the experimental colony. Indeed, it seems as if colonial representations against the division of New South Wales were studiously ignored by the metropolitan power throughout these deliberations.[5]

As an alternative solution, Grey attempted to circumvent colonial opposition to deported British felons by substantially reorganizing convict transportation. His system of exiles relieved penal colonies from a crippling financial burden by ensuring that every convict served a period of incarceration in Britain followed by enforced labour on public works either in Britain or at Gibraltar or Bermuda. Following completion of this second stage of punishment criminals were to undergo the third and final part of their sentences by being exiled to the colonies and absorbed there into the general work force.[6] Grey claimed that these arrangements were tantamount to the abolition of transportation; but Molesworth pointed out that if exiles were involuntary emigrants, then the exile system fell far short of abolition. Molesworth maintained that only convicts who wished to make a new start in Australia should be deported to the colonies, and that if the imperial power shipped all exiles there, it would be continuing transportation under another name.[7]

The debate over Britain's penal system therefore continued throughout the 1840s, and public interest remained lively. The conservative Stanley became a parliamentary spokesman for the pro-transportation forces, and although he was no longer in office, he put forward a persuasive case for its continuation in 1846. He appealed both to British self-interest and to the moral welfare of the felons themselves, though he ignored colonial claims that local interests ought also to be considered. Stanley argued that it was an inestimable advantage to the mother country to possess a means of relieving itself of the polluting presence of many thousands of criminals. He further maintained that to abolish transportation would be immoral since it would effectively deny convicted criminals any chance of rehabilitation. He did not believe 'that at the expiration of their sentence, men going out of prison stigmatized as felons by having been sentenced to what was equivalent to transportation, would have the remotest chance in this over-peopled country of obtaining employment'. Economic circumstances would compel a return to crime. On the other hand, the penal colonies had much to offer such men for they were situated 'in a country where the climate was good, the means of subsistence were ample, and there was plenty of room for employment'.[8]

Grey's system of exiles clearly satisfied Stanley, and both men agreed that it was economically impossible to persevere any longer with the probationary system. Yet Grey was not the only Englishman to realize that changes in British penal procedures were long overdue, and some elements of his plan of 1847 had already been foreshadowed the previous year. The *Globe* newspaper argued that transportation as it then existed was ineffective as punishment or reform, and had ceased to be an instructive warning to criminals. The paper claimed that criminal natures could not be reshaped in an environment where felons were herded together in a demoralized and gaderene fraternity. Some form of separate and reforming imprisonment was needed in Britain before convicts were transported.[9] The *Spectator* concurred; convicts inhabiting the penal settlements had become so debased that if Britain continued to transport new criminals to such a setting, she would be transferring moderately disreputable British felons to surroundings where all hope of reformation would be forsaken, and where they would swiftly and thoroughly complete their education in vice under the expert instruction of hardened recidivists already in Australia.[10]

Much of this disgust was aroused by imperial persistence in working convict gangs away from the centres of free settlement. All the vices and cruelties of which Molesworth and Whately had warned parliament in 1840 were reproduced in Van Diemen's Land and Norfolk Island in these gangs. The system had been initiated by Stanley and continued by his successors in a fruitless attempt to use fear as a means of lowering the rates of domestic crime in Britain. By 1846, however, many Englishmen believed that this attempt to control British crime by severity in Australia had irredeemably failed. The growing volume of propaganda in favour of emigration had stressed the exciting potentialities of the antipodes with the result, as Charles Rowcroft complained, that there existed a 'most mischievous' misconception, 'that a transportation to the penal colonies is not, as the law intends, a punishment, but rather a change of country to be desired, from the opportunity which it is supposed to afford for the rapid acquisition of large fortunes in many ways; and for the sake of the licentious liberty of action which the wilderness holds forth the promise of, and which, to restless minds, presents so fascinating an attraction.'[11]

Deterrence and reform were the twin poles between which British penal policy oscillated during the 1840s, and Grey's move away from severity of punishment meant that his scheme for exiles won only cautious public approval. The *Times*, for example, supported Grey's policies but expressed concern that his blueprint went too far in the direction of leniency. It would deprive transportation of all fear if the exiles enjoyed better or even equal prospects with honest, free emigrants.[12] This was by no means an isolated opinion.

Britain's reassessment of transportation under Grey even brought a call from the indefatigible propagandist, Samuel Sidney, for a reintroduction of the old system of assignment in New South Wales. Sidney suggested that assignment of exiles should be limited to pastoralists who occupied properties far beyond the spread of urban or agrarian settlement. Such men provided vital supplies of wool for British industry, and experienced continual difficulties in securing adequate labour. Exiles assigned to them would be removed from the contagion of fellow criminals and from the temptations of urban centres. Therefore, reform would be facilitated, and at the same time the solitude and isolation of a bush shepherd's life was a dreadful punishment, the prospect of which would appal and unnerve British criminals.[13] On the other hand, some critics continued to echo the arguments of an earlier decade when they described assignment as slavery. The essayist Henry Rogers, for example, dismissed proposals for a return to the old system by pointing out that settlers who favoured these were motivated solely by self-interest. His article surveyed nine parliamentary papers dealing with convicts and transportation between 1838 and 1847 and unequivocally demanded complete abolition.[14]

Events were soon to show that it was Rogers rather than Sidney who had correctly judged the direction in which the tide was flowing. Indeed, the long-standing exodus of free emigrant labourers to Australia guaranteed a growing and vociferous lobby against transportation in the Australian colonies themselves. Although in 1846 a select committee of the legislative council in New South Wales reported in favour of resuming transportation to the colony, the bulk of the settlers no longer supported this position. The select committee's report was therefore accompanied to the Colonial Office by a petition of protest against its recommendations, and similar petitions soon followed.[15] From Van Diemen's Land the lieutenant-governor, Sir William Denison, warned Grey that any British attempt to resume transportation to the island would be regarded as a breach of faith by the settlers there.[16] At the same time, the Cape, British North America, Ceylon, and the West Indies all refused to accept exiles unless subsidized by Britain, and to this Grey was unwilling to consent.[17] The colonies' unwillingness to accommodate Britain in her search for new convict dumping-grounds increased the pressure on Earl Grey. He reiterated that convict labour was an economic boon to colonies for which they should be prepared to pay. Most colonists, however, regarded convicts as endangering the moral fibre of their developing societies and demanded financial inducements if they were to place themselves at risk in such a manner. There was no common ground between two such attitudes; conflict was inevitable and unresolvable. Grey's stubborn persistence over this question poisoned good relations between Britain and her eastern Australian colonies until 1852, when the Whigs were defeated and a Tory secretary of state announced Britain's intention to abolish the deportation of exiles to New South Wales and Van Diemen's Land.

Britain was afforded a limited measure of relief in 1849, when the colony of Western Australia petitioned the Colonial Office that its status be altered from free colony to full convict settlement. Governor Charles Fitzgerald informed Grey that the economic benefits were most alluring to settlers in a colony where economic depression seemed perennial and development had been severely retarded. If the mother country wished to establish another outlet for convicts in Australia, the majority of the inhabitants of this cinderella settlement 'would gladly learn that Western Australia was chosen as the site'.[18] Western Australian colonists had requested convicts in 1847 and Grey had expressed his concurrence in principle the following year.[19] Thus on 1 May 1849 an Order in Council was passed transforming Western Australia into a full penal settlement. Later that same year Grey notified Governor Fitzgerald that since the home government did not wish to swamp the meagre population under a tidal wave of vice, free emigrants would be sent out equal in number to the convicts.[20]

Unfortunately for Grey, Western Australia lacked the capacity of the colonies on the eastern seaboard to absorb all British criminals sentenced to transportation. The colonial secretary therefore continued his efforts to persuade New South Wales to accept exiles accompanied by an equal number of free emigrants, and to maintain the same system in Van Diemen's Land. As Grey was aware, to send exiles to New South Wales unaccompanied by the promised free emigrants, or to send them under any conditions to Van Diemen's Land, would be considered by the colonists as a breach of faith.[21] Despite this knowledge Grey elected to make the attempt, and in so doing stirred up a hornet's nest in both colonies. Public meetings were held which excoriated the Secretary of State as a dishonourable double-dealer.[22]

Notwithstanding Grey's claim to have acted with the best intentions and with valid reasons, the fact remains that his actions were at variance with his earlier professions of intent to the colonists of New South Wales. Yet with paternalistic pique he chose to regard the legislative council's repudiation of transportation without free emigrants as intransigence. In November 1849 he told the Prime Minister, Lord John Russell, that it was 'highly important that we should make the Colonists feel how utterly unreasonable they have been and that they are not at liberty to change backwards and forward upon a question of this kind quite as often as they please'.[23] Later that same month Grey sent a despatch to New South Wales which announced with bad grace that, as a result of widespread remonstrances and an address from the legislative council, no more convicts were to be sent to any part of the colony.[24] Nevertheless, he obstinately refused to implement Russell's suggestion that, as a conciliatory gesture to the colonists, the Order in Council permitting New South Wales to receive convicts be immediately revoked.[25] In the face of overwhelming rejection Grey clung stubbornly to the belief that New South Wales might still be persuaded to take British exiles once colonists were in possession of a full knowledge of the facts.[26]

What is interesting in Grey's communications during these transactions is the evidence they provide of an increasing British awareness that the movement towards self-government in Britain's colonies of settlement was irrevocable, that even in convict colonies the consent of the governed was a prerequisite of successful imperial administration. Grey was opinionated and paternalist by nature, and could never fully bring himself to admit that it was no longer possible to coerce colonial societies in the search for British advantage. Russell, on the other hand, saw this quite clearly and recommended that Grey conciliate the settlers in New South Wales. Even the colonial secretary, however, was forced to admit, albeit reluctantly, that in suspending transportation to New South Wales in 1849 he was acting in direct response to pressure from a community of irritated settlers.[27]

Britain's new policy that the number of convicts transported to Australia was to operate in tandem with a synchronized system of assisted free emigration helped to allay much of the domestic concern over the social effects of continued transportation on colonial populations. The conservative *Blackwood's Magazine* carried an article by Archibald Alison which positively endorsed the convict system and emphasized the economic utility of the programme to Australia. Alison disregarded the free colony of South Australia and the previous non-convict status of Western Australia, and claimed that the great progress and prosperity in New Holland was due to convict labour. Transportation should therefore be continued and operated concurrently with free emigration. Alison represented the export of free but indigent British workmen as a form of preventative social medicine, for he believed that the living conditions of many English workmen were so wretched that they must inevitably lead to crime.[28]

Between 1846 and 1850, Grey's modified form of transportation won only moderate support in Britain, while at the same time it caused outrage in Australia. Anti-transportation leagues were formed in all colonies except Western Australia and a co-ordinated campaign was undertaken to secure the abolition of transportation throughout the antipodes. These associations were organized as a direct response to Grey's efforts and are further evidence that many colonists questioned the colonial secretary's sincerity and willingness to give sufficient weight to majority colonial opinion when it happened to oppose his own views.

Grey's reaction to these developments was to stress British convenience and to attach the colonial organizations which resisted him. He pointed out to Lieutenant-Governor Denison and to the House of Lords that Van Diemen's Land had been founded as a penal colony and had remained one ever since. Therefore, the free inhabitants—who had not been forced to go there—went in the full knowledge that it was a penal colony. It was illogical for them to begin complaining that its penal character was an intolerable grievance.[29] In the House of Lords, Grey argued that in any conflict between Britain and her colonies the interests of the mother country must prevail over those of the colonies. Consequently, residents of Van Diemen's Land could not expect that any sectional advantage of theirs should take precedence over imperial expedience. For Grey, the interests of the empire were obviously synonymous with those of Great Britain.

The agitation against convict transportation received an important fillip after 1850 from the discovery of the huge auriferous deposits in Australia. The comparative ease with which gold could be unearthed led Governor Charles Fitzroy to comment that 'there are few English criminals who would not regard a free passage to the goldfields of New South Wales, via Hobart Town, as a great boon'.[31] Grey consistently refused to accept the validity of this view,[32] though it was widely disseminated in Britain. The *Spectator* described transportation as 'a free passage to the goldfields of Australia', and the *Morning Chronicle* agreed;[33] C. B. Adderley, the founder of the Colonial Reform Society (1850), similarly pointed out that transportation no longer inspired fear, since it was well known that offenders were usually better off in Australia than remaining in Britain as free men.[34]

Gold turned the tide of public opinion in Britain against Grey and the supporters of transportation. The need to organize a domestic alternative to exile in Australia became more urgent and this caused concern. As has already been noted, the unskilled labourers seem to have felt considerable empathy with convicted criminals sent to the antipodes, but this feeling of fellowship did not permeate the entire labour force. The British working class was not homogeneous, and there were considerable social distinctions within its ranks. In 1851 Henry Mayhew, a discerning contemporary social commentator, depicted the arrogance with which skilled artisans disparaged unskilled labourers in urban London,[35] and this incompatibility of outlook was reflected in the attitudes of skilled workmen towards convicts. Such men found nothing to applaud in the prospective termination of transportation to Australia, for they feared the effects of unexiled convicts on the British Labour market. The decision to halt transportation was viewed as a direct threat to the livelihoods of many artisans and labourers since it was felt that the government would make use of convict labour on public works projects and that an alternative work force of this nature would help to keep domestic wage levels from rising: 'The very notion of compelling the British work-man to compete with the criminal is repugnant to all our ideas of justice, and will bring down upon the abettors of this project the censure of all good men'.[36]

There is evidence therefore, that although supporters of convict transportation were by now in a minority, Grey's was not a lone voice when he pressed for the current system to be maintained. The third Earl Grey, however, was a most obstinate man[37] who seemed consti-tutionally unable to yield gracefully to colonial demands for the abolition of transportation. When New South Wales rejected his attempts to reintroduce convicts, Grey resurrected Gladstone's old policy of separating the northern districts from the colony and forming with them a new penal settlement. Opportunism seems to have been Grey's chief motive, and he warned Governor Fitzroy that if the imperial government should once decide in principle that a new penal colony in northern Australia would best serve British interests, it would brook no interference from the legislative council in New South Wales. The possible dismemberment of the colony was to be a decision Britain would take alone. 'It is a pretension', lectured Grey, 'on the part of the Inhabitants of New South Wales which could not for a moment be listened to, that having themselves derived great wealth from Convict Labour, they should now claim to prevent a similar advantage being enjoyed by the Northern District, because they themselves no longer stand in need of such assistance'.[38]

Grey's tenacity alienated both colonial and domestic opinion. The *Times* expressed concern and maintained that the gold discoveries had made Australia too familiar to Englishmen for convict transportation to be anything but a self-defeating system. Australia was now so well known that it would become a positive inducement to crime if the imperial government should continue to send criminals there. Moreover, the newspaper claimed that British persistence would so outrage the colonists in Australia that they would resort to force in order to break the British connection. Although Grey was by then out of office, the paper savagely attacked him and his successor for what it described as their 'infatuated perseverance in the present system'.[39]

The Russell government fell from office in February 1852, and Grey's replacement at the Colonial Office was Sir John Pakington. Pakington was a conservative, but of a far less dogmatic frame of mind than Grey. When Colonel Jebb, the Surveyor General of Prisons, reported that the combination of gold and emigration propaganda had deprived transportation to Australia of all its terrors,[40] the new government was prepared to discontinue transportation to eastern Australia.[41] John M. Ward has claimed that this decision was motivated by British convenience and was little affected by circumstances in Australia: 'The final abolition of the system, like its beginning, its suspension and its renewal, owed nearly everything to British and little to Australian wishes or needs'.[42] While there is considerable evidence that British opinion had largely swung against transportation during the late 1840s and early 1850s, it would be a dangerous oversimplification to regard this as sufficient to account for a reversal of imperial policy. Indeed, Ward's somewhat uncompromising observation can be counterbalanced by an abundance of data which supports the more traditional interpretation that the decision taken by the imperial government in 1852 was a belated reaction to a campaign of defiant obstructionism in Australia.[43]

Contemporary statesmen and commentators in the mother country certainly felt that colonial objections to transportation had been paramount. Palmerston, the home secretary in Aberdeen's coalition ministry, openly linked Britain's promise of responsible government to the Australian colonies with the decision to abolish the convict system; 'we had conceded to those Colonies the principle and right of self-government, and, that cession being made we must adopt and submit to its consequences'.[44] It was the United Kingdom's misfortune if, having granted to the colonists the right of conducting their

own affairs, they should wish to abandon transportation. The principle, however, had been endorsed, and Britain had now no option but
'to alter the system which we had hitherto pursued'.[45] Grey was
convinced that the government's decision was a grave miscalculation,
and he accused the colonial secretary, the Duke of Newcastle, of being
too ready to allow colonial interests to prevail over those of the mother
country. Grey declared that it would be preferable to sever every
connection with the Australian colonies than to retain them with all
the burdens of defence, if they persisted in refusing to admit Britain's
right to exercise a 'substantial authority' over them.[46] Both Derby and
Newcastle disagreed: Britain had no right to force convicts on the
colonies if the bulk of the colonists were resolutely opposed to such a
course of action.[47] Outside parliament, the social critic and industrialist William Greg, reproached the Australian colonists for acting
'ungenerously' in declining to accept further shipments of British
criminals. Even so, he did admit the validity of the submission that
gold had rendered transportation inoperable, and expressed considerable uneasiness over the possible effects of retaining Britain's criminals at home.[48] The harmful repercussions of accommodating convicts in Britain concerned many Englishmen at this time, and Colonel
G. C. Mundy echoed the views of such people when he commented
that even if criminals could be disciplined more cheaply in Britain
than in a penal colony, it was better for the imperial authority to pay
the extra expenses of transportation; for 'the privilege of shooting so
much moral rubbish upon other and distant premises is cheaply
bought at such a rate'.[49]

After 1853 the issue of abolition was effectively resolved, and such
opinions were no longer relevant to British behaviour. But Mundy's
reference to convicts being the 'moral-rubbish' of the mother country
raises questions of British attitudes to the convict and the colonial
society in which he lived, as distinct from opinions dealing with
transportation as a secondary punishment. Convicts and former convicts formed a numerically significant segment of the populations in
eastern Australia,[50] and British thinking and comment on communities thus constituted tended to fall into patterns which had been
established during the early years of settlement. The common thread
uniting British attitudes throughout the years covered by this study
was an openly stated conviction that antipodean populations were both
inferior and morally tainted.

In 1828, however, the disability was not considered to be hereditary.
The Reverend Sydney Smith, for example, estimated in that year that
the total population of New South Wales was approximately 60 000, of
which only one quarter was female. Since it was believed that colonial
society could not reproduce itself until the sexes were in an almost

equal ratio, he called for 'a cargo of young women' to be sent to the colony, 'even though they should not be always of the most exemplary purity'.[51] Smith did not consider that such an emigration would degrade colonial society still further, because at that time he believed that the children of convict parents—the 'currency' lads and lasses—did not inherit the criminal predilections of their parents. Criminality was not a trait passed on to succeeding generations.[52]

If the sins of the fathers were not yet thought to be visited upon the children, emancipated convicts were regarded with all the odium which attached to their former condition. In 1832, for example, the *Globe* newspaper found the suggestion that emancipists be granted representative government 'revolting',[53] and several years later Archibald Alison described the emancipists in New South Wales as an 'unruly population'.[54]

In the contemporary state of ignorance concerning penology, such attitudes were not surprising, but not all sections of the British press were so unenlightened. At this time, the *Westminster Review* was under the editorship of J. S. Mill, and its treatment of New South Wales and emancipists reflected utilitarian belief in the reclaimability of man. The journal expressed the strongest sympathy towards the ex-convicts in New South Wales, and resolutely declared its opposition 'to those who would exclude the emancipists from the rights and privileges of citizens'.[55] This position, however, was a minority one. Mill's opinion may have been predetermined by his utilitarian outlook, but other attitudes tended to be far more prejudiced. Dr Thomas Arnold of Rugby School maintained that criminality not only marked an individual for the entire course of his life, but also would endow successive generations with the same evil tendencies:

> If they will colonize with convicts, I am satisfied that the stain should last, not only for one whole life, but for more than one generation; that no convict or convict's child should ever be a free citizen; and that, even in the third generation, the offspring should be excluded from all offices of honour or authority in the colony. This would be complained of as unjust or invidious, but I am sure that distinctions of moral breed are as natural and as just as those of skin or of arbitrary caste are wrong and mischievous; it is a law of God's Providence which we cannot alter, that the sins of the father are really visited upon the child in the corruption of his breed, and in the rendering impossible many of the feelings which are the greatest security to a child against evil.[56]

In 1837, *Blackwood's Edinburgh Magazine* carried an article by an unknown author which claimed that Britain had committed a 'shameful and unblessed act' in establishing a convict settlement in New South Wales, because such a community would ultimately spread its moral corruption to New Zealand and all the inhabited islands of the Polynesian and Indian archipelagos.[57] Nevertheless, on this occasion editorial prejudice did not denote a closed mind, and less than twelve months later the same journal printed a joint article by the writer George Groly and John Wilson, a professor of moral philosophy at Edinburgh University. The co-authors refuted the claim that emancipist populations were irrevocably tainted, and brought forward as evidence to substantiate their point of view the good behaviour of the convicts in Major Thomas Mitchell's exploring expedition into the interior of New South Wales. Character regeneration, the writers decided, was obviously taking place in New South Wales, and far from being a country infected with galloping moral deterioration the colony was actually the venue for 'a great experiment in the faculty of renovation in the human character'.[58]

Despite occasional references of this sort, most publicists continued to denigrate emancipists and the colonial populace in general. Lady Mary Fox described convicts and emancipists as 'the scum and refuse of mankind',[59] while even the working-class newspaper the *Operative* commented that the lower ranks of colonial society in Australia were corrupted by the high proportion of convicts and ex-convicts.[60] Such writers obviously believed what Dr Arnold had implied, that human nature was inherently wicked and that once a man trod the path of iniquity his evil nature could infect his children and all those who came in contact with him, whether convict or free.

Not all British criticism of colonial society in Australia took such a serious turn, and on occasion similar attitudes were expressed in a more light-hearted, if still intolerant, vein. Transportation was known to have caused a serious imbalance in the ratio of sexes in Australia and prostitution naturally flourished. In such a situation, the moral virtue of many colonial women of fashion was thought to be extremely dubious. The following vignette describes such a colonial belle:

> For the lady was young, and the lady was fair,
> And withal so wondrous gay,
> That wherever a ball was, she was there
> The Pride of Botany Bay.
> The First of her virtues was beauty you see,
> And the Hundred and second was chastity.[61]

Private individuals were not alone in perceiving a moral flaw in antipodean character during these years. On the contrary, Colonial Office documents reveal a similar preoccupation. In 1828 the Tory Colonial secretary, Sir George Murray, referred to the 'peculiar character' of the population in New South Wales,[62] and several years later

a Whig secretary of state, Lord Glenelg, maintained that transportation had produced a population in dire need of religious and
ethical re-education. According to Glenelg, the British government
was convinced that 'in no part of the World, is the general Education
of the People a more sacred and necessary duty of the Government
than in New South Wales'.[63]

The imperial authority was not solely concerned with the immorality of the New South Wales' population, because it also feared that
society there, in addition to or perhaps as a result of its moral depravity,
was politically unstable. As early as 1830, Edward McArthur had
warned a select committee on secondary punishments that in New
South Wales one result of transportation was that 'Republican sentiments are in active operation', and two years later this view was
endorsed by Archbishop Whately.[64] It was a measure of the colony's
growth and development that in 1836 the ambassador of the United
States of America to Great Britain should have requested British
recognition of a United States' consul in New South Wales. Colonial
Office officials, however, were hesitant and uncertain of the wisdom of
allowing a consul to represent the United States at Sydney:

> Lord Glenelg is however of opinion that, in the very peculiar state of
> society in New South Wales, and adverting to the Political dissen-
> sions by which it is agitated, it is not convenient to recognise any
> Inhabitant in a character carrying with it so much influence as must
> attach to a Consul of the United States of America.[65]

It was the republicanism of the United States which caused concern,
as one month later the Colonial Office returned a favourable answer to
a similar request for consular recognition for a representative of the
King of the Netherlands.[66]

Such requests from foreign powers were indicative of the rising
commercial importance of New South Wales. Social advance in the
colony under the stimulus of free emigration kept pace with economic
improvement, and led Horace Twiss—a former under-secretary at the
Colonial Office—to comment during 1838 that the colony had out-
grown its earlier character as a predominantly penal settlement and
had become

> a little English world, with flourishing cities and cultivated fields,
> and fantastic villas, harbours alive with the ships of every nation,
> and jostling crowds, and angry politics, and warring journals—all
> the savagery of a horde of buccaneers, and all the jealousies, vices,
> and vexations of the most civilized society.[67]

Yet Twiss (who had never been to Australia) refused to be misled by
the superficial resemblance to England, and went on to comment upon
the vice and depravity of convict and emancipist society, as well as the

debilitating effects on colonial virtue of exposure to such influences. He discerned character defects which had spread throughout the lower classes, irrespective of whether their origins were free or convict. The most notable of these faults was a partiality for strong drink and loose women.[68]

Not only were the lower orders in the convict colonies considered to be corrupt. Some British publicists believed that convict transportation and assignment were mutually degrading for masters and servants alike.[69] In 1835, an article in the *Quarterly Review* refused to distinguish between levels of depravation in the upper and lower classes of New South Wales. The *Review* claimed that immense corruption existed in New South Wales, 'even among the upper class of society in that colony', where vice was prevalent to a degree 'quite beyond the reach of an unsophisticated English imagination'.[70] Despite occasional comments of this nature, the great bulk of British prejudice was directed against the colonial lower classes. Typical of this underlying social bias was one critic's wry notation that the three appropriate and never-failing accompaniments of advancing civilization in New South Wales were 'racecourses, public-houses and jails'.[71]

British assessments of the effect of convicts on colonial society had a far more serious side, and Molesworth was not contradicted when he informed the House of Commons that transportation to Australia 'has given birth to the most depraved communities in the universe'. According to his assessment, the reputation of convict colonists was so bad that it produced amongst the British working classes a growing disinclination to emigrate there.[72] Some newspapers sought to turn Molesworth's arguments in favour of abolishing transportation against their proposer by agreeing that convicts did indeed deprave society in Australia and by deducing from this that penal deportation was an essential 'safety valve' for the United Kingdom. Otherwise, untransported criminals would similarly infect British society with their immorality.[73] Indeed, the *Globe* actually claimed that criminals were the best colonists Britain could supply, and that if infant colonies were to progress, supplies of convicts and other malcontents were indispensable. New settlements needed men prepared to gamble with their lives, to take desperate risks in the hope of bettering a desperate condition. 'Look at the junior branches of the American commonwealth; and say whether they may not more than compete with our penal settlements in every symptom of prevalent licentiousness and defiance of law. *On ne fait pas des révolutions avec de l'eau-de-rôse—* nor new empires neither'.[74]

This was an extreme statement from a newspaper which on this issue stood utterly opposed to Molesworth's views; yet both outlooks reflected the usual British opinions concerning the degeneracy of colonial populations in New South Wales and Van Diemen's Land. Colonial Office attitudes also shared this general consensus, and in 1845 the imperial authorities felt compelled to protect the New South Wales' community from itself. When in that year the colony's legislative council passed a bill designed to set up a public lottery, Stanley, the Colonial Secretary, withheld his consent on the ground that temporary financial advantage would be gained 'at the expense of morality and the permanent interests of Society at large'.[75]

The idea that the populace of New South Wales was morally defective even received support from Earl Grey. In 1848 he admitted that emigration had altered the balance of society in the colony and raised it into a 'free country'.[76] Yet the following year he described the population of the free country as more depraved than undiluted convict society. The occasion of Grey's outburst was news of a public meeting held in Sydney which opposed his proposals for the renewal of convict transportation to the colony. Grey vented his petulance in a minute which read: 'I think the apprehensions of the colonists as to being demoralized by convicts are not a little visionary and that the danger would be rather that even the worst of our convicts would find that they had something to learn from the members at the public meeting in despising truth and decency.'[77]

In 1848, however, the liberal *Fraser's Magazine for Town and Country* demonstrated that there was a further dimension to British criticism of society in Australia, which went far beyond an understandable distaste for communities of ex-criminals. The journal carried a long article on the free colony of Western Australia, which after describing the settlers as hospitable accused them of evincing a low moral tone. The tenor of the article was emotional and pejorative, and the sentiments it expressed were indistinguishable from the current British attitudes towards convict and emancipist society in the eastern colonies. According to this critic, the reason for the abject state of morality in Western Australia was that the bulk of the free emigrants came from 'the humblest ranks of life' in the mother country.[78] When the free populace of Western Australia was attacked in the same terms and for the same alleged shortcomings as were said to exist in the convict colonies, it becomes plain that much of the antipathy expressed in Britain towards Australian colonial society is explicable in terms of domestic class jealousies which convictism enabled Englishmen to parade as respectable moral concern.

Many members of Britain's middle and upper classes resented the success which sundry ex-convicts and lower-class free emigrants enjoyed in Australia. Envy was a constant feature of British attitudes in the period under review, and Grey's animosity was consistently aroused by emancipists and emigrants who attained affluence or self-sufficiency. In 1832, as the youthful parliamentary under-secretary at the Colonial Office, he informed the House of Commons that an emancipist petition from New South Wales which sought trial by jury and a representative assembly could not be taken seriously because it came from ex-criminals. In an effort to add bite to his speech, Howick used as an example the case of a large New South Wales' contractor named Girard. This man had in 1829 laid a complaint against Governor Ralph Darling. 'On investigation' Howick explained, 'it appeared that this Mr Girard was nothing more nor less than a respectable pickpocket', who had been transported for theft in 1821 and 'in 1829 was a great contractor'.[79] Howick was scandalized that a man with such a background should have become a successful entrepreneur within eight years of being transported. The possibility of rapid affluence for ex-convicts in Australia was offensive to some Englishmen who believed that wealth should be inherited or amassed slowly through several generations. In 1846, for example, the Bishop of Oxford implied that it was a violation of justice and natural law for emancipists to make money. How could crime be prevented, the Bishop asked, if the public were to be continually presented with the spectacle of vice 'not in chains, in fetters or in punishment, but prosperous and triumphant'.[80] Grey's disapproval that the labouring classes in Australia—whether emancipist or free in origin—should make such notable economic progress remained unaltered through the years, and in 1852 he attempted to justify the continuance of convict transportation to Van Diemen's Land by arguing that it would depress colonial wage rates which were 'extravagant' and 'not favourable to the moral improvement of the population'. In this matter Grey believed that transportation to Van Diemen's Land would provide a beneficial moral influence.[81] Victorian society during these years was economically and communally divided, and Grey and others of his ilk seem to have believed that the existing social order could be undermined by the acquisition of undue wealth by the lower classes. Grey's belief that poverty was necessary to ensure the moral rectitude of the proletariat was derived from his fear of social mobility and the political ambitions of the lower orders in Britain.

British criticisms of Australian society during the gold rushes indicate that this emotional substratum of British attitudes was significant,[82] but while convict transportation continued, economic envy and social jealousy could be safely disguised as moral concern. Grey advised Lord Yarborough that he would do well to dissuade any scion of the Yarborough family from going to Australia, which was a place where 'only working men thrive'.[83] Other critics continued to launch attacks on Australian society for its lower class origins, and to echo Grey by complaining that Britons of birth and education were discouraged from emigrating to Australia because of the inferiority of colonial minds and manners.[84] Indeed, hostility was so pronounced on occasion that colonial society's imbalance was blamed for having unnecessarily delayed the discovery of gold. Gold would have been detected years earlier if the rural population in New South Wales had comprised a higher class of immigrant. For such men would have been interested in scientific pursuits and in studying the geology of local rocks and mineral samples.[85]

British preoccupation with criminal taints and the moral and social imperfections of Australian populations constituted, as Frederich P. Werner points out, 'a gross injustice to the hundreds of thousands of free and decent colonists who populated the periphery of this vast continent'.[86] Little significant change of attitude towards the developing Australian community took place throughout the period under review; there were few Englishmen in 1851 who would have seriously disagreed with Frederick Engels when he described Australian colonists as a 'United States of deported murderers, burglars, ravishers and pickpockets'.[87]

Despite an apparently widespread British dissatisfaction with the constituents of society in Australia and the egalitarianism engendered by a colonial environment, British attitudes displayed a curious ambivalence. After all the charges stimulated by envious malice and detraction had been levelled at the antipodean populations, a feeling nevertheless persisted that in Australia Britain had created something worthwhile. In 1828 Sydney Smith had claimed that New South Wales could become in time an empire 'greater and more populous than that from which it sprung',[88] and the *Gentleman's Magazine* concurred that 'Australasia would become of great consequence to this country'.[89] During the 1830s even the hypercritical *Fraser's Magazine* admitted that 'at some future period' the settlements in Australia were 'destined to become great and flourishing nations'.[90] By 1838 the *Gentleman's Magazine* had become almost lyrical with enthusiasm: 'If there is a country in the world that could be independent of all others, that could furnish the various wants of all the inhabitants with all that Asia and Europe conjointly now afford, it is undoubtedly this—the land of the savage, the convict, and the slave'.[91] The following year the publicist George Groly added his voice to the swelling chorus of great expectations,[92] and the opinion was reinforced by the essayist Henry Rogers several years later.[93]

It is within the context of this eventual destiny that British strictures on colonial society and concern over the effect of convictism on future generations should be viewed and assessed, even though it must be remembered that much of the obsession with colonial morals was subconsciously motivated by economic envy and social jealousy. But

if vice and criminality were hereditary, as many Englishmen believed
them to be, then Britain had founded a nation, predestined to become
a powerful empire, from the very worst materials imaginable. Furthermore, Britons were apprehensive about the experiment of allowing
such a community to exercise self-government. Although such fears
originated in ignorance, they were plausible in their day. *Simmonds's
Colonial Magazine* echoed the sentiments of many Englishmen in
1849 when it expressed a general uneasiness that New South Wales
and Van Diemen's Land might become 'a great piratical republic', if
transportation was permitted to coexist with liberal electoral
suffrages.[94] At all times the convict character of the Australian communities affected the speed and direction of constitutional advance.

3: *Constitutional Advance I 1828–49*

When the first British settlers landed at Sydney Cove in 1788 there was no question of their fundamental human freedoms being protected by Royal Charter or some other rudimentary form of constitution. The colony was a gaol and the early colonists were the prisoners and their warders. A constitution in the political sense is usually a systematic compilation of the principles and customs according to which a people is governed. Such an arrangement implies that both governed and governing are subject to certain agreed rights, privileges and duties; very few eighteenth or early nineteenth century thinkers would have accepted the proposition that a convict colony was entitled to a constitution of its own. Convicted felons were understood to have forfeited, at least temporarily, most of the liberties enjoyed by Englishmen at home, and the commission of Captain Phillip R.N., the first Governor of New South Wales, placed full executive authority in his hands. This state of affairs remained unchanged for over thirty years.

In the years between 1823 and 1855, however, the colonies in Australia travelled the full gamut from convict dumps under gubernatorial autocracy to settlement colonies enjoying responsible government. During these years the apparently willing and amicable transfer of authority from Britain to the Australian colonists took place without violence and without seriously endangering links between the mother country and her colonies in the antipodes. Such a change implies an underlying alteration of quite major proportions in British attitudes towards Australia, and raises complicated wider questions concerning imperial trusteeship and the extent or practicability of the metropolitan authority's power of enforcement over maturing colonial societies.

During the early years of settlement, the all-embracing nature of a governor's rule does not appear to have unduly concerned the inhabitants of New South Wales or the mother country. It was not until 1823 that steps were taken in Britain to reduce the preponderant influence of the governor. By that year, an expanding flow of free emigration to New South Wales,[1] increasing agitation from the growing emancipist population in the colony, and the publication in Britain of the reports of parliamentary commissioner John Bigge's investigations into the administration of New South Wales,[2] forced the Colonial Office to take stock.

In July 1823 the imperial parliament passed an act for the better government and administration of justice in New South Wales and Van Diemen's Land[3] which contained the first restrictions on the powers of governors in Australia, though the limitations were of a relatively minor nature. Under the authority of this act, a nominated advisory legislative council numbering no more than seven men was set up in New South Wales. Moreover, the right to initiate legislation was reserved to the governor who in an emergency needed the consent of only one member of the council to enact laws. In 1825, under powers given to the crown by this act, Van Diemen's Land became a separate colony with its own distinct legislative council.

The concession of legislative councils was the first breach in the dyke of executive autocracy in the Australian colonies, and colonial agitation for more liberal institutions became progressively stronger during the two decades after 1823. Subsequent constitutional developments in the Australian colonies tended towards a gradual diminution in the powers of governors and in executive independence, a process which eventually resulted in executive subordination to colonial legislatures. The slow erosion of the authority of governors in Australia between 1823 and 1855 was not solely the result of colonial complaint and initiative: on occasion the British authorities gave added impetus to what was a continuing process in the colonies.[4] Nevertheless, in the years after 1825 the two settlements of New South Wales and Van Diemen's Land placed the British government squarely on the horns of a judicial and constitutional dilemma. What future governmental provision should be made for settlements composed of convicts and their descendants, as well as a growing population of free immigrants, particularly when the demands of free settlers conflicted with the requirements of a gaol? Should convicts be permitted to exercise their civil rights on the expiration of their sentences? Was it necessary to modify British institutions for Australian conditions? What sort of judicial system would best suit the needs of such a strangly mixed community? If election of members to a house of assembly was eventually to be allowed, how restricted a franchise should be granted? These were some of the thorny, intractable problems originating in the convict antecedents of antipodean settlement which beset the Colonial Office as it attempted to grapple with the constitutional development of Australian colonies in the period under review.

As far as pressures from Australia were concerned, the years between 1825 and 1828 saw the demands for constitutional advance intensify in New South Wales. This development was complicated by a split in the colonial populace which had divided into two irreconcilable factions—the emancipated convicts and their descendants on the one hand, and the exclusives or wealthy free settlers and their offspring on the other. In 1826 the exclusives petitioned the colonial secretary for an independent press, increased free immigration, the establishment of an executive council composed of the officers of government in New South Wales and enjoying all the powers of an upper house, and the extension of the existing legislative council to at least fifteen members selected by the crown from amongst the most respectable landholders and merchants in the colony. The petition also requested trial by jury as it existed in England, which would have neatly excluded emancipists from jury service.[5] Not to be outdone, the emancipists joined the fray in 1827 and applied to the imperial parliament for a system of juries which would include them, as well as for an elective assembly.[6]

A. P. Thornton in *Doctrines of Imperialism* maintained that 'all statements about rights are assertions of opinion with a defiance stamped on them. They declare that the condition of things is not what it should be. Something must be done to change it; if that something is not done, a great wrong goes unredressed'.[7] This aptly describes the emancipist frame of mind in New South Wales, where ex-convicts were demanding their birth right as free-born Englishmen, a familiar cry that the authorities in England had heard from other groups of colonists at other times. At the same time, many Englishmen perceived in such demands that element of defiance mentioned by Thornton and very clearly resented it.

The emancipists' position was a powerful one. They claimed that once their sentences had been served and their debt to society paid, they were entitled to enjoy again the rights and privileges of Englishmen. This argument was unanswerable; had their sentences been served in England, convicts automatically would have been reinvested with their civil rights upon release. Refusal to extend the benefits of the British constitution to ex-convicts and the lower classes in the Australian colonies could not be justified, and this explains the preoccupation noted earlier[8] of British publicists with the pseudo-scientific question of inherited criminality and a 'tainted' population.

Such a condition provided those in both England and Australia, who were unfavourably disposed towards an extended electoral franchise, with an unassailable reason for withholding it from the Australian colonists.

Initial British reactions to, and fears of colonial defiance during, the 1820s were probably rooted, consciously or unconsciously, in bitter memories of 1783. When the *Times* in 1828 raised the whole question of trusteeship in Australia, it warned members of the government that colonies should be handled tactfully and administered

> on a consideration of what best suits their local interests, and not of the manner in which they may be forced to yield the greatest sacrifice to the parent state; otherwise they will inevitably cast about for an opportunity of releasing themselves from the trammels imposed by English selfishness or pride, and the history of the United States will have become that of our entire colonial empire.[9]

The general precepts enunciated by the *Times* were those which common sense and prudence alike dictated, but other English critics were doubtful whether British institutions ought to be transferred unaltered to miniature colonial societies in penal colonies. Jury service in the mother country was dependent on property, and many Englishmen felt that additional safeguards were indispensable in New South Wales, and that colonial jury lists should also take cognizance of the character of potential jurors.[10] Similarly, some observers felt that a house of elected representatives in a convict settlement would only exacerbate existing social tensions, and that in this instance society in the Australian colonies was not 'wholesome' enough for the implementation of the British right to an elective assembly. As far as Englishmen in the 1820s were concerned, convicts and emancipists comprised too large a proportion of the colony's population for such a concession yet to be wise or necessary.[11]

The colonists were not discouraged in their demands by the initially unsympathetic response in Britain. In New South Wales and Van Diemen's Land the colonial press ensured that constitutional issues did not cease to be prominent and that constant agitation for administrative change was maintained by emancipists and their supporters. The press was crucial in this campaign and the role of the press in convict colonies was a matter of controversy. Some governors tended to see newspapers as unduly inflammatory and provocative, but in Australia they formed a critical and efficient lobby against both overbearing governors and the exclusives' pretensions to a monopoly of political power, and thereby ensured that colonial debate on civil rights and constitutions did not flag. Largely for this reason, Governors Arthur, in Van Diemen's Land, and Darling, in New South Wales, both attempted, though without success, to censor colonial newspapers. In 1827 Darling complained that a passion for constitutional change existed amongst the lower orders in New South Wales, and he blamed this on the colony's newspapers.[12] Such attempts to stifle emancipist newspapers were described by the *Times* as an exercise in excessive autocracy,[13] though Darling's delineation of the passionate, emotive nature of colonial journalism evoked anger and a sense of foreboding in some of the more conservative of British publicists.[14] The response of officials at the Colonial Office, however, reflected greater optimism. The value and beneficial influence of a free press in Australia were acknowledged by William Huskisson when in 1828 as secretary of state he introduced into parliament a new constitutional bill for the better government of New South Wales. Huskisson implied that in many ways colonial newspapers performed functions normally exercised by elected delegates. 'The existing government was neither arbitrary nor despotic, for there was a free press, which had a due influence and control over public affairs'.[15] Confidence in the value of the local press made imperial officials disinclined at that time to graft elective principles on to the constitution of New South Wales. Such an outlook, shared by Whig and Tory administrations, temporarily precluded further constitutional advance. When Major General Richard Bourke was sent to New South Wales in 1831 as Darling's successor, he was instructed to answer any address or petition for an elected legislative assembly with the simple reply that the imperial authorities did not intend to make any alteration to the week New South Wales Act.[16]

Under the act of 1828 the governors of New South Wales and Van Diemen's Land were authorized to nominate legislative councils of not more than fifteen nor less than ten members. In practice the councils were composed of the higher public functionaries and private colonists of wealth and respectability. The act also stipulated that a governor must seek the advice and guidance of an executive council to be composed of the leading public officials in the colonies. The process of paring away the arbitrary powers of Australian governors was at last under way. The arrangements of 1828 established a model which, with minor variations, remained until 1850 the standard form of government in the colonies of Van Diemen's Land, Western Australia and South Australia.

Nevertheless, agitation for an elective assembly in New South Wales continued. One technique favoured by settlers in many British colonies was the appointment of a member of parliament as a spokesman to protect their interests when colonial questions were under consideration. Accordingly, in 1830 emancipists and their supporters in New South Wales launched the Australian Patriotic Association, and subscribed sufficient funds to retain the services of a member of the House of Commons. When the liberal diplomatist, Henry Lytton Bulwer, agreed to represent the Association, his first task was, in June 1832, to present a petition from New South Wales' emancipists demanding the immediate grant of trial by jury and an elected legislature. Despite notable economic progress in the colony and an increasing population of free immigrants settling there, Bulwer noted that British attitudes were still coloured by the settlement's origins. It was, he claimed, a popular British prejudice to think of New South Wales in 1832 in the same terms as the Botany Bay settlement thirty years earlier, and still to regard it as 'a small penal settlement, exclusively inhabited by thieves and pickpockets'.[17] According to Bulwer, such a description no longer reflected the true character of society in New South Wales and he claimed that the colonists were more than ready for both trial by jury and an elective assembly. The task of reply fell to Howick. He had already pondered the question and come to the conclusion that because of their numerical preponderance emancipists would quickly dominate any house of assembly, and he held a low opinion of the moral character of ex-convicts, describing them as 'outcasts' with 'little improvement likely to be effected by the discipline they have undergone'.[18] In his parliamentary reply, therefore, Howick was prepared to concede that trial by jury would be introduced as quickly as possible, a popular decision that had already been taken before Bulwer brought forward his motion,[19] but he was adamant that emancipists and their descendants were tainted with criminality and therefore unfit to be given a legislative assembly. In Howick's view, the constitutional conflict between emancipist and exclusive in New South Wales closely resembled a struggle between the forces of good and the powers of darkness: 'A constant struggle ... was going on between those who had been once convicts, or who were the descendants of convicts, and those who were wholly untainted.[20]

Howick's facile reduction of colonial constitutional conflict in Australia to simplistic theological constituents was not uncommon amongst Englishmen of his day. Frequent comment on the tainted population of New South Wales was made throughout the 1830s and 1840s, and it may be relevant to note that the vast majority of the convicts came from the lower classes in Britain at a time when social disruption was prevalent, both in the years preceding the passage of the Reform Act of 1832 and later accompanying the activities of Chartists. Since upper class British emotions during these two decades were already aroused to resist demands from the lower classes at home for a measure of political democracy, claims of a similar nature emanating from the criminally tainted and suspect population at the antipodes[21] were bound to be deemed offensive. Molesworth's parliamentary inquiry into convict transportation during 1837 and 1838 reinforced British prejudices concerning the type of society emerging in Australia. Two of the main witnesses before the committee were James Mudie and James Macarthur. Both were exclusives and both had recently published books in Britain in which they denounced colonial society in New South Wales for the existence of a crime rate which, they alleged, was excessively high and evidence of the colony's obvious unreadiness for representative government.[22] Existing British prejudices against self-government for colonies could not fail to have been reinforced by this corroborative evidence from Australia.[23]

The advisability of conceding elective assemblies in Australia again arose during 1834 when parliament passed an act establishing the free colony of South Australia. The excuse of a tainted population could not be used on this occasion, and in addition most of the colonial reformers and other supporters of the South Australian scheme were socially respectable men. For these reasons, and because the parliamentary opponents of the measure concentrated their attack on the speculative nature of the project and the impracticality of the theory of systematic colonization which underlay the new colony,[24] there was little debate over a provision in the act which pledged self-government at some future date when the population should reach 50 000.[25] The experience in Western Australia, where the inhabitants still numbered less than 3000 five years after the first settlement, suggested that such a promise to South Australia would not have to be redeemed for many years to come.

Throughout the 1830s emancipists and their sympathizers continued to demand an elective assembly with a liberal franchise for New South Wales. In 1833 Governor Bourke proposed to enfranchise emancipists and to this end he suggested that the lists of colonists eligible for jury service could also serve as electoral registers.[26] Bourke's design implied what Lytton Bulwer stated explicitly to parliament during 1835, that to deny ex-convicts and their descendants the right to vote for an elected legislature because they were somehow untrustworthy, made a mockery of the earlier decision to allow them to serve on juries.[27] Bourke put forward another plan for a colonial legislature in December 1835 and again he refused to make constitutional distinctions between exclusive and emancipist in New South Wales.[28] After 1840 when convict transportation to New South Wales ceased and an influx of free immigrants permanently altered the demographic balance, wealthy emancipists and exclusives discovered common ground in protecting squatting interests and property against the increasing attacks mounted by urban and rural colonists of a more radical hue.

Agitation in the Australian colonies and in Britain by emancipist sympathizers did not fall on altogether infertile ground. Opinion at the Colonial Office apparently regarded representative government in Australia as an eventual certainty, and in the late 1830s officials discussed several draft schemes for constitutional advance which showed that Englishmen were not indifferent to the problem and which illustrate their preconceptions about colonial government. During 1836 and 1837 James Stephen, now permanent under-secretary at the Colonial Office, tinkered with proposals for a new constitution in New South Wales, and when Francis Forbes, the colony's chief justice, returned to England in 1836, Stephen sought his counsel and advice. The under-secretary favoured a scheme whereby representation in a colonial assembly would be elective but indirect. He proposed to establish municipal corporations in New South Wales, the members of which would be elected on a wide suffrage. When the elected councillors in each municipality met they would select one of their own number to represent their area on the colony's legislative council. Forbes replied that such proposals were unwieldy and inefficient and suggested a simple enlargement of the existing legislative council with half of the total members elected and half remaining crown nominees.[29]

Despite such unambiguous rejection of the principle of indirect representation by men with personal experience in the colonies, other imperial politicians and administrators continued to regard such a system of government as most desirable for Australia. Even Charles Buller, who in December 1837 had replaced Bulwer as parliamentary agent for the Australian Patriotic Association, was affected by this climate of opinion. In 1838 he submitted his own plan for a constitutional settlement in New South Wales which also envisaged secondary representation by way of municipal corporations.[30] At this time Buller was much under the influence of James Macarthur, the London representative for the New South Wales' exclusive faction. Macarthur played on the former's antipathy to convict transportation and influenced him against a directly elected legislature in New South Wales which would be dominated by the numerically superior emancipist group. Needless to say, the Australian Patriotic Association lost no time in rebuking Buller for his unbidden initiative.[31]

Although unpalatable to the people he was ostensibly representing, Buller's suggestions interested Lord Howick who warned that complete control over the purse would have to be withheld from any representative assembly established in New South Wales. Howick believed that Australia's distance from the mother country was a serious impediment to constitutional advance. To allow colonial assemblies in such far off places to exercise a substantial control over finances would amount to a *de facto* grant of independence. In a conflict with the local legislatures, Australia's remoteness would effectively preclude the metropolitan power from rendering forceful support to the executive authorities. Distance would materially reinforce the real power which representative bodies would wield in Australia. Howick therefore concluded that management of the purse would make a representative assembly in Australia 'as completely the supreme authority in the colony as the House of Commons in this country'.[32]

Howick had his own distinctive ideas concerning the best method of handling the constitutional problems of New South Wales, and in many ways they foreshadowed the unworkable settlement that he and Stephen were to impose upon New Zealand in 1846.[33] Financial considerations featured prominently in Howick's scheme for New South Wales. Six municipal councils were to be set up and given power to levy local rates thus ensuring that taxation did not become a responsibility of the central colonial assembly. Members of the assembly were to be elected by the councillors, and the assembly would have no power to appropriate money. On matters of finance it would be restricted to making recommendations which the governor would be under no obligation to accept.[34]

British preoccupation with indirect representative government for New South Wales which all these schemes embodied, also seems to have reflected a desire to keep a suspect population as far removed from the exercise of political power as was possible. Even the contemplation of direct elections for a legislative assembly in New South Wales made Howick uneasy. He and Stephen felt that in New South Wales a strong case could be presented to justify the modification of British practice and precedent to harmonize with colonial conditions. Howick preferred good government from Britain to giving the colonists what they desired. Indeed, in 1839 he is reported to have supported a motion then before cabinet to abolish all the legislative assemblies in the West Indian colonies and replace them by direct crown colony government from Britain.[35] It is not surprising therefore to find him opposing two successive governors and the former chief justice of New South Wales who had pointed out that an assembly based on municipal government was unsuited to the needs of the colony and the desires of a majority of the colonists. In the face of colonial criticisms Englishmen persisted in advocating the bestowal of such unwelcomed institutions on the colony. The Australian Patriotic Association firmly rejected innovations like indirect representation and maintained that there was nothing in colonial society which would justify the adoption of so unusual a form of government.[36] When Russell undertook the task as colonial secretary of framing a bill for the government of New South Wales,[37] he does not appear to have shared the predilections of Stephen and Howick for imposing an unpopular form of government on the colonists. The bill of 1840, in line with the suggestions made by Governors Bourke and Gipps, provided for an increase in the existing legislative council to thirty-six members, two-thirds of whom were to be directly elected by the colonists. The franchise was set on a non-discriminatory property basis of freehold valued at £500 or rental of a dwelling worth £10 per annum. Subject to deductions for a civil list, the entire colonial revenue, with the exception of the proceeds of sales of crown-lands, was to be appropriated by ordinance of the governor with the advice and consent of the legislative council. This bill was never adequately debated, because the government withdrew the measure before the second reading on the plea that it was imperfect.[38]

Until Russell's bill came briefly before parliament, all the draft constitutions and administrative theorizing in Britain concerning a constitution for New South Wales had been the private occupation of a handful of influential men with direct interests in Australian affairs. But Russell had made the question public and some interested observers took the opportunity to propound their own solutions. In 1841 Henry Chapman, the colonial judge and long-standing resident of Canada, drew clear distinctions between the various Australian colonies and the degree of civil liberty which could with safety be offered to each. According to Chapman, the convict populations in New South Wales[39] and Van Diemen's Land presented an insuperable barrier to the grant of representative government. On the other hand, he did recognize that South Australia had a promise under the terms of the South Australian Act of 1834 that it would be granted an elective assembly when the population reached 50 000. 'The great Australian jails', he continued, 'will require checks upon the elective franchise which to the people of South Australia and New Zealand would be unnecessary and even insulting'.[40] Sir John Barrow voiced similar sentiments, and refused even to consider the possibility of representative government for New South Wales. Self-government might be acceptable in Canada, but 'The time is not come even for discussing *this* question as to Australia'.[41]

The prevalence of such opinions and the years of fruitless debate over a constitutional settlement for New South Wales indicate that many Englishmen both in government and out entertained doubts concerning the wisdom of conferring representative government upon a colony to which criminals were still being transported. The cessation of transportation to New South Wales in 1840 cleared the way for self-government there, but Van Diemen's Land was specifically excluded, as it had been in Russell's bill. 'The continuance of its character as a penal settlement', Russell informed Lieutenant-Governor Franklin, 'has rendered it inexpedient in the opinion of Her Majesty's Government to propose at present any material change in the institutions of the colony'.[42] This opinion was shared by the conservative Lord Stanley, whose comments in 1842 echoed those of his Whig predecessor in office

> The sole reason for which Her Majesty's Government have not felt justified in proposing to Parliament the extension to Van Diemen's Land of a similar form of Legislature [i.e. elective assembly] as in New South Wales is the incompatibility which they consider to exist between the grant of such a form of constitution and the continuance of transportation to the Colony.[43]

Accordingly, when Stanley introduced a bill into the House of Commons in May 1842 for the better government of New South Wales, its provisions were largely based on Russell's earlier measure[44] and it passed with little debate. A straight property franchise heralded the end of open conflict between exclusive and emancipist in New South Wales and met with Stanley's cautious approval, as did the prospect that emancipist influence would be progressively weakened: 'Looking at the great increase of the free population, and the cessation of transportation, Her Majesty's Government have not thought it necessary to introduce into the Act any exceptional provision in reference to emancipists'.[45]

Accordingly, after more than a decade of agitation in New South Wales, representative government was finally granted. Certain similarities can be discerned between the New South Wales Act of 1842 and the Canadian Act of 1840. Most strikingly, British distrust of colonial legislatures was indicated by provisions in both acts that certain specified sums—set out in detail in the schedules of the acts—were to be set apart from the colonies' consolidated revenues for the maintenance of various public services and the payment of official salaries. New South Wales received a legislative council of thirty-six members, one-third nominated by the crown and two-thirds elected on a highly restricted franchise. Six of the twenty-four elected members were to come from the Port Phillip district, from whence settlers had petitioned the imperial parliament for independence from New South Wales and the grant of a representative legislature of their own. Voters were limited to those possessing freehold property worth £200 or a rental of £20 per annum; and council members had to own freehold valued at £1000 or live in £100 per annum tenements. The legislative council was empowered to make laws for the colony and to appropriate all colonial revenues except that which colonists most wished to control, the income from sales of crown-land. In addition, an annual civil list of £81 600 was placed beyond the reach of the council. The governor no longer possessed a monopoly of the right to initiate legislation, though he alone could introduce finance bills. Finally, the act sought to give expression to British proclivities for municipal institutions, and contained provisions for an elaborate system of municipal local government through district councils.[46]

A crucial provision in the new act was the crown's retention of full control over the New South Wales' land fund. British management of the price and revenue of colonial waste lands had been a grievance of which the squatter-dominated legislative council in the colony had complained before 1842; it was destined to remain a bone of contention until the crown finally renounced such rights in 1852. Indeed, a major stimulus to constitutional agitation in New South Wales during the 1830s had been provided by the dissatisfaction felt by New South Wales' pastoralists with British land policy.[47] Since the new act did nothing to assuage colonial discontent in this vital area, it thereby ensured unflagging agitation throughout the 1840s from the united front of wealthy exclusives and emancipists. They made repeated attempts to exert financial and constitutional pressure on the executive officers in the colony in an endeavour to force the British authorities into relinquishing imperial control over crown-lands. The imperial government remained adamant. In 1840 a Colonial Land and Emigration Commission had been established to manage these related spheres of activity and to promote uniformity of practice throughout the Australian colonies. In 1842, in the interests of administrative regularity, Stanley accompanied the Constitutional Act by a companion measure designed to standardize crown-land administration throughout Australia, and set a uniform price of £1 an acre on all crown-land on the continent.[48]

In the course of this general review, South Australia also received a constitutional regeneration in June 1842 when Stanley introduced into parliament a bill for the better government of the colony. In effect, Stanley was mounting a rescue operation. South Australia had gone bankrupt; and following the recommendation of the select committee on South Australia in the previous year,[49] this act vested authority in the governor and a nominated legislative council of not less than seven members. The earlier promise of a legislative assembly when the population reached 50 000 was withdrawn. The crown now reserved the right to introduce an elective assembly at a time considered propitious, and, when that moment came, to deduct a civil list from the colony's revenues and place it beyond the jurisdiction of the legislature.[50] Colonists were informed that further constitutional advance was conditional upon fiscal recovery and the provision of an annual revenue sufficient to meet the civil list,[51] and many settlers resented the implication that representative institutions had to be paid for.[52]

While Van Diemen's Land was automatically excluded from constitutional change in 1842 because it continued to function as a convict repository, Western Australia was also denied representative government due to a paucity of population and revenue. There were less than 5000 settlers in Western Australia in 1842, nowhere near the target of 50 000 which had previously been considered an essential prerequisite for representative institutions in South Australia. Moreover, Western Australia's land revenues were practically non-existent.[53] Receipts from colonial revenues in Western Australia were so low that government functionaries were paid their salaries from British parliamentary grants until well into the 1860s.[54] Such problems, however, had not inhibited enthusiasm for representative government from surfacing in the colony, and settlers claimed that they were being subjected to taxation without representation.[55] Despite an apparently deliberate attempt to play upon British fears by echoing the rebellious American colonies of 1774, Western Australia was not considered eligible for even minor constitutional adjustment until 1868. The fact that between 1849 and 1867 the colony was a regularly constituted penal settlement strongly reinforced the economic arguments against the conferral of representative institutions.

As these discussions indicate, the irascible Stanley was always resolute and often insensitive and tactless in his enunciation of colonial policy or in his dealings with troublesome colonists. In 1843 the newly-elected legislative council in New South Wales met for the first time at the height of a severe economic depression, and immediately sought to relieve the colony's financial burdens and assert itself against the metropolitan power by affirming that the financial responsibility for the maintenance of prisons and prison staff in New South Wales belonged to the British Treasury and should not be charged to the colony's land fund.[56] This attempt to assert colonial control over crown-lands' revenue was vigorously rejected, though on this occasion Stanley was understanding and conciliatory, if a trifle patronizing:

> Meeting as they did for the first time with no practical experience of the inconvenience of insisting on extreme rights and doubtful claims a large allowance is due for any such indiscretion brought together as they were under circumstances of widespread and urgent distress among their constituents it is no matter of great surprise that their zeal for retrenchment of public Expenditure may have given birth to demands against the British Treasury and in aid of the Local revenue to which the confidential Advisers of the Crown cannot accede.[57]

Similar complaints emanated from Western Australia and Van Diemen's Land during these years and the related areas of imperial land policy and control over colonial revenue proved to be a fertile breeding-ground for local protest in the colonies and provided Colonial Office administrators with a series of intractable and controversial problems throughout the 1840s.[58]   Conflict between the legislative council and the governor in New South Wales continued, as the pastoralists who dominated the council attempted to force the executive authorities into financial dependence on the legislature. The schedules to the 1842 Act, however, guaranteed sufficient funds to make this impossible. Alienation between the executive and the legislature was increased in 1844 when the council rejected the governor's proposed reorganization of crown-lands' administration.[59] Stanley was sufficiently displeased to refer ominously to the council as an 'experiment', and to complain that it showed a 'restless and innovating Spirit' in attempting 'to assert and exercise powers expressly withholden from that body by the Act of Parliament under which they [sic] sit.[60]

Stanley became even more irate in December 1844 when the 'experiment' petitioned the Queen that the government of New South Wales 'be conducted on the same principle of responsibility as to Legislative Control which has been conceded in the United Canadas'; and also requested that a tribunal of impeachment be set up in the colony.[61] Stanley's reply was typical of British views at this time, and he refused to admit that Canada created a precedent for New South Wales, or that the settlement in North America embodied principles which were valid for other parts of the empire:

> In Canada Her Majesty has commanded Her Representative to conduct the administration of the local Government in strict accordance with the terms and the spirit of the Statute by which the Provincial Legislature is constituted. In New South Wales Her Majesty had commanded you to conduct the Administration of that Government in strict accordance with the terms and the spirit of the Statute by which the Legislature in New South Wales is constituted. In neither case has the Queen entered into any statement of any theory or abstract principles of Colonial Government; nor is Her Majesty advised that to discuss such theories, or to propound such abstract principles, forms any branch of the duties which the Laws and Constitution of the British Empire call on Her to discharge.[62]

Stanley, in this instance put the claims of practical experience above those of constitutional theory and despite the blueprints and tinkering of men like Howick, Stephen and Buller, insisted that abstract principles of government had no relevance to the day to day affairs of imperial administration. This was an outlook shared by Russell, his Whig predecessor in office, and there was much in common between

Russell's attitude during the debates of 1839 and 1840 on a political settlement for Canada, and Stanley's reaction to protests and appeals to general maxims of government from New South Wales in 1843.[63]

Here the matter lay for the moment, until the Whigs returned to office in 1846 and Grey became Secretary of State for War and Colonies. Unlike Stanley and former colonial secretaries, Grey revelled in abstract theories and their application to colonies. He imposed a constitution involving indirect election on New Zealand that same year, and in 1847 gave notice that he intended to extend a similar constitution to New South Wales. He planned to establish Port Phillip as a separate colony and to revivify the moribund municipal corporations established on paper by the act of 1842. Under his scheme the corporations would elect representatives to a legislative assembly, the lower house of a bicameral constitution. There was a further component to his delight in the consideration of such hypothetical speculations, for Grey also aspired to federate the colonies in Australia. To this end he suggested that the same form of government with which he proposed to endow New South Wales might be extended to the other colonies at the antipodes, thereby creating constitutional machinery which would enable them 'to cooperate with each other' and regulate their common interests through membership of 'a central Legislative authority for the whole of the Australian Colonies'. Grey expected colonial reactions to his scheme to be favourable, and he assumed that he would soon be 'in the possession of the most complete local intelligence, and supported by the opinion of the most eminent local authorities'.[64]

Although Grey hoped to gain colonial support for his project, scholars have noted that his proposals bore very little relation to demands for constitutional reform made in the colony or to suggestions put forward by successive governors in their dispatches.[65] But Grey tended to distrust governors' opinions which did not coincide with his own prejudices, and to claim that governors were too prone to local influences. In 1832 he told Spring Rice that 'Governors as you know are apt to take their notions too much from those about them'.[66] This predisposition, when allied to a paternalist attitude towards colonial administration, left Grey open to the criticism that he was an autocratic doctrinaire, prepared to ride roughshod over colonial opinion in order to see his own peculiar theories implemented.

Unfavourable reaction was by no means limited to Australia. In 1847 and 1848, even before Grey heard of the widespread discontent caused in New South Wales by his attempt to impose so unpopular a form of government on the territory, British critics savagely attacked the imperial government for indulging in abstract theorizing when legislating for the colonies, and for paying insufficient attention to colonial realities when it contemplated legislation for New South Wales. Observers pointed out that colonial conditions and opinions did not favour the creation of district councils as envisaged in the act of 1842; the settlers 'could neither *be bothered* with them to the neglect of their affairs, nor could they stand the local taxation with which they threatened them'. On the other hand, 'they liked a voice in their general legislature at the seat of government'. Commentators expressed no objection to local municipalities as such, but the British government was in error when it sought to impose this mode of organization on underpopulated districts whose few inhabitants were opposed to the plan.[67]

During the period covered by this study Englishmen tended to regard New South Wales as synonymous with Australia, and as a general rule British response to claims of injustice and constitutional agitation in the smaller Australian colonies was submerged in reaction to events in the oldest colony, but occasionally restlessness in the other Australian settlements provoked attention. In March 1848, for example, *Fraser's Magazine* descanted on Western Australia. It argued that the free society of Western Australia was unfitted for self-government because of its immaturity and because its populace came predominantly from the lower orders in Britain. 'What', the magazine asked rhetorically, 'can societies like that in Western Australia do with self-government except abuse it?' The journal amplified its disparagement of immature societies in Australia by denying that even the governor and a nominated legislative council were competent for legislative activity:

> The Governor, with his council, though they should in no case be authorised to make new laws, may surely be left to administer the laws which exist with a wide margin; but to commit to them, much more to a rabble which shall be dignified with the appellation of a Legislative Assembly, prerogatives more extensive than any which the British Parliament itself can claim, is surely monstrous.

Resentment was expressed that Western Australia, 'the very feeblest of our settlements' had already begun to talk of its rights, and the magazine expected before the passage of many years to see New South Wales asserting these same rights 'by separating altogether from the mother country and becoming a humble imitation of the United States of America'.[68] In a further discussion entitled 'Australian Colonies or Republics?', *Fraser's Magazine for Town and Country* accused the colonial populations of New South Wales and the other Australian colonies of contemplating an appeal to Holland for a number of Dutch regiments to aid an attempt to throw off allegiance to Britain and take control of the continent.[69] Journalism of this type in reply to a colonial demand for 'rights' is surely an indication of the degree to which Britain's unfortunate American experience almost a century earlier still coloured British attitudes to empire.

Opinion in the mother country that colonists planned a forcible overthrow of the British yoke probably resulted from taking the extreme rhetoric used in New South Wales at its face value. During 1848 antagonism to Grey's proposed constitutional settlement had been expressed with a great deal of colourful invective throughout New South Wales. At a public meeting in Sydney colonists had listened appreciatively to speeches which described the £81 600 civil list as taxation without representation, and referred to Grey's attempt to force a constitution on the colony which involved indirect election as a 'damning proof of Colonial Office tyranny'.[70] The legislative council echoed these sentiments and Governor Fitzroy advised Grey that if he persisted with his proposals for a new constitution with indirect election he 'would excite throughout the colony a resistance which would in all probability render it inoperative', while it could not fail to create a degree of ill feeling towards the imperial government which would not easily be allayed.[71]

Earl Grey was an obstinate but not a foolhardy man. In the face of New South Wales's antipathy to indirect election, and perhaps because a similar constitutional settlement had failed in New Zealand, Grey backed down. He informed Fitzroy that although he still believed such a reorganization would greatly benefit New South Wales, he would not impose his design on an unwilling population.

> But I can have no wish to impose upon the inhabitants of the Colony a form of Government not in their judgment suited to their wants and to which they generally object, and shall therefore not think it necessary to advise the carrying of this proposal into execution.[72]

Grey intended therefore to introduce a bill into parliament which would separate the Port Phillip district from New South Wales and allow it a mixed legislative council similar to that in New South Wales. The same concession would be extended to Van Diemen's Land and South Australia. Colonial legislatures in these four colonies would be empowered to originate and discuss alterations to their constitutions subject to confirmation by the Queen in Council, though Grey, an ardent free-trader,[73] hastened to warn that the imperial government would not permit the establishment of differential customs and tariffs that would interfere with intercolonial trade.[74]

But this dispatch was noteworthy for other reasons: it indicated that Grey had reversed the policy enunciated by Stanley in 1842: the British government no longer believed that representative assemblies were incompatible with continuing convict transportation. It was convenient for Britain to expatriate her criminals to Australia, however, and for this reason Grey seems to have been prepared to override both colonial opinion and considerations of long-term colonial welfare in order that Britain might take advantage of an opportunity to rid herself of her undesirables. In the event, Grey's attempts between 1847 and 1852 to impose his will on the colonies over the matter of transportation led opponents of the system in the colonies to view representative government as a necessary protection against the autocracy of British colonial secretaries who had manifestly placed Britain's interests above those of her colonies in their scale of priorities. The result in Australia of the association of important areas of imperial statecraft like land policy and convict transportation with the narrower questions of constitutional settlement was to lend an added stridency to colonial demands for self-government which led the *Times* to comment gloomily:

> We are ready to grant that our new colonies are better and more British than our old ones, and that we have profited somewhat by our American experience. But we cannot divest ourselves of the thought that Australasia will one day be the seat of a vast federal union, independent of this realm, possibly hostile to this nation, and exhibiting in the great southern archipelago a maritime variety of the American character and species. To look forward at all is to despair of an agreeable or honourable result.[75]

The American model, however, did not strike every British observer as inappropriate. Grey's provision in the constitution of 1847 for a federation of the Australian colonies has been attributed by some recent writers to the influence of United States' political institutions as described by Alexis de Tocqueville in *Democracy in America* (1835).[76] Grey was a Whig not a radical, and his desire to federate the Australian colonies was a pragmatic measure to ensure uniform tariffs and to provide a basis for colonial co-operation in areas of common interest. It did not imply an ideological commitment to the political values enshrined in the United States' constitution. On the other hand, radicals who wished to preserve the empire were attracted to and inspired by the constitutional arrangements in the United States of America. They felt that Britain could learn some profitable lessons for imperial reorganization from the American experience in designing an administrative model which encompassed within a vast territory a strong central authority and constituent states enjoying local self-government. They suggested that forms of government in the settlement colonies should be recast in order to allow imperial relations with them to be restructured in the American manner.[77]

While the organic nature of United States' institutions and the democratic form of American government were admired by British radicals, most Britons from the governing classes remained opposed to manhood suffrage or even an enlarged franchise in domestic and colonial politics. Nevertheless, all shades of British political opinion had conceded that government ought to be predicated on the consent of the governed. The situation in Australia made this difficult. The New South Wales' legislative council was the only representative assembly in Australia and it was elected on a very limited franchise. How then was the British government to discern what the Australian settlers really wanted?

While Grey was not especially interested in giving the settlers what they desired, he was sufficiently astute a politician to seek wider support for his own particular theories concerning the type of constitution best suited to Australia. To this end, in 1848 he secured the appointment of a committee of the Privy Council for Trade and Plantations to report on the constitutional position of the Australian colonies.[78] Although the committee's findings predictably supported the proposals made by Grey, superficial appearances of unity were deceptive.[79] In fact there had been considerable debate between James Stephen and Herman Merivale over the form of constitutions to be granted to Australia, and the draft reports of both men show that Grey's federation proposals were a major area of disagreement.

In a rough synopsis submitted to Grey in February 1849, Stephen recommended that a general assembly of Australia should be constituted to handle matters of common interest, and that one of the governors should be elevated to the rank of governor-general with powers to convene this assembly composed of members elected by the various colonial legislatures. Stephen's report also made it plain that self-government had to be paid for. Western Australia should not be included at this time because, in contrast to the other Australian settlements, its colonists still were incapable of sustaining 'the whole expense of their own civil government'. The draft also affords further concrete proof of a common British tendency to judge all the Australian colonies by what was known of New South Wales. Since public opinion in New South Wales had expressed itself in favour of a unicameral legislature, Stephen concluded that all the other Australian colonies would want the same: 'For although it is not actually known, it may reasonably be presumed that on such a subject as this the state of public opinion is the same throughout all the Australian colonies'.[80]

Grey appears to have passed the draft on to Merivale who appended his comments in March 1849. Merivale's outlook was similar to that enunciated by the *Times* the previous January. He expected that 'the

great Australian Republic' would eventually break the British connection, but this would not happen in the immediate future unless the
imperial government persisted with the plan to legislate for a general
assembly in Australia. Merivale felt that such a body would attempt to
imitate Frankfurt or Washington; and that if Britain persevered in this
matter it would amount to a premature 'infliction of political agitation'
on the Australian colonies, and greatly accelerate the final severing of
the nexus between Britain and her antipodean settlements.[81] He did,
however, advance other more substantial practical arguments against
the proposed general assembly when he referred to the problem of
venue and the huge distances between Sydney and the other colonies.
Who would be delegates for the other colonies at Sydney, when so
much time would be taken up by travelling and the transactions of the
general assembly that there would be no time for the conduct of private
business? Merivale foresaw that the inevitable result would be the
payment of salaries to members of the central legislature and this, he
felt, would attract 'that class which lives by political agitation . . . and
it is a class I think there is little reason for encouraging'.[82] The most
weighty reason put forward by supporters of an Australian federation
was that a general assembly would ensure uniformity of customs and
tariffs, thereby facilitating intercolonial trade. Merivale attempted to
diminish the impact of what was a powerful theoretical argument only
two years after Britain herself had embraced free trade. He took the
short-term view and maintained that there was not enough local trade
to warrant such complicated constitutional machinery. According to
Merivale, the colonies all produced the same staples and exported
them to Britain rather than to one another. Furthermore, he was
unconcerned over the prospect of differential tariffs between the Australian colonies because he claimed they could never adequately be
enforced on the long uninhabited colonial frontiers.[83]

In the event, Merivale was overruled and the committee's report
favoured a federation of the Australian colonies, uniform tariffs, the
extension of representative government as established in New South
Wales to Port Phillip, Van Diemen's Land and South Australia, as
well as the endowment of the representative legislative councils in
Australia with the power of constitutional amendment subject to the
royal veto. A bill was quickly prepared for presentation to parliament
which incorporated these suggestions, though the recommendation in
favour of uniform tariffs was abandoned in favour of a provision which
forbade the introduction of differential tariffs but permitted the colonies to set their own tariffs within that restriction.[84]

It soon became obvious that this major bill, unlike Stanley's
measure in 1842, would provoke considerable public debate. Even
before it reached parliament critics initiated discussion by cautioning

the imperial government to proceed with circumspection and to remember that the populations of New South Wales and Van Diemen's Land were criminally tainted. The degree of self-government granted to the Australian settlements would need to be sharply limited—in short, representative government without ministerial responsibility. To illustrate this argument, the *Times* drew a parallel between self-government for colonies and municipal government in Manchester or Birmingham. These two cities assessed their own local taxation for municipal objects, but for all national purposes were subject to the central executive and the British parliament. In the same way, the paper claimed, 'New South Wales, South Australia, Prince Edward's Island and Newfoundland might administer their own local government and assess their own local taxes, subject to certain definite rules and limitations of the Imperial Parliament'.[85]

When the bill was submitted to parliament in June 1849, it generated considerable debate. Grey had underestimated the degree of interest the measure would create, and the discussion was so critical that he was persuaded to withdraw it for resubmission the following year. Widespread suspicion also existed concerning Grey's motives for bringing the bill forward so late in the parliamentary session, and he was reprimanded by some newspapers for trying to ram it through parliament with little or no debate.[86] The time had finally passed when major alterations in the constitutional affairs of the colonies of settlement in Australia could be effected by the exercise of prescriptive authority by a secretary of state in Britain.

4: Constitutional Advance II 1850–55

Earl Grey had discovered to his surprise in 1849 that colonial affairs could no longer be handled secretively, and it is illuminating to note the extent of public interest in the antipodean colonies prior to the enormous publicity generated by the gold discoveries a few years later. Moreover, the Russell government's hold on power between 1846 and 1852 was tenuous indeed, and the administration could not have survived in parliament without the support of either Sir Robert Peel and his followers or the radicals.[1] Throughout this period opponents of the government tended to debate colonial questions with party political advantage foremost in mind rather than on their own intrinsic merits.[2] This fact alone ensured that Grey's Australian proposals would receive close critical attention. At the same time, the 1830s and 1840s had been decades in which a significant revival of public as well as parliamentary interest in colonial affairs had taken place in Britain. During these years large numbers of British emigrants left the mother country and settled in various parts of the empire. Controversies over slavery and the Canadian rebellions produced parliamentary repercussions in Britain, as did the frequent complaints of the advocates of retrenchment who denounced the financial burdens of empire. Furthermore, the long debate preceding the repeal of the Navigation Acts and the end of preferential imperial tariffs had accustomed Englishmen to thinking of the problems of individual colonies in a wider and more abstract imperial context.

This tendency was observable in contemporary discussions in many newspapers and journals of opinion. Both the *Examiner* and the *Times* wholeheartedly supported the Australian bill. The former appeared to have learnt nothing from the Canadian rebellions and the Durham Report and seemed a somewhat old-fashioned paper expressing views more typical in outlook of the 1830s and early 1840s than of 1849. The *Examiner* equated self-government with independence and believed that if colonies were self-supporting they ought to be self-governing. The newspaper, however, was obviously referring to a degree of self-government far greater than that offered by Grey's bill, since it proclaimed a desire to sever all constitutional links between Australia and the mother country and to replace them with a more informal connection based on the common heritage of a mutual language, literature, trade and affection.[3] The *Times*, on the other hand, was more flexible and supported the settlement as outlined in Grey's bill. The paper stated its opinion that physical conditions in Australia ideally suited a confederation of the colonies there, and made the startling discovery that there was no intercolonial jealousy between one Australian colony and another.[4] This was a misunderstanding of quite major proportions. In fact a tariff war between New South Wales and Van Diemen's Land had lasted throughout the 1840s and was one of the contributing reasons for the proposal to establish a central legislature to set uniform tariffs throughout the Australian colonies.[5] Moreover, the bill contained provision for separating Port Phillip from New South Wales precisely because the two areas had proved unable to coexist amicably within the one governmental structure. Nevertheless, the *Times* believed that the principles enshrined in Grey's bill were 'those which liberty sanctions and experience approves'.[6]

Such approval was the very opposite of the sentiments espoused by the *Spectator* which generally reflected the views of the colonial reformers and took a far more critical line. It favoured the grant of representative government to the Australian colonies and defined what was envisaged by drawing a parallel between municipal government in Britain and self-government overseas. Grey's bill was criticized because it did not distinguish adequately between imperial and colonial spheres of competence, nor did it protect the colonies sufficiently from officious interference by the Colonial Office. The paper also indicated that some of the colonial reformers were aristocrats *manqué* when it supported bicameral legislatures for Australia and claimed that these would attract scions from British aristocratic families in sufficient numbers to fill the colonial upper houses.[7] Such a suggestion that branches from Britain's noble families be transplanted to provide members for upper houses in the Australian colonies was decisively rejected by other contemporaries like the propagandist Samuel Sidney:[8]

> I am no admirer of republican institutions for British colonies. An aristocracy, that is to say, a refined educated class, would be an undoubted advantage among a British race, instead of the mere Plutocracy, or the plated imitations of nobility, who condescend,

while enjoying colonial salaries, to bestow their tedious insolence on the natives; but such an aristocracy can neither be created by backstairs intrigues with a governor, nor transplanted from England helpless in ignorance. It must be grown in the soil. In the meantime the best aristocracy would be an aristocracy of education.[9]

Discussion progressed from such general matters of principle to specific proposals contained in Grey's bill when it was reintroduced into parliament during February 1850, and from the beginning debate was spirited. Colonial reformers, Sir William Molesworth and John Roebuck, even found fault with the form of the bill. Its preamble listed existing legislation bearing upon the constitution of New South Wales, with the purpose of indicating that this legislation was not to be repealed but merely amended by the enactments which followed. As followers of the utilitarian philosopher, Jeremy Bentham, colonial reformers like Roebuck and Molesworth preferred to strip away irrelevant complications and reduce problems to their ultimate simplicity.[10] They insisted that all constitutional legislation affecting the Australian colonies should be repealed, thus enabling the problem to be tackled from fundamental first principles.[11] Molesworth even suggested that a convention should be called in the colonies to voice the real aspirations of the colonists,[12] and he denounced administration by the Colonial Office as 'government by the misinformed with responsibility to the ignorant'.[13] In reply, under-secretary Henry Labouchere maintained that the government did not intend to draw up a new constitution for New South Wales and the rest of Australia, but merely to confirm and extend the constitution to which the colonists were already accustomed.[14]

While initial British reactions to the debates were mixed, the general feeling emerged that the bill was timely and that some form of settlement was long overdue.[15] Such sentiments were not unanimous, however, although the ultra-Tory *Standard* was quite out of step, even with prevailing conservative sentiment, when it predicted disaster from any attempt to impose on the Australian colonies governmental institutions modelled on those of the mother country. British institutions were admirable at home, but overseas colonial populations consisted of an unpromising mixture of deported paupers, decayed tradesmen, impoverished gentry, and land speculators. As a result of the manifest inferiority of society in Australia the colonial populace could not be expected to handle its affairs with the requisite degree of common sense and level-headedness necessary to make the British system of government work. The paper favoured the exercise of prescriptive authority in Australia until emigration from Britain had improved the colonial stock. To initiate constitutional alterations in the present situation could only end in democracy and the triumph of popular rights. In any case, new constitutions should be withheld until colonial populations had greatly increased in numbers, because representative government at Australia's present state of development would mean the election of delegates to represent nothing more than 'a few square miles of desert'.[16]

The debate, both in parliament and out, revolved around a small number of constitutional points. The main concern was whether the new legislatures in Australia should be unicameral or bicameral, and whether nominated members were acceptable in either case.[17] The government argued that the blended council of nominees and elected members on the model of New South Wales would be both familiar and acceptable to the colonists.[18] Opponents of the bill denied that such was the case, and that even if it were true of New South Wales, insufficient pretext existed for extending equivalent arrangements to the other colonies.[19] The *Times* plumped pragmatically for unicameral legislatures since New South Wales already had such a system and it appeared to work reasonably well. The paper supported the continuance of nominees in the legislatures for the same reason.[20] The *Times* also echoed the government's position when it pointed out that under the provisions of the bill the colonies could draw up any form of constitution they chose, and if they preferred bicameral legislatures they could easily secure them. C. B. Adderley, the founder of the Colonial Reform Society, cautioned the House of Commons, however, that the much-vaunted permissiveness of the bill was misleading because the Colonial Office would retain over-all control through the provision 'which reserved a veto to the Crown'.[21]

Both William Gladstone and the conservative parliamentarian and future home secretary, Spencer Walpole, favoured bicameral legislatures, though the former believed that both chambers should be elected, where as the latter proposed a nominated upper house, the members of which would hold their seats twice as long as elected representatives in the lower body.[22] Paul Knaplund argued that Gladstone developed an increasingly liberal attitude towards colonial administration as the range and depth of his experience broadened.[23] During the years of the Canadian crisis between 1835 and 1840 he had favoured nominated upper houses for colonial legislatures, but by 1850 he had changed his mind. He now regarded nominated bodies as divisive elements because they established a *de facto* British or Loyalist party which opposed the wishes of the general populace. If both houses were elective, the mother country would avoid this pitfall and 'make the whole colony a British party'.[24] Other speakers endorsed Gladstone's stand. Francis Scott, the parliamentary agent for the New

South Wales' legislative council, took the popular view in the colonies when he also favoured a bicameral legislature without nominees.[25] Roebuck and Molesworth both attacked the nominee system as a thinly disguised method of retaining power in the hands of a privileged few.[26] To all criticisms, however, the government replied that the bill was permissive, and that if the colonists sincerely wished to modify the existing system, they would have the machinery ready at hand to undertake the task.[27]

Arguments in favour of a bicameral legislature were generally popular amongst Englishmen because they were based on an appreciation of Britain's own system of government and a sincere wish to extend the benefits of the British constitution to Australia. 'The colonies do not want Whig government or Tory government. They want a constitution upon the English model, in which their own political factions—Whig, Tory, and Radical—may fight their own battles in their own way, as we do in this country'.[28] While the appeal to British precedent and practice was common, the debate produced an interesting confrontation between Tory traditionalists and those Whig and radical reformers who favoured imaginative innovation. Parliamentary liberals like Roebuck and Molesworth, who argued in support of bicameral legislatures with upper houses elected on a restricted franchise, were seeking to protect the position of their own class in the colonies against advancing democracy on one side and an incipient squatter aristocracy on the other. They maintained that a second chamber was necessary to guard against democractic legislation from the lower house, and that a restricted franchise would ensure a meritocracy of equal opportunity and ability which would particularly favour the professional and mercantile classes. On the other hand, parliamentary conservatives like Spencer Walpole or William Gladstone, who favoured bicameralism sought to approximate colonial government as closely as possible to the British model. Britain's institutions were the embodiment of centuries of slow evolution and embalmed the knowledge and experience of the race. Consequently, they could not be significantly improved upon, and the mother country could do no better than to preserve and reproduce traditional forms of government in Australia.

Only slightly less controversial was the bill's provision for the establishment of a general assembly of the Australian colonies. On a practical level, Russell explained that such a body was needed to ensure uniform tariffs between the various colonies and prevent widespread smuggling.[29] Grey, on the other hand, while not discounting arguments that federation would bring important utilitarian benefits, sought a nobler vision. He was very conscious that in federating the

Australian colonies he would be creating a new nation of Englishmen at the antipodes:

> that if these clauses were adopted, they might not make any extensive or very important alteration in the first instance, but they would be the beginning of a system which would swell and develop itself with the growing wants of these colonies, and tend to bind them into one great nation, intimately and closely connected with this, and subjects of the British Crown.[30]

Grey's theoretical abstractions on the principles of empire-building do not appear to have carried much weight with his parliamentary colleagues, and members who supported the federal proposals generally did so because of the immediate practical advantages which might be gained. The ministry itself was prepared to avoid an inconvenient source of colonial discontent and to meet pastoralists' demands for control over the waste lands of Australia by vesting such authority in a federal assembly. This would have eliminated a major source of friction which had impaired relations between Britain and the Australian colonies for nearly two decades. One reason for the refusal to allow individual colonial legislatures to control their own crown-lands had been the fear that intercolonial competition to attract immigrants would lead to reduced prices for all waste lands and to a consequent diminution in the total amount of money available to pay for British emigration. Since uniform control would preclude such a possibility, however, the imperial government was willing to permit the central legislature to administer the waste lands of the entire continent on a non-differential basis.[31]

In general, the federal proposals were not welcomed. Molesworth shared Merivale's earlier fear that a federal assembly in Australia could lead to separation from the mother country;[32] an attitude also endorsed by Vernon Smith, a former Whig under-secretary at the Colonial Office in Russell's time, who professed to find the federal principles 'republican'.[33] It was a perplexing question of constitutional theory: even the colonial reformers disagreed. Roebuck, a former parliamentary agent for the house of assembly of Lower Canada, was so enthusiastic a proponent of federation that he urged that an amendment be tacked onto the Australian bill which would extend the right of federation to all the British colonies in North America.[34] More realistically, he also advocated the establishment of some sort of Supreme Court to settle 'matters of dispute arising between the different colonies'.[35]

Roebuck's enthusiasm did not prove contagious, and the general consensus in the press mirrored parliamentary opposition to the federal sections of Grey's bill.[36] *Fraser's Magazine for Town and*

Country expressed the common and ultimately prevailing view when it criticized the bill for containing federal proposals that were unduly weighted in favour of New South Wales which, due to its large population, would enjoy a preponderating majority in any federal assembly. The magazine emphasized that this favoured position would be reinforced by a provision stipulating that in areas where federal and provincial legislation conflicted federal laws would prevail. In such circumstances the other colonies seemed 'to gain very little from federation and lose a great deal to New South Wales'. The government's intention of surrendering control over Australian waste lands to the general assembly was roundly denounced as a bribe to encourage colonial acceptance of the federation proposals. Despite the high level of parliamentary interest in the bill, the journal depicted the climate of contemporary opinion as one of 'sad indifference to colonial politics' and called upon the 'really honest Colonial Reformers' to defeat the confederation proposals and thereby save Australia from proceeding along the same republican road as the United States of America.[37]

With the widespread lack of concern about, and some hostility towards, the federation clauses in Australia, Grey was unable to appeal to domestic enthusiasm to counterbalance hostility to his proposals when he had to defend them in parliament.[38] The general feeling of the House of Lords seems to have been that in the light of colonial indifference Grey's plan to federate the Australian colonies was premature. The government's majority in the Lords was reduced to one on a motion of Stanley's that the federation clauses be expunged from the bill,[39] and rather than endanger his measure Grey agreed to withdraw the troublesome sections. He claimed to have been motivated in part by doubts raised in his own mind by the barrage of opposition and by arguments in the House that many defects existed in the proposed machinery which would have prevented the federal sections of the bill from coming into practical operation. He now concluded that 'as the clauses stood they would have been a dead letter'.[40] Even in defeat, Grey refused to acknowledge that colonial opinion in Australia influenced his change of mind, yet one of the main arguments used by critics against this portion of the bill was its failure to reflect the aspirations of any significant section of the Australian populace. Grey's arrogant paternalism had in this instance led him into flagrant violation of the consultative principle upon which Britain's colonial administration of settlement colonies was properly based. In this matter he had failed to obtain the consent of the governed to a major constitutional alteration, and his parliamentary colleagues were unwilling to support an attempt to impose on Australians an unwanted form of government.

The idea that colonial consent was necessary to legitimize British administration received a somewhat different application when *Fraser's Magazine* again discussed the bill. On this occasion it was the bill's failure to include Western Australia amongst the beneficiaries which brought charges of misgovernment. The magazine launched a major attack on the imperial authorities and charged them with denying 'constitutional government' to Western Australia, and of indulging in gross economic exploitation by placing a monetary price on constitutional concessions:

> The even partially free institutions which the other communities are to enjoy are to be withheld from Western Australia, until the present civil list is guaranteed out of the colonial revenues. It is argued, that until the colony can support her own government she ought not to govern herself. England, it is said, pays so much towards the government of the colony, and has, therefore, a right to govern it. The mother-country ought to get something for her money, so she takes out the change in despotism.[41]

This attitude was described as a trampling under foot of all the most cherished notions of constitutional right. According to the journal, the main object of free institutions was to maintain a check upon administrative expenditure and to ensure that public money was not paid out to sinecure offices or incompetent officials. But in the case of Western Australia, the imperial government had dictated the size of the colony's governmental establishment and its salary levels and was holding the dependency to ransom until it could guarantee the full sum.[42]

The question of a financial price for constitutional concessions was also raised by Molesworth in parliament. The draft bill contained financial schedules which placed the civil lists byond the control of the colonial legislative councils, and Molesworth argued that this was inconsistent with the government's avowals that colonists in Australia should control their own government. Such inconsistency also extended to the retention of the royal veto over colonial legislation and other powers of a similar nature. Accordingly, he moved a major amendment to disallow all sections of the bill which empowered the Colonial Office to reject colonial legislation, force renewal of existing colonial acts, or instruct colonial governors.[43] The speech received little support, however, and the amendment was lost.

Nevertheless, Molesworth had raised an important point when he referred to colonists controlling their own government, and it was with the intention of increasing this control that the House of Lords altered the electoral franchises contained in the bill, and applied the more liberal enactment to South Australia, Victoria, and Van Diemen's Land as well as to New South Wales. The government accepted an amendment which halved the existing qualifications in New South Wales and extended the right to vote to all who owned freehold worth £10 per annum. Originally the bill had proposed to continue the existing franchise regulations in New South Wales, and to give the various colonial legislative councils the power to adopt more liberal qualifications if they thought them necessary. It was realized in Britain, however, that the legislature in New South Wales was unrepresentative and dominated by wealthy pastoral interests; and it was felt that bodies so constituted would seek to perpetuate the power of their controlling interests by denying liberal franchises to their fellow colonists.[44] In every colony, the newly-elected councils were authorized to alter these arrangements should they think fit, and to draw up their own electoral boundaries.[45] This was a noteworthy provision because the *Times* was later to accuse the legislative council in New South Wales of gerrymandering the electorates in favour of the proprietors and squatting interests.[46]

The act for the better government of the Australian colonies received the royal assent on 5 August 1850 and was forwarded to the colonies later that month. Though it received a favourable welcome in the other colonies, the measure did very little to redress the grievances of that small class of wealthy settlers which exercised political power in New South Wales. The franchise had been lowered, which they had not requested: they had desired to control the crown-lands and the revenues therefrom, and these remained under imperial administration; they had hoped to ensure that the governor and his executive would be at least partially responsible to the legislative council, yet the independent position of the governor and his executive council vis-à-vis the colonial legislature remained unchanged. Earl Grey justified this lack of initiative by stating that the imperial government believed that it was not parliament's job to make constitutional alterations in Australia, but rather to transmit powers whereby needed changes could be enacted locally.[47]

The resentment of New South Wales' pastoralists was expressed in two remonstrances which affirmed their 'deep disappointment and dissatisfaction' with the new constitution, declared that the reasonable expectations of the legislative council had been 'utterly frustrated', and petitioned the British authorities to surrender the management of all revenues, restrict recruitment for local administrative posts to local settlers, and allow a constitution similar to that enjoyed by Canada. In return the legislative council promised to meet the entire cost of colonial government and guarantee a generous civil list.[48] The wealthy colonists in New South Wales agreed with those domestic critics of Britain's imperial administration who argued that constitutional concessions could be obtained by offering the metropolitan power large amounts of money. Yet Grey was activated by principle, not by mere greed and his reply to such venal representations was uncompromising. He reiterated his contention that colonial crown-lands and their revenues were held in trust for the empire as a whole and consequently could not be passed to the control of individual colonial assemblies. Official appointments in the colonies were another area of wider imperial concern rather than the province of the local legislatures in the colonies. For this reason Grey refused to admit that appointments to customs posts and other governmental positions in the colonies should be filled from local applicants, and he reserved the right to bestow such situations on any of 'Her Majesty's Subjects'.[49]

Grey had great breadth of vision, and worked within an ideological framework of far-ranging imperial responsibilities. He seemed to view the empire as an organic unity, the interests of which he had incurred a duty to protect. Thus Grey could rebuff the legitimate ambitions of Australian colonists to control their own destinies, in the name of his responsibility to consult the welfare of the larger unit. In his case, colonial welfarism—the idea that each colony should be administered in a way which best suited its own individual development[50]—was subordinated to imperial trusteeship. The benefit of the monolith took precedence over any advantage of its components. This was a not unintelligible or indefensible position. The problem was that it appeared to settlers in Australia, that when particular questions like convict transportation or control over colonial waste lands were under consideration, imperial trusteeship too often became a euphemism for British advantage. When Sir John Pakington took over the seals of the Colonial Office during the short-lived Derby-Disraeli ministry, he had quite a different ideological outlook from his predecessor. There was a public awareness that with Grey out of office the way was cleared for further constitutional concessions to Australia. One interested journal outlined its conception of the difference between Tory colonial policy, which it claimed tended to be pragmatic and empiricist, and Whig colonial policy, which tended to be more ideological. The commentator suggested that the Whigs would never have granted responsible government to Australia because they believed Britain had a clear moral duty to protect the interests of future generations of colonists, and such an outlook was incompatible with the grant of full self-government.[51]

Throughout the period of these exchanges, the British press had not been altogether uninterested, though the *Times*—obviously influenced by the newly-returned ex-colonist Robert Lowe[52]—devoted considerably more attention to constitutional affairs in Australia than did other contemporary British newspapers. In May 1852 the *Times* began its attack on the manifold shortcomings of the act of 1850. This criticism stood in sharp contrast to its avid support for the bill during the debates in 1850, and provides some indication of the extent of Lowe's ascendancy with John Delane, the newspaper's manager and editor. Forceful editorials now pointed out that Britain took upwards of £150 000 a year in civil lists from the Australian colonists before they were permitted to touch a single shilling of the revenue they raised by taxing themselves. They were also compelled to support customs departments whose members were appointed and whose salaries were set by the home government. This, the *Times* claimed, was too heavy a price to extract from colonists before they were eligible to exercise the right of appropriating the remainder of their revenue.[53] Furthermore, the imperial government came under attack for attempting to retain control over the land revenues of New South Wales, and was accused of sacrificing constitutional probity to a greedy appetite for a continuation of colonial subsidies for British emigration.[54] These arguments were buttressed in June by the *Morning Chronicle's* support for the constitutional demands of settlers in New South Wales.[55] Later in the year the *Examiner* entered the fray with cautious remarks upon the impossibility of distinguishing satisfactorily between imperial and colonial spheres of interest. The paper suggested tentatively that the answer might not lie in that direction but rather in some form of colonial representation in the House of Commons.[56]

Colonial dialectic was undoubtedly persuasive; and the gold discoveries in New South Wales and Victoria placed the financial viability of independent Australian settlements beyond doubt. But the main reason for the shift in attitudes expressed in the daily papers, from considering Grey's settlement timely and helpful in 1850 to describing it as ill-considered and unduly restrictive in 1852, may have been British fear of an Australian uprising to secure the independence withheld in 1850 and further denied by Grey in 1852. As has been already noted, colonists in Australia appeared to make a conscious attempt to frame their complaints in the emotive terminology of the rebellious American colonies, and the second remonstrance from New South Wales[57] made pointed reference to the disastrous results of Britain's intransigence with the American empire during the eighteenth century. The *Times* fully appreciated the analogy:

> A stern necessity will shiver to atoms the Acts of Parliament by which we have sought to fetter the colonies, will give to them the management of their lands, their revenues and their laws, and give them, whether we wish it or no, the fullest powers of self-government. It only remains with us to say whether they shall be peacefully conceded or wrested from us by tumult and agitation.[58]

By December 1852, the pragmatic Pakington had decided that it would be more expedient to surrender to the colonists than to provoke them into rebellion. The Colonial Office after Grey's departure had come to the realization that in a conflict with the settlement colonies it could really only advise. If colonists were determined on a course of action, Britain had no means other than moral pressure to compel subjection to British policies. In the last resort the Colonial Office lacked the power to enforce.[59] In his surrender to the demands of New South Wales as well as those of South Australia and Victoria, Pakington referred to the huge influx of population into eastern Australia caused by the gold discoveries, and to the firmness and good sense of the local colonial authorities in keeping order on the goldfields. In this task the people of New South Wales had 'given signal evidence of their fitness to regulate their own affairs'. If the legislative councils of those colonies drew up constitutions, he would submit to the imperial parliament all the measures necessary to ensure that they became operative. In deference to earlier demands for a constitution like that of Canada, Pakington indicated that he envisaged bicameral legislatures in Australia with nominated upper houses on the model of British North America. Moreover, Britain was ready to surrender unreservedly its control over crown-lands and their revenues, and was willing to consider colonial proposals for the better regulation of the customs service and governmental appointments in the colony.[60]

The secretary of state's reference to the praiseworthy handling of the goldfields as a contributory reason for no longer withholding responsible government was ironic, because the *Times* drew a contrary lesson: the breakdown of law and order on the goldfields formed a major inducement for Britain at once to concede responsible government. The *Times* affirmed that a huge influx of population into New South Wales and Victoria had greatly strained the governmental machinery in those colonies, and alleged that this had resulted in the collapse of local administration. The newspaper laid responsibility for this breakdown directly at the door of the metropolitan power, and held that the act of 1850 had paralysed effective government in Australia. When Britain had reserved to itself control over 'imperial' aspects of colonial government it had been interfering in the 'parish matters of the Antipodes'. The functions of government had been divided and a paralytic equilibrium had resulted. Readjustment was vital because, as things stood, 'the colonial Legislature, which has the knowledge, has not the power, and the Imperial Parliament, which has the power, has not the knowledge'.[61]

When the Duke of Newcastle succeeded Pakington at the Colonial Office at the end of 1852, he no longer insisted on the creation of colonial upper houses full of nominees, but he did instruct colonial legislative councils in Australia to frame constitutions which embodied the principles of ministerial responsibility. As a justification for this bold step, he maintained that it was unwise to give British subjects in Australia a different political status from British subjects in Canada.[62] Such a concession went further than most politically ambitious pastoralists or proprietors had bargained. Although during the 1840s they had used responsible government as a catch-all demand to coerce the British government into giving up control over crown-lands, the pastoralist oligarchies which exercised power in the legislative councils in Australia did not want the divisive element of political parties and ministerial government introduced to disturb their own enjoyment of ascendancy.[63] Moreover, the political parties on which cabinet government was predicated had not yet emerged, and in this instance Newcastle was forcing the pace of constitutional development in Australia in order to give effect to his own theories of colonial government. The fact that he was moving in a more liberal direction than had Grey only serves to emphasize the freedom which British statesmen exercised in using the Australian colonies as an arena for the implementation of their own constitutional preferences.

Although the legislative councils in New South Wales, Victoria, and South Australia occupied themselves during 1853 preparing draft constitution bills for submission to the imperial parliament, Van Diemen's Land had not at first been included in these concessions. But dispatches from Pakington and Newcastle had announced the cessation of transportation to the island, thereby clearing away the barrier of convictism which Stanley had earlier described as an insuperable obstacle to constitutional advance.[64] A recent study has argued that once the Colonial Office had decided to confer responsible government on New South Wales, it was inevitable that identical arrangements would be made in the other Australian colonies, because the British authorities believed that concessions granted to one colony must be extended to all.[65] It is interesting to note, therefore, that this did not occur with respect to Van Diemen's Land: here the initiative came from the lieutenant-governor who successfully requested in 1853 that Van Diemen's Land should be placed on an equal footing with the mainland colonies and granted the right to devise a constitution of its own.[66]

Some degree of doubt was felt in Britain, however, over the *modus operandi* under which the draft constitutions were created; and of particular concern were the motives which activated Australian legislative councils. After all, these bodies were only two-thirds elected on a very restricted franchise. Should such unrepresentative agencies be entrusted with the responsibility of drafting constitutions for entire colonies? The *Times* thought not. The newspaper appeared to have the

McArthur family in mind when it contended that in New South Wales there was real danger that the colony might fall under the domination of a family compact: 'There are strong symptoms that those who have at present possessed themselves of political power are seeking so to form their new constitution as to perpetuate in their own hands the authority they have obtained'.[67] By late 1853, it was evident from the paper's discussion of constitution-making in Australia that former doubts had hardened into certainties.

The *Times* pointed to both South Australia and New South Wales as examples of what could happen when the rapacious and self-interested cliques which controlled the colonial legislative councils were permitted to draft their own constitutions. In South Australia, the majority of elected members in the legislative council reflected public opinion in the colony in favouring an elected upper house for the new legislature. But a few opponents of the elective principle allied with the reactionary governor, Sir Henry Fox Young[68] and, supported by the governor's nominees in the legislative council, forced provision for a nominated upper house into the draft constitution. According to the *Times*, all that had been gained by allowing the South Australian legislative council to frame the constitution had been 'a constitution manufactured by resident officials, instead of by the English House of Commons'.[69]

The state of affairs in South Australia afforded ample grounds for concern, but it was against the legislative council in New South Wales that the *Times* levelled its biggest guns. Here the newspaper reiterated its earlier charges of electoral malpractice in favour of the wealthy squatter class and expressed concern at the unfitness of such a body to devise a new constitution. Moreover, the legislative council had originated a scheme to establish an hereditary aristocracy in the colony based on ownership of land, which would elect fellow aristocrats to the upper house of the proposed new legislature. Such contrivances were rejected in Britain as absurd. Ownership of land did not constitute a sufficient ground for public honours, and certainly there was no genealogical basis for such a claim. To the *Times*, the device was indicative of 'the most grasping selfishness, the most narrow and illiberal ambition, and the most vulgar and ridiculous misconception of the estimate of public honours and dignities in this country'.[70] Only the previous year Grey had already rejected suggestions for the establishment of a colonial baronetcy in New South Wales in less violent but nonetheless unequivocal terms. The most he would concede was that governors in the Australian colonies might be authorized to honour private citizens with knighthoods and in very special cases by a baronetcy, though he had made it quite plain that such honours 'could not be bestowed according to any fixed rate on persons who have purchased lands and settled in the Colony'.[71] Since the bulk of the colonial populace in New South Wales was also irrevocably opposed to the patrician pretensions of the 'bunyip aristocracy', the proposal was ultimately dropped in favour of a nominated upper house. In contrast to such preoccupations over the existence of a colonial nobility in New South Wales, the draft constitutions from Victoria, Van Diemen's Land, and eventually from South Australia displayed democratic tendencies, and envisaged elected upper houses in preference to a second chamber filled with crown nominees.

When constitutional bills from New South Wales, Victoria and South Australia arrived in London during 1854, they were subjected to extensive scrutiny by the law officers of the crown to ensure that they contained nothing which might unwittingly violate the British constitution. The *Times* pursued its seemingly indefatigable interest in Australian affairs with an extremely harsh disquisition on the bill from New South Wales and the legislative council that had produced it. By implication the criticism also encompassed the bills from Victoria and South Australia, for the *Times* traced the source of all the faults in the New South Wales' bill to the unrepresentative nature of a legislative council containing one-third nominees: 'The measure obviously emanates from the majority of a body which does not represent the wishes of the people, and seeks to perpetuate by means the most unscrupulous and indefensible the domination of one party and the humiliation of another.'[72]

Complaints that the legislative councils in Australia were not sufficiently democratic did not cause undue concern to the imperial government which itself had been elected on a restricted franchise. In May 1855, after minor modification by the law officers of the crown,[73] the bills were introduced into the House of Commons. The parliamentary debate was stormy. Russell, who had now become colonial secretary, claimed that the bills had been drawn up by the colonists and therefore carried the hopes of a majority of the settlers in Australia.[74] Robert Lowe, the newly-elected member for Kidderminster in the House of Commons, disagreed with this presumption. His criticisms, which were endorsed by Lord Monteagle in the House of Lords,[75] closely followed those in the *Times*. Lowe argued that the nominated upper house provided in the bill from New South Wales represented a device by 'a small oligarchical clique' anxious to maintain its political position,[76] and that the draft constitution amounted to a conspiracy by those who owned property in the colony.[77] Russell's line of defence against these attacks was to exploit the ploy he had found so effective during the debates in 1850 and to point out to parliament that the bills were permissive. He replied that if the New South Wales' colonists really did find a nominated second chamber repugnant, they could always alter their constitutional act to make the upper house elective. Russell did not profess a preference for the superior merits of either nominated or elected upper houses, but he did realistically point out that deadlock between two elective houses presented far more difficulties and dangers than did deadlock involving elected and nominated chambers of government. In the latter case the conflict could be resolved by the addition of further nominees. Finally, he declared that as the bill stood, simple majorities in both houses could alter provisions through which the pastoralists had sought to inhibit constitutional change by requiring approval from two-thirds of the sitting members in each chamber before such adjustments could come into effect. Above all, he believed that British statesmen should not meddle: 'I think, therefore, that it is best to allow the people to judge what may be the form best suited to the interests of the colony'.[78]

Russell's sensible pleas were successful, and the bills from Victoria and New South Wales were passed with little alteration. The *Times* remained doubtful whether the new constitutions bestowed any benefit on the colonies. The old controlling interests would still be in command under the new arrangements and some form of class struggle could result when the innate selfishness of this group had alienated the majority of the colonial populations.[79] On the other hand, the *Globe* applauded the fact that the draft bill from New South Wales was not too democratic and commented that despite the objections of Robert Lowe the bulk of the colonists appeared anxious to retain the imperial connection.[80] The radical *Leeds Mercury* added a further dimension to the debate and provided evidence that some Englishmen still persisted in regarding the Australian colonists as fit subjects for political experimentation. It noted that Australia would prove to be of great interest to students of comparative government, since an intriguing situation had been created whereby it would now be possible to view the separate workings of the New South Wales' upper house of nominees and the Victorian elected upper house in almost identical societies.[81]

The existence of two distinctly different types of upper house in the contiguous colonies of New South Wales and Victoria is indicative of the latitude and freedom of action extended by conservative colonial secretaries after 1852 to the legislative councils of the various Australian colonies. It is inconceivable that the tidy mind of Earl Grey would have permitted such variations to exist. In his apologia for the colonial policy of the Whig ministry between 1846 and 1852 Grey claimed that the Russell administration had always been activated by a desire to forward the best interests of the Australian colonies.[82] But such an affirmation was not compatible with his record, which had shown an authoritarian personality intent on securing maximum advantage for the mother country. Prolonged colonial agitation had been necessary to impress on the metropolitan power the necessity of change; and even on occasions when ferment in the colonies had convinced British administrators of the indispensability of adjustments, the solutions propounded by the Colonial Office during Grey's tenure had more often than not borne little relation either to advice from authorities in the colonies or to petitions from interested colonists. British discussion of constitutional development in the antipodean colonies during the 1840s and 1850s dealt with the grand and the far-reaching. Its participants usually lacked precise and detailed knowledge of colonial conditions, and preferred to ponder abstractions like the universal laws governing the course of political development in settlement colonies and the possible implications of such processes for the imperial structure.

Responsible government was only one of a number of different theories or schemes in circulation which attempted to grapple with the problem of constitutional development for colonies. During the debates on the 1832 reform bill, for example, the radical Joseph Hume and the Tory Sir George Murray had proposed that settlement colonies elect representatives of their own to the House of Commons at Westminster.[83] Such a possibility had obvious attractions, and in 1849 Russell submitted a similar scheme for Grey's consideration. Russell believed that responsible government for colonies was the precursor of a republican independence which he hoped to avert. In supporting his blueprint, he argued that if Britain retained a political connection with the colonies through the House of Commons, the empire could become a free-trade *zollverein* in which British goods and merchants could move without fear of hostile tariff barriers. Ethnic kinship with particular reference to Australia and Canada was stressed, and he also adverted to Britain's prestige without empire. Russell feared that Britain's position as a world power would deteriorate vis-à-vis other European nations once the process of allowing colonies to become independent had begun, and 'the vultures would soon gather together to despoil us of other parts of our Empire'.[84]

Russell's solution was to obviate the need for colonial independence by permitting colonies direct representation in the imperial parliament, and to place the colonies in an identical constitutional relationship with England as that currently enjoyed by Ireland. He calculated that Ireland had 105 members in the House of Commons and provided an annual revenue of £3 500 000 per annum, and on this basis he devised a formula that Ireland possessed one member of parliament for every £33 000 the country contributed to the general revenues of Great Britain. Russell proposed that this ratio be extended to the settlement colonies and that they be permitted to select as many representatives to the House of Commons as they wished, provided that they paid an annual sum of £33 000 to Britain's general revenues for every member sent to Westminster.[85] Grey's reaction was one of waspish discouragement. He had little respect for Russell's judgement[86] and even less for the prime minister's amateurish interference in the affairs of the colonial department. Grey regarded the idea of colonial members sitting in the House of Commons as thoroughly impractical; he described Russell's suggestions as 'startling' and commented that 'many difficulties' prohibited their application.[87] In the face of so marked a lack of enthusiasm from his colonial secretary, Russell quietly allowed the question to drop.

Other proposals were also advanced—many of them probably influenced by proponents of systematic colonization—which sought to formalize Britain's connection with the colonies before they became completely independent.[88] Such plans generally made provision for the appointment of colonial agents in Britain or for the establishment of some form of consultative council of colonial delegates which would be empowered to discuss British colonial policy and make recommendations to the imperial government. Since these councils could not be vested with legislative powers as they would then usurp the prerogatives of the House of Commons, it was usual to allocate purely advisory functions to them.[89] An underlying assumption, common to all these projects and often advocated by Molesworth in parliamentary debates, was the need for a definitive separation of imperial and colonial spheres of interest. These designs all envisaged something less than self-government with ministerial responsibility for the colonies, and gave expression to the collective attitudes of many Englishmen when they persistently maintained that the imperial government should continue to supervise and legislate in imperial areas of administration and that to this limited extent colonies should remain dependencies.

The prevalence of this theorizing suggests that many Englishmen wished to subject the untidy conglomerate of territories which constituted the British empire to some much-needed rationalization. Many Benthamites, radicals, and other doctrinaires approached this task and devised their solutions as though all the component parts of the empire were at the same level of constitutional sophistication. This erroneous conception illustrates a characteristic that underlay British attitudes to the Australian colonies and to the empire at large during these years, namely impatience with or ignorance of colonial realities. Blueprints of colonial reform were essentially utopian or romantic since they were based on an unreal or at best a partial view of the world. Schemes for the general management of empire which attempted to force settlement colonies into a preconceived and unitive intellectual framework had their roots in an irrelevant perception of reality. At the same time, such plans had concrete origins in a fundamental dissatisfaction with Colonial Office administration, and were evidence of a desire to make administration honest and responsible, to establish order out of seeming chaos, and to make all the colonies of settlement develop at the same rate and in the same direction. Such a thing was manifestly impossible. Nevertheless, Britons from the prime minister to newspaper and periodical publicists seemed to imagine that settlement colonies could be treated unitively if only the essential general principles of such imperial management could be discovered.

The effect of such beliefs on constitutional development in Australia was profound. While some British administrators had occupied themselves in searching for and seeking to apply universal laws and theoretical maxims of government, all had been inclined to regard the Australian settlements as immature societies in need of firm guidance. The result was long periods of drift[90] interspersed by short bursts of paternalism. Englishmen tended to undervalue colonial opinion and the views of colonial officials on the spot, or at best to grant their relevance only grudgingly. When this tendency is allied with what seems to have been an aversion to change inherent amongst officials at the Colonial Office, a propensity for shelving difficult problems in the hope that they would solve themselves,[91] and difficulties of distant communications, it is not surprising that Australian colonists regarded British attitudes to constitutional advance as vacillating, inconsistent, exploitive and infuriatingly paternal.

5: Emigration 1828-55

Between 1828 and 1855 British attitudes towards emigration to the Australian colonies were in a state of flux and subject to considerable debate and modification. The convict antecedents of antipodean settlement caused many Englishmen from different social backgrounds to look askance at the idea of cohabiting with former criminals. Such an outlook led some commentators during the period under review to regard emigration to Australia as a form of self-inflicted transportation, while others saw it as a social corrective which merited British subsidy. The two points of view were not necessarily exclusive, and when assisted passages to Australia became common after 1831 there was a tendency amongst some Englishmen to denigrate the characters of working-class emigrants who took advantage of such financial inducements and to regard emigrating workers as little better than convicts. Distrust of emigration to Australia was a widespread phenomenon which transcended class barriers, and emigration figures make it plain that the majority of British expatriates preferred to seek their fortunes in a North American environment rather than chance their luck in far off Australia.[1] Nevertheless since most observers were reasonably well inclined towards Australian development, the country and the colonies therein tended to lose their primary reputation as the unhappy abode of England's penal exiles and began to take on the public character of a land of opportunity. These alterations in consciousness were part of a continual reassessment of antipodean potential during these decades, and the kaleidoscopic evaluations of the benefits of emigration to Australia reflected the divergent needs and aspirations of the main social divisions in the British body politic.

The United Kingdom experienced considerable economic dislocation following the Napoleonic wars. The immediate cause was the cessation of government orders for materials of war. The resultant unemployment in the manufacturing districts was aggravated during 1816 by a post-war economic depression, and unemployment was further increased by the discharge of large numbers from the nation's armed forces. The underlying cause of economic disruption and widespread indigence, however, was the continuing process of economic and social transformation under the influence of which Britain was moving inexorably away from her historical agricultural and mercantile economy to become a predominantly manufacturing country.[2] When the swollen ranks of the unemployed proletariat sought redress for their grievances through political agitation, successive British governments found themselves facing a potentially explosive situation which was destined to remain a constant problem throughout the next four decades. Laissez-faire economic doctrine held that man should not oppose the laws of nature and that government interference in the economic process could only make matters worse. Moreover, during the first half of the nineteenth century British governments lacked the knowledge to interfere with the mysterious workings of the economy in attempts to control or mitigate the effects of the periodic cycles of boom and depression to which industrial economies are subject. Nevertheless, contemporary Englishmen felt instinctively what modern scholarship has proved, that there was a direct correlation between cyclical recessions and outbreaks of rioting amongst the working classes.[3] Concern over the growing radicalism of the lower orders was a contributory factor when the imperial government undertook several experiments between 1819 and 1827 designed to relieve pauper distress by providing free passages to the colonies for impoverished workers and their dependents.[4] Such schemes were expensive and the benefits doubtful, and assisted emigration financed by the British taxpayer remained out of favour with successive governments despite continued distress.[5]

Such governmental reluctance to underwrite the costs of pauper emigration did not necessarily imply selfish unconcern amongst the ruling classes. During the war years the National Debt had quadrupled and by 1815 stood at £861 million. Taxation, including a 10 per cent income-tax which had been introduced as a war-time measure, had also increased, and overall government expenditure had risen four-fold.[6] Nevertheless, in 1816 income-tax was abolished and the country's interest payments and current expenditure had to be met from the income derived from customs and excise, the traditional sources of British government finance. Furthermore, between 1816 and 1822 Britain experienced severe currency deflation in addition to widespread unemployment, and these developments combined to produce an unwillingness on the part of British statesmen to undertake activities which would involve the government in increased expenditure. Common contemporary opinion held that this was an age of retrenchment. Consequently, a state-assisted scheme of emigration, whereby penurious labourers might travel to the Australian colonies, was not considered an economically viable remedy for distress. Parsimony precluded Australia from participating in the experimental schemes mentioned above. The price of a passage to the Australian colonies during the 1820s varied between £20 and £30, while that of a voyage to North America was sometimes as low as 30s.[7] Moreover, Australia's great distance from Britain, together with the primitive state of the New South Wales' and Van Diemen's Land' economies precluded the possibility of shipping firms being able to obtain a return cargo without which shipping to Australia was an uneconomical proposition.[8]

A further factor which militated against pauper emigration to Australia was that British labourers were advised by their leaders to eschew emigration if they could; in the event that this should prove impossible they were instructed to look to the democratic United States of America and to avoid all British colonies where they would be subject to the autocracy of colonial governors.[9] But particularly were they instructed to shun Australia, the entire extent of which was considered to be synonymous with the Botany Bay penal settlement. William Cobbett described the continent as a 'horrid Country'[10] and seemed unaware that Swan River, New South Wales, and Van Diemen's Land were three quite separate colonies, and that the Swan River settlement had no convicts.[11] Cobbett, however, did point to one of the main problems faced by a working-class emigrant to Australia: both past and current imperial policy discouraged such an emigrant by making it extremely difficult for him to acquire colonial lands. Before 1831 land in New South Wales and Van Diemen's Land was gratuitously granted by the authorities in proportion to the amount of capital a settler possessed. The smallest grant usually made was 320 acres, to qualify for which a colonist had to produce a minimum of £250.[12] This placed land effectively beyond the reach of lower-class immigrants from Britain. Peter Burroughs has argued that such regulations were the result of colonial conditions and did not constitute a conscious imperial policy to deprive emigrants from the lower classes of ownership of land in the Australian colonies;[13] though this is not to say that local administrators in the colonies did not desire such a restriction and use the regulations to effect it. But to an uninformed propagandist like Cobbett these British policies must have represented a perpetuation in Australia of British social distinctions and prejudices against upward social mobility from the labouring classes. It is in this context that his advice to English paupers that they would do better to endure their hovels and potatoes in Britain rather than go to Australia should be understood.[14] There was little during these years to attract the interest of British workers to the Australian colonies, even those who may have felt disposed to emigrate. Even Cobbett's description of the prospects which awaited well-to-do emigrants in Australia was extremely gloomy:

> When arrived you depend on the public authorities for a grant of land. If you have money to purchase pieces of ground already cleared and cultivated, your servants are convicts, and you are at the joint mercy of them and the murdering natives. Even for the services of the convicts, your sole dependence is on the pleasure of the public authorities.[15]

In addition to the unattractive aspects of Australia and the general reluctance of the lower orders to emigrate except as a last resort,[16] there was a further argument put forward by opponents of emigration in the years between 1828 and 1855 to the effect that it was neither wise nor economical to send people overseas when they could add to Britain's prosperity by staying at home. So much waste land existed throughout the British Isles which could be reclaimed and brought into production if it were granted to paupers on easy terms. This was a not uncommon point of view and Rowland Hill made it the subject of an influential pamphlet in 1832 which he revealingly entitled *Home Colonies*.[17] In effect, the supporters of such schemes were attempting to reverse the drift of population and to reestablish an agrarian economy by returning a dispossessed peasantry to the land. Such ambitions were chimerical and contrary to the movement of the age, but they were nonetheless influential. In 1828 George Groly had categorically stated that it was unnecessary to send paupers overseas: 'There is *no excess* of population in the British Islands . . . the surface of these islands has acres enough to feed, clothe, and employ, *five* times their present number'.[18] Groly believed that instead of encouraging paupers to leave the country the government should allocate areas of Britain's waste lands to indigent labourers entirely free of charge. Once such people possessed their own land they would make it fruitful.[19] During the 1830s and 1840s some working-class commentators continued to voice this opinion. The radical newspaper the *Operative*, for example, claimed in 1839 that so long as any chance remained of the workers obtaining land in England 'we will not quit our fatherland to companion with demi-savages and kangaroos';[20] and a return to the land in Britain was a prominent demand of Feargus O'Connor and the Chartist movement during the 1840s.[21]

When indigence or political persecution did force members of the working classes to emigrate, the vast majority of them appeared to share Cobbett's preference for the United States of America. Between 1828 and 1855 there were only four years when emigration to British North America was at a higher level than that direct to the United States, and it was well known that many emigrants moved on from Canada and looked on British North America as a temporary way-station *en route* to the United States. Even during the height of the Australian gold rushes in the early 1850s British emigration to the United States was approximately four times greater than emigration to Australia.[22]

Nevertheless, working-class antipathy towards emigration to Australia did not seem to be shared by commentators from the middle and upper classes. In 1828 Sydney Smith compared Australia with the United States as venues for British emigration, and maintained that Australia offered greater opportunities to the free emigrant with capital, even if the longer and more expensive sea voyage were taken into account. Upon arrival in the United States, the would-be settler was faced with a protracted and arduous journey into the interior before he reached the frontier of settlement where land sold at a reasonable price. Such an expedition more than offset the tedious sea trip to the Australian colonies. Smith pronounced Australia superior for the emigrant because land there was still free and convict labour very cheap; whereas in the United States land had to be purchased and labour was scarce being obtainable only 'at the most enormous wages'.[23] The Scottish economist J. R. McCulloch agreed that the antipodes were superficially attractive but he also stated his belief that Australia was too distant from Europe for a *'natural'* European connection, obviously feeling that as things stood the bulk of emigration there would continue to consist of convicts and their families.[24]

The imperial government was faced with a dilemma. There was an apparent redundancy of working-class population throughout the United Kingdom, and the simplest and most straightforward remedy was emigration. Yet how was an excess population of paupers to depart unless some outside agency made sufficient money available to finance this relief? During the 1820s colonial under-secretary Robert Wilmot Horton championed the cause of state-assisted emigration, and suggested that parishes be permitted to mortgage their poor rates and use the revenue thus provided to send their excess labouring population to Canada or the Cape. The third report of a parliamentary committee which under Horton's chairmanship studied redundant population and related topics and advocated government aid for emigration was published in 1827. J. R. McCulloch supported this recommendation though he preferred directing the stream of evacuees to South America.[25] Nevertheless, state assistance for emigration roused the ire

of many other observers. Some newspapers opposed Horton's proposals on ideological and emotional grounds. The conservative *Standard*
held that the concept of state interference was 'jacobinical',[26] while the
Whig *Courier* felt that emigration was contrary to nature and a deser-
tion of the fatherland.[27] The *Times* was very cool and opposed to
Horton on the basis of expense, though it did not deny the urgency of
the domestic situation nor the need for some redress:

> At first sight it appears very plausible to recommend the trans-
> porting, to other countries, of large bodies of the King's subjects,
> who possess no means of decent subsistence at home. When,
> however, we proceed a little further into the subject . . . One hun-
> dred thousand emigrants to Canada would cost two millions of
> money. But it would take a half million of people, at least, to
> accomplish any sensible relief to the United Kingdom, and a prime
> cost of no less than ten millions sterling.[28]

Despite such powerful opposition, Horton's views received widespread support. In 1829 John Barrow endorsed the idea of assisted
emigration in an article for the *Quarterly Review* dealing with the new
Swan River colony in Western Australia, and inferred that such emigration could profitably be directed to the new settlement.[29] The
settlement at Swan River afforded topicality to discussions on the
wider implications of pauper emigration, and several other publications availed themselves of the opportunity thus provided to bring
emigration again before the public's notice. One newspaper described
emigration to Swan River as 'exile', thereby vesting departure to the
new colony with all the unsavoury connotations of convict
transportation;[30] though other commentators agreed in principle that
some form of government-assisted expatriation was required for the
relief of distressed labourers.[31] A contributor to the *New Monthly
Magazine and Literary Journal* suggested a somewhat modified version of Wilmot Horton's plan. He acknowledged that the country was
under a deep obligation to Horton, although he did not agree that
emigration was necessary for the relief of want in England. He distinguished between temporary redundancy in England, caused by
improvement in the extended use of machines, and permanent redundancy in Ireland. Fears were expressed that a government-assisted
emigration of paupers from England would only create a vacuum into
which Irish emigration into England would flow, and the article
commented that it would be infinitely more desirable to promote a
government-assisted emigration to the colonies from Ireland.[32] Emigration, therefore, was a subject very much in the air when Edward
Gibbon Wakefield published his first work on colonization in 1829.
Beginning in the *Morning Chronicle* of 21 August 1829, there appeared

a series of anonymous letters purporting to have been written by a settler in New South Wales. Wakefield's analysis of New South Wales society and its problems revealed that the fictitious settler wrote from a socially elevated position. His main criticism was that artisans in the colony became landowners too quickly; yet it has already been noted that few British workers could have afforded the fare to Australia let alone the £250 necessary to qualify for the minimum land grant. Any shortage of labour in New South Wales was caused not by the undue availability of crown-lands, but by the fact that British working men were not emigrating there in substantial numbers. During the 1820s an increasing number of small capitalists had set themselves up in New South Wales, and they soon exhausted the colony's supplies of convict labour. Fortuitously, the shortage of artisans and farm labourers in Australia occurred at a time of obvious redundance of labour in Britain, and Wakefield proposed to ameliorate both situations by a method of financing the settlement of British workers in New South Wales. This scheme of systematic colonization will be discussed in a later chapter, and it is sufficient to note in this context that the fund was to be provided from sales of colonial waste lands in Australia. British distress would thereby be relieved and the capitalists of New South Wales and Van Diemen's Land would receive a much needed augmentation of the work force; at the same time the British taxpayer would not have to bear the financial burden of the emigration.[33]

Wakefield's proposals were given a partial application by the Colonial Office in the so-called Ripon Regulations of 1831, which provided for the sale by auction of crown-lands in New South Wales and Van Diemen's Land, and stipulated that part of the money thus produced should create a fund with which to defray the costs of carrying free British emigrants to the colonies.[34] The Colonial Office was initially unsure whether the sale of crown-lands would produce sufficient revenue to make free emigration a viable prospect, and so it also contemplated imposing a tax on all convict servants in private employment in the colonies. The proceeds of this tax were in like manner to be appropriated for free emigration.[35]

Throughout the 1830s the question of emigration was widely canvassed and it is against the background of this preoccupation with the subject that the eventual success of Wakefield's theories should be viewed. Although it has been argued that Wakefieldian ideology had captured the Colonial Office by 1831,[36] neither public nor official acceptance of Wakefield's thesis was ever complete. In 1830, the *Quarterly Review* carried an article by Thomas Bruce, the seventh Earl of Elgin, on the causes and remedies of pauperism in the United Kingdom. The *Review* withdrew its earlier support for Wilmot Horton's proposals, but Bruce did not pronounce in favour of Wakefield's plan. Perhaps he was a prey to doubts similar to those troubling Colonial Office officials who were originally sceptical whether land sales alone would provide a sufficient revenue for emigration purposes. In any event, Bruce put forward his own theory on the best method of ensuring a self-supporting export of labourers to the Australian colonies. He believed that a labourer's passage to Australia should be paid initially by the imperial government, which could then recompense itself by instituting a tax on the wage differential between what a labourer could earn in Britain and what he did earn in Australia. This tax was to be paid by the employer in Australia, and thus the labourer 'would never be aware that he was paying it; the wages he would still receive would be affluence compared to his condition before his removal from Britain'.[37] Meanwhile, the *Edinburgh Review* continued loyal to Wilmot Horton's views, and the influential economist J. R. McCulloch stated that it was impossible for anyone who was interested in pauperism and emigration to make too high an estimation of Horton's services.[38] In 1835 John Barrow returned to the pages of the *Quarterly Review* in an article on emigration, and the journal swung again to support for British assistance for pauper emigration and urged the government to provide up to £1 000 000 for payment of such passages to Canada. British North America was usually favoured to receive this type of emigrant because it was much closer than Australia, costs were cheaper, and therefore more paupers could be sent on a limited budget. Barrow did admit that the free Swan River settlement appeared to be progressing satisfactorily, but added that 'these are not the colonies to which any sensible person will mainly look for the sort of relief which forms the object of this paper'.[39]

In June and July of 1834, parliament debated a scheme proposed by the South Australian Company for the colonization of South Australia on Wakefieldian lines, and opinions were sharply divided concerning the efficacy of the plan as a method of relieving domestic distress in Britain. Arguments tended to relate to wider questions of policy rather than to emigration *per se*, but opponents of the proposed colony did allege that labourers who took advantage of offers of free passage to the new colony would not be bettering their condition.[40] Naturally, supporters of the plan claimed that emigration to South Australia would be extremely beneficial to Britain and to the emigrants themselves whether they were labourers or capitalists.[41]

Despite the wide publicity given to Australia as a result of the South Australian venture and the ostentatious public relations campaign preceding settlement, doubts continued to be expressed—even by some of those in favour of emigration—concerning the advisability of promoting emigration to the antipodes. One observer voiced a common working-class sentiment when he approved of pauper expatriation but expressed doubt about claims that the stream should be directed to the Australian colonies. This critic favoured the United States of America as the best and cheapest venue to which such an emigration should be directed, and he accused the British government of advocating emigration to Australia in an endeavour to bring about a decline in the rate of British emigration to America, because emigration to the United States was a direct augmentation of the strength of a country obviously predestined to become Britain's chief rival.[42]

Throughout the 1830s, emigration of British labourers to New South Wales and Van Diemen's Land gathered momentum as sales of colonial waste lands continued to provide a substantial revenue. Under the terms of the Ripon Regulations, first preference was to be given to women and mechanics as these were in shortest supply in the colonies. After the gazetting of the regulations in 1831, several shiploads of female emigrants were dispatched to the colonies in anticipation of the forthcoming revenue, but the colonists made numerous complaints to the Colonial Office concerning the undesirable characters possessed by many of these women, a great number of whom were former residents of female penitentiaries and workhouses. The colonists of New South Wales and Van Diemen's Land had hoped for wives and household servants and were quick to express resentment that their money should be spent on such a poor class of female emigrant.[43]

Although the Colonial Office controlled the expenditure of the funds which became available for emigration to Australia under the new regulations, governmental preoccupation with retrenchment at this time resulted in the Colonial Office's refusal to accept liability for ensuring that the money was wisely spent or that the background of prospective emigrants was adequately investigated. Between 1832 and 1836 the entire management of emigration to the Australian colonies was overseen by a committee known as the London Emigration Committee, which became the official representative of the Colonial Office and controlled the selection and dispatch of emigrants on free passages to Australia.[44] The secretary to the London Emigration Committee was the shipping agent John Marshall, and as Sir William Molesworth pointed out, Marshall had a vested interest in ensuring that his ships were not delayed while emigrants were properly investigated. Molesworth claimed that this conflict of interest was directly responsible for the streets of Hobart and Sydney being crowded with prostitutes.[45] Certainly the advertisements placed by the committee in the public press to attract female emigrants made it easy for women of ill-repute to disguise their calling. The women were expected to provide £5 towards their fares, but the broadsheet advertisements stated that this stipulation could be waived and that the committee would accept promissory notes 'payable in the Colony within a reasonable time after their arrival, when they have acquired the means to do so'.[46]

Marshall escaped the consequences of such sharp practice because the government had no supervisory machinery to scrutinize the committee's activities. In June 1831 the Colonial Office had appointed an emigration commission which was empowered to collect and dispense useful information to correspondents interested in emigration, but its functions were severely restricted and the government freely admitted that it did not wish to become involved in this field of administration.[47] For this reason the emigration commissioners were dismissed in August 1832 on the ingenuous ground that the commission had succeeded so well in the fourteen months since it had been established that it had rendered its own existence unnecessary. Nevertheless British officials were sensitive to criticism that they were neglecting their obligations in not closely policing emigration and the results of such neglect were blamed on the colonial authorities in the colonies. The Colonial Office reacted to the inevitable public complaints which accused the imperial government of being uninterested in the irregularities and improprieties of female emigration to Australia by abusing the local governor. In 1834 Spring Rice wrote to Governor Richard Bourke in New South Wales commenting on the unfavourable publicity generated by the complaints of immigrants to New South Wales. Bourke was instructed to ensure that no grounds for future recrimination remained unredressed and that 'every requisite attention' had been paid to the comforts and feelings of emigrants.[48] A fuller degree of involvement by the British government, however, was ultimately inevitable. Crown revenues were being collected in Australia for disbursement on emigration in Britain and the Colonial Office was answerable to parliament and the Treasury for such activities. Money spent in assisting the departure of excess population from Britain had to be accounted for and this together with the enforcement of the Passenger Acts was eventually to force the home government into an unwilling involvement in the administration of emigration. For this reason the decision taken in 1831 to adopt assisted emigration on a regular scale has wider implications than its immediate effect on the future and progress of the Australian colonies. It illustrates the increasing involvement of the State during the nineteenth century with areas of activity which previously had been the province of private enterprise.[49]

Emigration to Australia financed from colonial funds meant a change in the type of emigrant attracted. Hitherto, only wealthy capitalists or well-to-do bourgeoisie could afford to pay their own passages to New Holland. Assisted emigration put Australia within reach of the non-criminal British lower classes and the social status of free emigrants after 1831 was generally lower than that of emigrants prior to the Ripon Regulations. Although overall British emigration to Australia rapidly increased, some would-be emigrants from the middle and upper classes were dissuaded from settling in Australia once it became official policy to sell crown-lands and to discontinue free grants proportioned to capital.[50]

Although a few of Britain's monied classes became temporarily disenchanted with Australia in the early 1830s opinion from the lower levels of society in the mother country slowly became more favourably inclined towards emigration to Australia as the 1830s and 1840s progressed. Between 1831 and 1834 the English labour movement underwent a great upheaval as Robert Owen, one of the first syndicalists temporarily succeeded in organizing British workers into a single Grand National Consolidated Trades Union (G.N.C.T.U.).This potentially powerful structure was designed to place both economic and political power in the hands of the workers, and while the G.N.C.T.U. lasted the attitudes of labour spokesmen to emigration remained generally unfavourable.[51] By 1834, however, the movement had collapsed in chaos and fragmentation, Owen's influence waned and a more pragmatic leadership emerged. The failure of Owen's union caused some of labour's new leaders to revalue the strike weapon and to realize that other methods of improving the lot of British wage-earners ought to be tried. They believed that there were too many labourers and too few jobs. The superfluity of labour kept wages low and made strikes ineffective. The remedy therefore was to lessen the numbers of workmen competing for jobs, for if a scarcity of labour could be engineered the strike would once again become a useful weapon. Thus emigration funds became a constant feature of many of the large trade unions, and emigration benefits one of the rights of union members.[52] This was a point of view which was shared by prominent observers from the middle and upper classes who feared that large-scale emigration from the lower classes would lead to strikes and labour unrest. J. R. McCulloch, for example, commented in 1854 that the great exodus of workers to the Australian goldfields was the direct cause of an outbreak of strikes and combinations to raise wages.[53] Thomas Carlyle also believed that emigration would lead to higher wage-levels, and in 1849 he had harangued Earl Grey, then colonial secretary, claiming that 'I would do in a single year all that needs to be done for emigration, tho' officialism pronounces it impossible in any number of years'. Grey is reported to have blushed, which Carlyle interpreted as a sign that he had more conscience than was usual amongst politicians.[54] The irascible Carlyle maintained that the

real reason the British government consistently refused to vote financial aid for emigration was because the cabinet was the tool of the
manufacturers whom it feared to offend; for the one thing sure about
emigration was that it would tend to raise wages.[55]

While British workmen during the 1830s gradually came to a realization that emigration could offer advantages both to the individual
and the labour movement, New South Wales continued to experience
an endemic shortage of labour. Free British emigration was only one
of a series of proposed remedies. Wakefield had claimed that if labourers were not sent out to New South Wales under his scheme, then
the imperial government should allow an importation of Chinese or
Indian coolies.[56] Similar suggestions emanated from the Australian
colonies themselves during the 1830s, but the Colonial Office
remained resolutely opposed. In 1837, Thomas Frederick Elliot,
newly-appointed agent-general for emigration, wrote to the economist
J. S. Mill and explained the British government's thinking on the
question of coolie emigration to the Australian colonies. Elliot felt
that if such an experiment were undertaken unsuccessfully it would
cause a great deal of misery and suffering to the uprooted coolies; and
if it worked, it would either depress British and colonial labourers, or
else white labourers would refuse to do the same work as coloured. In
the latter eventuality there would be unfortunate social consequences:

> the labour of the country would settle into the hands of an inferior
> class, marked by a distinct colour, and instead of the vigour, enter-
> prise and unexampled progress which have hitherto been seen in
> this colony [i.e. New South Wales], we should have the old and
> vulgar spectacle of a lazy and proud aristocracy of the skin, served by
> a listless race of helots. A few individuals might make their fortunes
> faster, but the prospect of national greatness would be gone.[57]

The question of non-British emigration was not only raised in
connection with coolies, and the Colonial Office actively discouraged
emigration from Europe to Australia unless it was specifically to
introduce a skill or occupation which could not be supplied from
Britain. Thus German vignerons were allowed into New South Wales
and the colonial government was even permitted to pay a bounty for
their passages,[58] but a general emigration from Europe assisted from
colonial land funds was inadmissible. During the 1830s and 1840s the
Colonial Office regarded the land funds of the Australian colonies as
palliatives for British domestic distress and as a means of relieving the
British Treasury from the heavy costs of administering police and
gaols in the colonies. Revenue for emigration provided from the sales
of Australian land did not appear to be viewed by the Colonial Office
primarily as a means of empire-building or of accelerating colonial

expansion. British priorities not colonial necessities were stressed, and the record gives a clear indication that ideas of trusteeship or the notion that colonies might have had a right to an immigration tailored to suit their own development had little relevance to imperial practice in this period. Governor Bourke in New South Wales was instructed not to pay the passages of immigrants from Europe who settled in the colony, because such payments would diminish the funds available for British emigration and leave larger numbers of British paupers to remain a burden on the rates.[59] After 1838, when George Fife Angas wished to send out several ship loads of German Lutherans to South Australia, he had to pay the entire cost of their passages from his own pocket.[60]

Although the money to finance British emigration to New South Wales or Van Diemen's Land came from sales of lands in the respective colonies, the mechanics of emigration were not so straightforward, and two different systems of emigration existed side by side. Firstly, under the government's system the imperial authorities paid from colonial funds for the charter of emigrant ships and the expense of emigrants' passages. Secondly, under the less formal method known as the bounty system, local officials in the colony paid a fixed amount per immigrant from the land fund to reimburse those responsible for introducing them into the colony. Bounties were raised during the 1830s to the extent that carriage of emigrants on bounty to eastern Australia became a source of lucrative profits, and shipowners began to compete for the trade. Shipping-agents in Britain were involved in widespread irregularities and were accused of practising a twofold deception, by publishing falsely optimistic reports concerning conditions in Australia,[61] and by forging credentials and making fraudulent declarations concerning the occupations and ages of the emigrants they carried.[62] In 1840, the office of agent-general for emigration was superseded by the establishment of the Colonial Land and Emigration Commission, which was charged with controlling the allied matters of land sales in Australia and emigration from Britain to Australia. This new organization was also given a measure of control over the bounty system, in that bounties were no longer to be paid on immigrants arriving in the colonies who were not equipped with a certificate from the commission stating their occupations and ages.[63]

The implementation of free emigration to Australia which provided a measure of pauper relief at no cost to the British taxpayer caused many publicists to look again at the prospects of antipodean colonies, and some quite favourable reassessments began to appear. The rising economic importance of the wool industry made Australia a valuable acquisition and the establishment of the free colonies of Swan River and South Australia helped to render the country respectable. This progress towards respectability was greatly hastened by the cessation of convict transportation to New South Wales in 1840. Yet even before this occurrence, Horace Twiss, a former under-secretary from the Colonial Office, had publicly foreshadowed changing attitudes in an article for the *Quarterly Review*. Twiss commented that the complexion of colonial society in New South Wales was undergoing transformation as the free labouring segment of the colony's population slowly increased due to assisted immigration from England.[64] The improving status of New South Wales, however, was not sufficient to make the colony the automatic first choice of the press when emigration was under discussion. The *Times* refused to name the colony it thought most suitable for emigration, but at least New South Wales was no longer excluded when such subjects were canvassed.[65]

Free colonies in Australia offered a convenient alternative for those who favoured emigration to Australia but were doubtful whether it should be conducted side by side with convict transportation. In 1839, for example, George Groly decided that emigration to New Holland was not an inherently bad thing provided that free emigration could be kept separate from convict transportation. He appeared to contemplate a continuing influx of criminals into New South Wales and Van Diemen's Land, and advocated that the stream of free emigration be directed to the colonies of South and Western Australia.[66] His was not an isolated opinion when he proposed that free British emigration should be restricted to the free colonies,[67] though at this time Western Australia was still not self-sufficient in foodstuffs, and its population was destined to remain below 4500 for another ten years.[68] Working-class commentators, however, did not seem to be particularly impressed with the manifest advantages of the free colonies in Australia, nor were they overly enthusiastic towards emigration *per se*. Nevertheless, even when editorial policy was distinctly averse to the emigration of British labourers, working-class interest in emigration to Australia was so widespread that the workers' press published reports setting out the advantages of such a course of action. In 1839 the *Operative* carried two articles in praise of South Australia, which it claimed to print in response to public interest in the subject.[69] The second of these articles contained a direct refutation of the paper's editorial policy, and maintained that emigration to South Australia was the workers' only hope:

> But how are the poor to obtain the land? . . . If they are to wait the working out of all your Utopian schemes of political economy, or, mayhap, of revolutionary reform, or to look to the removal of the imposts on corn for a cheap loaf and more wages, or to the development of the thousand and one panaceas for the drying up of the sources of our national discontent which every political demagogue

is ever and anon propounding, *usquam ad nauseam,* they may at once pillow their heads upon the sod, and quietly moulder into their parent earth.[70]

By 1840 the obvious success of emigration financed from the sale of colonial crown-lands had apparently convinced even the doubters that there was no obligation or necessity to spend British revenues on assisting emigration. The *Edinburgh Review,* long a supporter of Wilmot Horton's, became a partial convert to the rival theories propounded by Wakefield. James Spedding—then an official at the Colonial Office—wrote an article which marked the journal's first favourable mention of systematic colonization. Of course systematic colonization was no longer a new thesis. First made public in 1829, Wakefieldian theories of colonization had already been responsible for two new settlements on the Australian coast, the colony of South Australia in 1836 and the Australind settlement in Western Australia in 1840. Spedding held that systematic colonization was 'sound in principle' and refused to support schemes for British-assisted pauper emigration on the ground that such plans had proven too expensive in the past to be considered economically feasible. Besides, Wilmot Horton's programme was only a remedy for the day, 'a violent effort to relieve an extreme pressure', not a natural and continual source of relief for a pressure also natural and continuous.[71]

Unfortunately for the peace of mind of such arm-chair theorists, the colonial source of relief was soon to dry up. In 1841 the economic boom in New South Wales and Van Diemen's Land came to an end, and the colonies on the eastern coast of Australia began to slide into a serious economic recession. By the end of the 1830s most of the available areas of good grazing land in the colonies had already been occupied and further expansion seemed to offer little prospect of increased profit.[72] Furthermore, at this stage in its development Australia had a one-crop economy which apparently had reached the limit of its capacities given the industry's techniques of production and the effects of a recent drought. Moreover, wool prices in the United Kingdom were falling and British banks began to restrict credit in the colonies. The result was a dislocated money market and depression. Little money was available for the purchase of crown-lands and consequently the emigration funds were drastically reduced.[73] At the same time, the South Australian bubble burst and that colony was bankrupt, while Western Australia continued to be the impoverished poor relation amongst the British colonies at the antipodes. Land sales in the eastern colonies and in South Australia fell alarmingly, and emigration assisted from colonial funds was indefinitely suspended. Although small numbers of emigrants still went to Australia each year, large-scale assisted emigration was not renewed until 1847.[74] Consequently, throughout the worst period of Chartist disturbances, Britain was without even the very limited safety-valve provided by assisted working-class passages to Australia.

Colonial depression was not the only factor responsible for a decline in the amount of colonial revenue available for emigration. In 1840 the imperial government had ordained that transportation of convicts to New South Wales should cease, and had transferred the costs of the convict establishment, police and gaols in both New South Wales and Van Diemen's Land to the land funds of the respective colonies. The colonists were incensed. The essence of systematic colonization, as understood in the colonies, was that the entire land fund was sacrosanct for immigration. This principle had been affirmed by the 1831 Ripon Regulations, but the Earl of Ripon in June 1840 recanted in the House of Lords and explained that the imperial government of 1831 had had no idea that sales of colonial crown-lands would prove so popular or bring in such a huge revenue. He had never intended in 1831 to deprive future administrations of control over the expenditure of such large sums of money, and in the circumstances did not feel that the British government was bound by his earlier promises to the colonists.[75] Such artful political sophistry was not appreciated by British supporters of emigration any more than it was by settlers in the colonies, and the government received a savage mauling from the press.[76] As far as New South Wales and Van Diemen's Land were concerned, the result of this reallocation of their land funds was that the little revenue which did accumulate from sales of land during the depression was used to meet expenses other than emigration. The situation in South Australia was not much different, in that the new governor, George Grey, under instructions to cut expenditure to the barest minimum, decided to levy the costs of the land office, surveys, Aboriginals, stores, emigrants, one-half of the police, and two-thirds of the medical department on the colony's land fund.[77] The combination of widespread Chartist disturbances and lack of colonial revenue to underwrite the costs of British emigration caused some observers from the middle and upper classes to reassess systematic colonization as a method of relieving British distress through emigration. It is against the background of this activity that demands for a return to the former system of direct British grants for emigration should be viewed.

The opinion that it was necessary to relieve British distress by spending British revenue on emigration remained anathema to the imperial government. During a debate in 1842 on emigration and the Land Sales Act, Stanley resolutely stated that the government had no intention of encouraging emigration which it considered large enough already. The government would direct the current emigration but

would not support steps to increase it.[78] Old attitudes were reviving,
however, and the following year a contributor to *Fraser's Magazine*
observed that the obvious remedy for Britain's overpopulation, with its
concomitant evils of indigence and unrest, was for the home government to provide financial assistance for emigration. Expenditure for
such a purpose would aid the relief of the mother country and at the
same time hasten colonial growth.[79] Sentiments in favour of systematic colonization, or rather of that portion of the thesis which stipulated that the proceeds of colonial land sales should be made available
without reserve for emigration, were expressed during 1842 and 1843
in a series of parliamentary debates on Australia which dealt with
South Australia, emigration and the Land Sales Act, and came to a
climax on 6 April 1843 with the debate on Charles Buller's motion on
systematic colonization.[80] Buller was a close associate of Wakefield's,
and in his speech claimed that Britain could relieve its distressed
population by giving systematic colonization a fair trial. Huge tracts of
waste lands existed in the colonies, and if excess British capital, which
lowered interest rates on the home market, was to be invested in
colonial lands and farms, the return to the capitalist would be higher
than he could hope to obtain at home, and at the same time emigration
funds from the colonies would be increased and British distress would
thereby be relieved.[81] Some of the daily newspapers found Buller's
reasoning attractive, and in particular they were pleased with the
prospect of pauper emigration being continued without cost to the
British taxpayer. The Whig *Courier* was the most nakedly opportunis-
tic, because it favoured emigration to Australia as a means of relieving
domestic indigence only as long as the imperial government did not
have to bear the cost.[82]

Prior to colonial economic recovery in 1847, however, public debate
on the merits of systematic colonization was doomed to be arid and
fruitless. Proponents of systematic colonization claimed that the colonies would benefit equally with the mother country from a resumption
of British emigration, but such special pleading took no account of
actual conditions in Australia during these years. Unemployment was
rife, and life in Australia during the depression had been grim for
many working men and their families. In 1841, for example, several
hundred immigrant labourers had found existence in Sydney so
intolerable that they had re-emigrated to Valparaiso in South
America.[83] South Australia was no better off, and that same year the
governor was ordered to save money by shipping unemployed workers
to the eastern colonies and to stop relief payments to those who refused
to leave Adelaide when offered rural employment.[84] Systematic colonizers and colonial reformers in Britain had little conception of the
severity of this Australia-wide depression, nor did they seem to realize

that until economic recovery began in the depressed colonies all talk of emigration revenue from colonial land funds was hopelessly speculative.

There was a further variable which greatly affected British attitudes to emigration—namely, the health of Britain's domestic economy. When the economy was in a boom phase it proved difficult to attract emigrants to Australia even with free passages. The land and emigration commissioners claimed that although they had funds for renewed emigration to South Australia in 1845-6, they could only send out one shipload of labourers. They reported that the railway boom in Britain had created an inordinate demand for labour, and workers could not be persuaded to leave.[85] The following year, Irish distress and a slackening of the railway boom led to a large increase in the number of applications for free passages to South Australia, and the commissioners were forced to ask prospective emigrants whether they would consent to go to other Australia colonies.[86] Even when times were bad in Britain, an immense reservoir of emotion militated against emigration:

> Oh! Emigration! thou-rt the curse
> Of our once happy nation's race!
> Cannot our Fatherland still nurse
> Its offspring without taking place
> Of dislocated men to make
> More cause for thy disturbing sake.
> Thou art an enemy to peace,
> The restless hope but ends in grief
> When comforts in the mother cease
> How can we hope step-dame's relief?
> Better to bear the ills we have
> Than seek in foreign climes a grave![87]

By 1847, extensive emigration to the Australian colonies had been resumed, and as before the great majority of such emigrants came from the working classes. The theory of systematic colonization, insofar as it affected the lower classes, was predicated on the proposition that labourers who emigrated would be forced to remain workers for wages in the colonies. About this time, however, a new school of colonial theoreticians and popularizers appeared in Britain, who entirely rejected Wakefield's theories and openly claimed Australia's crownlands for the labouring classes of Great Britain. Samuel Sidney published *A Voice from the Far Interior of Australia* in 1847, and this became the first section of *Sidney's Australian Handbook* published the following year. The handbook was a publishing phenomenon going through seven editions of 1000 copies each in five months.[88] Sidney became the main spokesman for the new approach:

> Australia can never be colonized on a national scale, until the impolitic and unjust regulations founded on Mr Wakefield's theory are completely reformed. To bring about this most important of all Australian reforms, and, having effected it, to enable my labouring fellow-countrymen to exchange their state as ill-paid, ill-fed workmen in England, Scotland and Ireland, for that of comfortable free-holders in Australia, are the principal objects of this publication.[89]

In 1847, Alexander Harris's *Settlers and Convicts* had taken a similar line. Writing under the pseudonym of an emigrant mechanic, Harris had stated that Britain's workers and labourers had a greater moral right to the lands of British colonies than anybody else.[90] Sidney and Harris, however, did share with Wakefield and the systematic colonizers one very important attitude: Australia was still seen as a property to be exploited for Britain's benefit. The new school viewed the Australian colonies as palliatives for the radicalism of the British working classes. If workers did emigrate and become contented and well-fed farm labourers or peasant farmers in Australia, the theory seemed to run, they would lose their stimulus to revolution.

The insurrectionary potential of Britain's lower orders also concerned Caroline Chisholm, nineteenth century Australia's foremost social worker and self-appointed protector of the morals of British emigrants, who had travelled to Britain in 1848. Her purpose was to organize in the mother country a scheme for the colonization of Australia by encouraging family emigration. With the transfer of complete family units rather than of individuals, Mrs Chisholm hoped to avoid the immorality which had characterized previous attempts to systematize female immigration into New South Wales and at the same time to help redress the unnatural balance of the predominantly male populations of New South Wales and Van Diemen's Land.

In Chisholm's view the government system of emigration had serious shortcomings and she favoured a renewal of a modified bounty system of emigration which would be cheaper than the government emigration and would allow 'parties to select their own ship and proceed direct from the nearest port'.[81] In 1850 she met Charles Dickens[92] and found that they shared an interest in emigration and an attitude of profound apprehension concerning the dangers of revolutionary Chartism.[93] This similarity of outlook resulted in collaboration on a joint article which appeared in *Household Words* and contained an excerpt from a letter written by an emigrant Chartist from New South Wales. The letter gave clear evidence that good wages and regular employment had led him to renounce his earlier acceptance of the desirability of revolution.[94] *Household Words* was also used to publicise Chisholm's Family Colonization Loan Society which implemented the great Victorian ideal of self-help in the field of emigration. The society's object was to lend money to deserving families or suitable single people which would enable them to emigrate to New South Wales. The loan was to be repaid when the emigrants had established themselves in the colony.

Household Words was very much the personal voice of its editor Charles Dickens, and was far and away the most popular and widely read periodical of its time. Consequently, when the journal began to indulge in virulent criticism of the official emigration scheme and to contrast it most unfavourably with the emigration conducted by Chisholm's society, the government became concerned. Earlier criticism of the Colonial Office by Wakefield and the colonial reformers had usually been loftily ignored, and it is a measure of the importance of *Household Words* that its criticisms elicited a personal and private reply to Charles Dickens from Earl Grey then secretary of state for colonies. Grey stated that the emigration commissioners had his entire confidence, and that they had sent out more than 50 000 emigrants to Australia since 1847. With such large numbers it was unavoidable that a few mistakes would be made and some unsuitable emigrants would escape detection. Grey then launched into an attack on the character of those working-class people who made up the bulk of the emigration:

> It must be remembered that the latter [i.e. voluntary emigrants] are necessarily far below the average of the working population in respect to steadiness and strictly moral conduct. They are generally perhaps above the average of their class in respect to energy and intelligence, but in every rank of life it is not the steady and well conducted that are the most disposed to emigration, and amongst the labouring class it is remarkably the reverse ... Hence I believe it will be found that whether sent out by the commissioners or emigration in private ships a large proportion of the emigrants of the working class would be found to be men of somewhat unsteady habits.[95]

Caroline Chisholm was not the only colonist from Australia who embarked on a campaign to promote British emigration during these years. The Reverend John Dunmore Lang arrived from New South Wales in 1847 on a mission to persuade Scottish Presbyterians to emigrate to Australia. Although Chisholm and Lang detested one another,[96] their combined propaganda in favour of emigration to New South Wales could only have advanced the growing public interest in Australia and its prospects.

The period after 1847 was a time when emigration was very much a matter of public interest in Britain as a result of the devastating social dislocation caused by the great famine in Ireland. The huge population of indigent Irish placed a great strain on Britain's resources and social conscience, and to many observers emigration financed by the home government seemed the only solution.[97] Nevertheless, the British government continued to refuse all requests for such assistance, which led Dickens to comment that the Whig authorities seemed to have a secret belief in 'the gentle politico-economical principle that a surplus population must and ought to starve'.[98] Grey led the opposition to imperial expenditure on emigration, and his resistance was not solely on the grounds of expense. He refused to admit that Britain suffered from over-population and he held that if the full agricultural and industrial potentialities of the United Kingdom were to be realized Britain would need all her labourers at home.[99] Furthermore, Grey believed that if the government were to make money available for free emigration to the colonies it would be undermining the self-reliance of the British people, for he maintained that 'in ninety-nine cases out of a hundred, even in the worst times, it would be found, on strict investigation, that some fault or imprudence on the part of the labourer' was the real cause of unemployment.[1] In such circumstances assisted emigration would tax the honest and sober for the betterment of the lazy or slothful, and this was morally unacceptable. Finally, Grey described the suggestion of a government loan for Irish emigration as 'the most pernicious proposal ever made with regard to Ireland', because 'borrowing dulls the edge of husbandry'.[2] If the administration were to outlay money for pauper emigration it would quickly find itself responsible for the entire costs of the exceedingly large emigration already in progress. At present this outflow was entirely financed from private sources and Grey felt sure that the majority of such emigrants would throw themselves upon the government for relief if once they knew funds were available for emigration. Thus a British loan for emigration might actually lead to a decrease in the overall numbers leaving Ireland which was the very opposite of what supporters of such a loan had in mind.[3]

Emigration had become a matter of general concern and Australia received more favourable publicity from Sir Thomas Mitchell's published reports of his explorations in New South Wales between 1845 and 1847 which painted a glowing picture of the new lands he had traversed.[4] Under the combined stimuli of favourable colonial propaganda, the renewed prosperity of the pastoral industry, and domestic necessity, British interest in Australia continued to grow. The *Times* began to include letters from Australian settlers which outlined the opportunities created by the urgent need for labour at the antipodes,[5] and Henry Rogers, the popular essayist, reassured prospective emigrants that they would not find a completely alien invironment upon arrival in Australia. British emigration to that part of the world was already so great that there were 'comparatively few families at this day in Great Britain who have not some relation—brother, sister, son, daughter, nephew—in those colonies'.[6] The following year George Groly advised that England was overcrowded and counselled his readers that emigration to the Australian colonies was the best and most obvious remedy.[7]

Opinion in favour of Australia, however, was still far from unanimous. The *New Monthly Magazine and Humorist*, refused to rule which particular colony or continent best suited emigration. It discoursed upon competition between Canada, Australia, Nova Scotia, New Brunswick, Natal, and other British dependencies for the privilege of receiving more labour. Individual colonies were said to press their own claims by denouncing other colonies, and people were becoming confused. Moreover, the article expressed the sensible view that different colonies required different types of emigrants:

> The emigrants who prosper best at the Cape and in North America, in Canada, New Brunswick, Cape Breton, and Prince Edward's Island, are very small capitalists, men who land with £10 or £20 in their pockets, and enter upon a few acres at once, or those who make £10 and become proprietors forthwith. Australia requires generally speaking a different class of emigrants; capitalists of from £2000 to £10 000, or of nothing but health and willingness to work.[8]

A series of stanzas by the minor poet J. E. Carpenter illustrates the shift in British attitudes towards emigration and indicates a very different outlook from that espoused by the writer of the 1844 poem 'The Emigrant Ship'. Carpenter set out to describe some of the reasons which might prompt a man to quit his native land, and his doggerel reveals a tendency which recurred in the works of more important literary figures to romanticize the colonies and see them as a promised land. The third and fourth stanzas represent the appeal of emigration to an impoverished working man with a family.

> Let us go forth—a light is round me breaking,
> A star of hope points brightly to the West;
> Others have gone before—they now are making
> The quiet homesteads where their sons shall rest;
> For thousands more there is a mighty space
> Of fertile plains whereon no corn-fields grow;
> *Here* in life's future not *one* hope I trace,
> *There* is the land of promise—let us go!
> Let us go forth—behold our children's faces
> Radiant with joy—without mark of care;

A few more years, when time has left his traces
On those bright forms—no smile will circle there;
the same dull round that we have run before them
Must be their future if we linger still,
Let us the freedom they should know restore them,
Hence from life's valley—let us climb the hill![9]

Minor versifiers were not the only writers who indulged themselves with idealized fantasies concerning the prospects of emigrants from Britain to the colonies; and even intelligent and popular novelists like Charles Dickens and Bulwer Lytton shared similar attitudes to those enunciated by Carpenter. The theme of emigration to Australia was used in several ways by both novelists, but the Australian colonies proved particularly serviceable in two ways. Lytton found emigration to Australia convenient as a sort of social purgatory, and he used the experience as a literary device through which defects of character could be burned away in the fires of adversity and hard labour. Dickens, on the other hand, found that emigration to the Australian colonies proved helpful as a method of disposing of awkward characters. In *David Copperfield*, for example, Little Em'ly loses her virtue after her seduction by Steerforth, and mid-Victorian literary convention demanded that she die an unhappy and miserable death traditionally by suicide in a convenient river.[10] Em'ly is permitted to live, but is banished to Australia; ' "They will emigrate together, Aunt," said I. "Yes" said Mr Peggotty with a hopeful smile. "No one can't reproach my darling in Australia".'[11] After such a backhanded compliment to colonial society the reader is unsurprised that earlier in the book the golden-hearted prostitute Martha had been rescued from the brink of the orthodox suicide[12] and packed off with the other emigrants to Australia. Even Wilkins Micawber made a fortune in Australia and also became a magistrate, a fact which has led a recent critic to remark that for Dickens success in Australia was in itself an admission of failure in England.[13]

Dickens was not alone in his feeling that emigration was somehow synonymous with failure, particularly with moral failure. Steven Marcus has stated that mid-Victorian society recognized four ways by which prostitutes could enter respectable life again, and emigration was one of them.[14] Indeed, the aristocratic author of the contemporary scatological autobiography *My Secret Life* relates how, during the 1840s, he disposed of two sisters he had seduced and made pregnant by arranging for them to emigrate to Canada.[15] Between 1847 and 1858 Dickens himself was personally involved in this aspect of emigration when he co-operated with the philanthropist Angela Burdett Coutts in obtaining and administering a home for 'fallen women' where they were prepared for emigration and sent to the colonies. By 1853 fifty-seven girls had passed through the home, thirty of whom had done well in Australia or elsewhere.[16]

Bulwer Lytton also viewed Australia as a fit receptacle for Britain's failures, though his rejects came from the upper ranks of English society. Lytton found Australia useful as a place to which members of the upper classes could travel and by hard labour regenerate both their morals and their fortunes. In *The Caxtons*, Vivian de Caxton, a seducer of helpless heiresses, is caught in the act by his father and cousin, Pisistratus Caxton, and dutifully repentant, agrees to seek atonement by accompanying Pisistratus to Australia.[17] Guy Bolding another fallen aristocrat agrees to go with them as he is bankrupt from the excesses of his 'fast' life at Oxford.[18] There is an interesting difference between these three young men which indicates Lytton's conception of Australia as a reception centre for Britain's moral cripples. Pisistratus has committed no crime and consequently does not have to remain in Australia indefinitely. His sole object is to make a fortune and he takes £3000 which he hopes to treble within five years and return to England. Pisistratus has no intention of settling permanently in Australia: 'Our object, I take it,' he says 'is to get back to England as soon as we can'.[19] They are successful and the morally unstained Pisistratus returns with his fortune to Britain. The other two, however, remain. It is in his treatment of Guy Bolding and Vivian de Caxton that Lytton reveals that for him, as for Dickens, emigration to Australia still had overtones of transportation. Guy Bolding stays behind in Australia as a prosperous and happily married settler, and Vivian de Caxton having recovered his moral probity in the hard bush life, accepts a commission and dies bravely fighting for queen and empire in the Indian army. Both men, however, were unable to return to Britain.

When all the diverse sources of favourable publicity for emigration to Australia during the 1840s are considered together, they must have reached a very wide audience. Nevertheless, the problem of Australia's distance from Britain raised serious difficulties to the development of a numerically large emigration from the mother country. Colonial money was limited, the British government would not itself pay passages to Australia, and private charities tended to prefer the much cheaper emigration to North America. As Earl Grey explained to Governor Charles Fitzroy in New South Wales, the government was aware of 'the superiority of the inducements to a working man to proceed to Australia', but he added that even with a free passage paid from colonial land funds, the would-be emigrant had still to find £5 or £6 for bedding and other supplies. This additional money had often to be provided by private individuals or charitable institutions, and such people were usually aware that the total cost of emigration to North America was only £5 or £6. Australia therefore should not expect private supplementary help for emigrants to exceed the total cost of emigration to North America, particularly when such help was generally an attempt at relief.[20]

Such worries were soon destined to be allayed. Emigration to New South Wales and the newly constituted colony of Victoria received a great fillip from the discovery of vast auriferous deposits in both colonies. The British press now devoted even more attention to Australia and the colonies received a huge influx of population.[21] British publishers and commentators were preoccupied with the Russian war during these years, but many detailed descriptions of the Australian goldfields and their unusual way of life nevertheless appeared. Despite the war, the discovery of gold nuggets like the Welcome Stranger which melted down to 2284 ounces of gold and sold for £9436 captured the imagination of the British public. The existence of such nuggets caused a proliferation of popular melodramas on London stages in which emigrant fortune-hunters from England found affluence on the diggings at the antipodes.[22]

For all that, extensive emigration to Australia was not regarded with unalloyed joy, even by those very journals which had earlier proclaimed such emigration to be necessary. In 1852 the writer D. T. Coulton warned readers of the *Quarterly Review* that Britain was losing the cream of her population. Coulton recognized that the most valuable commodity Britain could export to the Australian colonies was people, but he went on to express concern that the bulk of those emigrating were 'the youngest, the healthiest, and most energetic of the adult population',[23] a somewhat higher opinion of British emigrants than that which Grey had propounded to Charles Dickens that same year. In the case of Ireland, Coulton applauded the loss of this section of the populace, but he was concerned that the result in England would be a declining population, for there was no surplus of that class from amongst whom the emigration commissioners chose their emigrants.[24] He believed that the wrong people were leaving for Australia. Britain had a superfluity of 'ingenious and educated men' who ought to seek their fortunes in Australia, though he did recognize that such men would more than likely lack the physical strength and stamina for gold-digging.

In the same year another journalist R. H. Patterson extolled the gold discoveries in New South Wales and Victoria and forecast that the long-term effects would be beneficial, as the endemic labour shortage in the colonies finally would be solved by a huge immigration of Chinese who were known to be hard workers and were also inured to a tropical climate.[25] Patterson realised that the goldfields formed an

irresistible attraction for European labourers, and an emigration of
Asian workers had obvious attractions. The imperial government was
loath to jeopardize the Australian wool industry upon which British
manufacturers had become dependent, and for this reason the Colonial
Office reversed a long-standing policy and reluctantly agreed to the use
of money from the New South Wales' land fund to provide financial
assistance for the immigration into the colony of Eurasians from
India.[26]

On the other hand, a contributor to *Fraser's Magazine for Town and
Country* enthusiastically welcomed the boost British emigration
received from gold discoveries in Australia, and commented favourably that the current rate of British emigration to Australia was then
5000 a week, although some reservations were expressed concerning
those who took advantage of the free passages. The magazine warned
that these came from 'the dregs of the lower classes', who were
credited with opposite characteristics to 'the young, the healthy, the
sober, the frugal, the industrious, the energetic' who came from the
middle or upper classes and paid their own way.[27] Stories of the great
wealth which could be obtained at the goldfields led the journal to
describe Australia as an El Dorado 'whose surface is so thickly strewn
with gold as to excite wonder how men, not destitute of eyes, could
avoid seeing it'.[28]

British agricultural labourers were informed that there could never
be a more propitious time for emigration to Australia. Colonial pastoralists complained that their labour force had decamped en masse for
the gold-diggings thereby creating a chronic shortage of all forms of
labour in the primary industries. It was said, that a man with a
knowledge of farming or livestock could become independent in a very
few years.[29] Moreover, British statesmen were reminded that the
mother country had a vested interest in ensuring a massive augmentation of the work force in the colonies or else production would suffer
which in turn would cause unemployment in the textile industry at
home.[30]

Perhaps it was for similar reasons that the British working-class
press exhibited so decided a preference for emigration to Australia
during these years. In 1852 *The Operative* claimed that 'Australia is
emphatically the poor man's country. The capital of the labourer and
the mechanic—viz., the strong arm, combined with skill, are always
wanted, and produce an immediate return'.[31] It is somewhat ironic in
the face of such enthusiasm to find that both Karl Marx and Frederick
Engels were profoundly irritated by the Australian gold discoveries
and the massive emigration from Britain which resulted. They felt that
the predicted commercial crisis and the onset of revolution would

thereby be delayed. Hence Engels described the discoveries as 'the Australian gold-shit',[32] and complained to Marx:

> Australia, too, does damage. First, directly through gold and the cessation of all its other exports, as well as through the increased imports of all commodities conditioned thereby, and then through the departure of the local surplus population, at the rate of 5000 a week.[33]

Between 1828 and 1855 therefore, British attitudes towards emigration to Australia underwent considerable change. Working-class leaders began by being exceedingly hostile to an emigration which smacked of convict transportation and placed labourers under the autocratic rule of a colonial-governor. The stigma of felonious exile made emigration to Australia appear undesirable to British workers and their spokesmen, particularly when the passage cost so much. After the Ripon Regulations had removed the barrier of expense in 1831, and convict transportation to New South Wales was abolished in 1840, working-class enthusiasm for Australia discernibly increased until by the end of the 1840s and the beginning of the next decade many British workers had come to look upon Australia as peculiarly their own, though a few of the more politically minded opposed all emigration as detrimental to the class struggle at home. For spokesmen from the middle and upper classes, emigration to Australia appealed as a quick method of making money, and also as a social corrective when widespread unemployment amongst the labouring classes led them to political and revolutionary activities of a threatening character.[34] There was considerable agreement that when distress was very severe the British government should assist emigration as a method of relief, but this was a sentiment rejected by both Tory and Whig governments in an age which stressed that governments must curb expenditure and encourage the Victorian ideals of self-reliance and private initiative. It was reasons of cost as well as of choice which led the vast majority of emigrants to head for North America rather than the antipodes. Once it became the practice during the 1830s to sell Australian crown-lands and make available a portion of the proceeds of such sales to meet the costs of free emigration, the major objection was removed. As the 1840s progressed and propaganda in favour of the Australian colonies reached a wide audience, it came to be recognized that the colonies in Australia were quite capable of absorbing a much larger number of emigrants than they were receiving. To this end some influential sections of public opinion even proposed a systematic renewal of direct financial assistance for emigration by the British government in an effort to supplement monies raised in Australia and to increase the effectiveness of the Australian colonies as one of Britain's major social safety-valves.

6: Native Affairs 1828-55

While the British commentators and statesmen devoted considerable attention to the rapid growth of emigration during the period under review, Australia's indigenous inhabitants were not entirely ignored. New South Wales had become a British possession by right of discovery and utilization. The first settlement was entirely governmental in character and all territorial rights were vested in the crown. There was no treaty with the native populace, and Aboriginals were deprived of the right to their own laws and the ownership of their lands. In return they acquired—unbeknown to themselves—the somewhat hazy status and privileges of British subjects. Between the first settlement in 1788 and the successful conclusion of the anti-slavery agitation in 1833, British authorities took little interest in the native population of Australia. The instructions given to Governors Phillip, Hunter, King, Bligh and Macquarie, insofar as they referred to the Aboriginals, were identical and involved the incorporation of a stereotyped formula that had originated in the days when the thirteen American colonies were still within the empire. Governor Phillip was instructed

> to endeavour by every possible means to open an intercourse with the natives, and to conciliate their affections, enjoining all our subjects to live in amity and kindness with them. And if any of our subjects shall wantonly destroy them, or give them unnecessary interruption in the exercise of their several occupations, it is our will and pleasure that you do cause such offenders to be brought to punishment according to the degree of the offence.[1]

Undoubtedly many of the early governors were men of good will, but their dealings with the Aboriginals of New South Wales and Van

Diemen's Land reflected an underlying assumption that British civilization and the European way of life was innately superior.[2] Consequently, their method of civilizing the natives took the form of repeated attempts to encourage permanent settlement by breaking up the pattern of tribal society and assisting Aboriginals to establish themselves as peasant farmers on small agricultural allotments. Education of native children was another area of life in which a policy of Europeanization was followed, and here also repeated attempts were made to wean Aboriginal children from the wild life of nomadic hunting or from a life of parasitical begging on the fringes of settlement, and to inculcate in them the necessary skills and desire to work the soil. Such schemes, whether governmental or missionary in initiation, were complete failures.[3]

It was not until 1825 that the British missionary societies devoted serious attention to converting the Aboriginals. Previously, the efforts of most clergymen in New South Wales and Van Diemen's Land had been fully occupied in ministering to the manifold needs of the white flock, particularly the convicts.[4] In 1824, the Reverend D. Tyermann and George Bennet, en route to the London Missionary Society's fields of endeavour in the South Seas broke their journey at Sydney, and were shocked at the extent of the 'wretchedness and degradation' in which they found the Australian Aboriginals. They notified London headquarters that one of the South Sea Island missionaries had expressed a desire to work amongst the Aboriginals and they had given provisional assent to the Reverend Threkeld's suggestion.[5] In 1825, therefore, the London Missionary Society founded a mission at Lake Macquarie in New South Wales to which the colonial government made a conditional grant of 10 000 acres. By 1828 the mission had failed and the land reverted to the government. The Church Missionary Society's mission at Wellington (1831–42) also received 10 000 acres, the Wesleyan Buntingdale mission at Geelong in the Port Phillip district (1838–48) 64 000 acres, and the Presbyterian Mission at Nundah near Brisbane (1838–42) 640 acres. The result of this surge of activity from British missionary societies was most discouraging and the effort to detribalize Aboriginals and convert them into christian peasant farmers in New South Wales failed to produce a single Aboriginal settler. Nor were the British missionary societies more active or successful in the settlements at Swan River and in South Australia. Small missions did exist in both colonies, but the impetus came from the colonial governments and colonial clergy rather than from the headquarters of missionary societies in Britain.[6]

There appears to be adequate evidence to support Paul Hasluck's claim that 'little of the missionary zeal of middle-class England seemed to be attracted towards the Australian savage. He stood a poor chance against the picturesque African and South Sea Islander.'[7] Nevertheless, this shortage of missionaries to attend to the welfare of the Australian native population should be seen in perspective, and one should keep in mind that as late as 1846–7 insufficient clergy resided in the colonies to minster effectively to the European population, and fears were expressed that by reason of this deficiency the settlers were backsliding into paganism.[8] Furthermore, the few missionaries actively interested in evangelizing the Aboriginals were genuinely convinced that the corruption of the native tribes was directly attributable to the pernicious influence of settlers and their convict servants.[9] Since contact between settlers and Aboriginals could not be avoided, the Society for the Propagation of the Gospel (S.P.G.) obviously felt that native conversion could best be served by first reconverting the European settlers and convicts, thereby eradicating the root cause of the moral corruption, rather than dealing only with the secondary symptoms of iniquity as exhibited by the behaviour of Aboriginals.

If this attitude seems strangely lacking in enthusiasm during an age of evangelical missionary fervour, one should remember that the S.P.G. was not evangelical in inspiration and that, by and large, it did not share in the burgeoning missionary movement then underway in Britain. Indeed, the society's realistic decision to concentrate on the recovery of the European population in Australia followed logically from similar policy decisions already taken in regard to British North America and other areas of English emigration and settlement overseas.[10] On the other hand, these priorities did not appeal to other British missionary societies who preferred to send at least an occasional missionary to work directly upon the task of winning Australia's natives for Christianity.[11]

Contact between settlers and Aboriginals provided colonial administrators as well as missionaries with a continual stream of insoluble problems, and it was in Van Diemen's Land that they loomed in their largest and most intractable form. Conflict between colonists and natives had been incessant on the island colony since the earliest days of settlement. By the 1830s this had resulted in the virtual extermination of the entire native race. The imperial authorities were not indifferent to the fate of the Van Diemen's Land Aboriginals, but neither the strictures of various secretaries of state nor the threats of colonial governors could be adequately enforced on the frontiers of settlement. In the final analysis it was the settler with his gun who decided whether native policy as enunciated by the Colonial Office was practicable or not. Moreover, native resistance to British settlement in Van Diemen's Land raised awkward wider questions which might have proved embarrassing to the Colonial Office if the extirpation of the native populace had not intervened. British possession of Australia and Van Diemen's Land rested on a claim to ownership of land previously unoccupied.[12] Yet the imperial authorities were also aware that the troubles in Van Diemen's Land rested squarely on a native refusal to recognize British sovereignty over their lands or persons. In 1829 Sir George Murray admitted that the Aboriginals of Van Diemen's Land did fell a sense of proprietorship over the lands of their island, and resented European attempts to drive them away from what they regarded as their own property. His answer to the difficulty, however, was the use of force:

> I am aware of the extremely difficult task of inducing ignorant Beings of the description of those alluded to, to acknowledge any authority short of absolute force, particularly when possessed with the idea which they appear to entertain in regard to their own rights over the Country in comparison with those of the Colonists.[13]

The British failure to give sufficient attention to the native problems caused by European settlements in Australia was not confined to the colonies on the eastern seaboard. Further evidence of a seeming inability to profit from experience can be seen in the lack of detailed or specific directions concerning Aboriginals in the Royal Instructions to Lieutenant-Governor Stirling upon the foundation of the Swan River colony in 1829.[14] Clashes between settlers and Aboriginals soon occurred, and were undoubtedly exacerbated by a disposition on the part of some settlers to discharge firearms at natives on sight.[15]

By this time, however, humanitarian sentiment was becoming increasingly influential in Britain. In 1829 the *Westminster Review* carried an article which publicly rejected the popular notion that Australian aborigines constituted 'the last link in the chain of humanity', and repudiated other writers who likened Aboriginals to apes, or claimed that they exhibited no aspects of civilization at all. The *Review* pointed out that 'The time has been when some liberal Roman wrote thus of the inhabitants of Britain.'[16] Two years later, another observer found merit in the suggestion that the administration and settlers in Australian colonies should follow the 'excellent policy which has gained us the vast empire of India', namely treating the natives kindly.[17] This was an attitude entirely in keeping with the predispositions of the Colonial Office, but that department was unable to ensure that its native policy was put into practice in Australia. After trouble had broken out between settlers and Aboriginals in Western Australia, Lord Goderich informed Stirling that peace between settlers and natives was essential to the prosperity of the colony, and that he hoped Stirling would be able 'to convince those under your Government that it will be only by observing uniformly a great degree of forbearance that they can expect to relieve themselves from further annoyance.'[18]

The pattern of settlement in Western Australia made Stirling's job a difficult one. He lacked the manpower to provide adequate protection for individual colonists and their families who lived in widely separated areas, and as in the eastern convict colonies, the burden of protection fell upon the settler himself. Militia was available to protect the colonists wherever possible, but in cases of emergency the European population exercised the right to defend itself. The Colonial Office endorsed this right in a dispatch of 1831 which instructed the settlers that they could only rely upon the government to repel a 'serious or combined attack from the natives' and that they were 'expected to defend themselves against any petty assaults of a predatory nature to which they may be exposed'.[19] Such permission was of course open to wide abuse, and settlers honoured the legal status of the Aboriginals as British subjects more in the breach than in the observance. Between 1829 and 1834 a state of continual friction existed similar to that which had occurred in the earlier settlement of Van Diemen's Land, and this culminated in 1834 in a punitive expedition led by Stirling himself, which was responsible for the massacre at Pinjarra of between twenty-five and thirty natives.[20]

The butchery at Pinjarra occurred at a time when British attitudes towards the Aboriginals in Australia were becoming increasingly polarized. In July 1834 the House of Commons unanimously passed an address to the crown which called on Britain to remember the duty,

> of acting upon the principles of justice and humanity in the intercourse and relations of this country with the native Inhabitants of its Colonial Settlements, of affording them protection in the enjoyment of their civil rights and of imparting to them that degree of civilization and that religion with which Providence has blessed this nation.[21]

Nevertheless, the unanimity of the House of Commons was not the reflection of a consensus of British opinion. The *Westminster Review* carried a long article on Van Diemen's Land that same year, in which it struck an attitude that was the very antithesis of those sentiments embodied in the address of the House of Commons. According to the article, the Aboriginals of Van Diemen's Land were the most debased and barbarous of all beings having human form. Their physical appearance was 'hideous' and their intellects were said to be as degenerate as their bodies. 'In a word, they possess in a remarkable degree the highest attributes of brute instinct rendered more powerful and more pernicious by the perverted glimmering of reason, with which even the lowest in the scale of humanity are to a certain extent endowed.'[22] The conservative *Quarterly Review* shared these sentiments and described Australian aborigines as 'scarcely human' and far inferior, both intellectually and morally, to the worst of the New Zealand Maoris who at least had the saving grace of being a handsome race, whilst the Aboriginals were 'among the most hideous of all living caricatures of humanity.'[23]

Despite the evident popularity of such views with a significant segment of the British public, they were not shared by the Colonial Office and Stirling's punitive slaughter of 1834 earned him severe censure, though not recall. A dispatch of July 1835 sternly pointed out that it was the governor's duty to impress upon settlers the determination of the British government to punish severely acts of injustice or outrage committed against the Aboriginals, and to ensure that the native victims of such violence would receive adequate compensation. 'You will make it imperative upon the officers of police', the dispatch continued,

> never to allow any injustive or insult in regard to the natives to pass unnoticed, as being too trifling a character; and they should be charged to report to you with punctuality every instance of aggression or misconduct ... Whenever it may be necessary to bring a native to justice every form should be observed which would be considered necessary in the case of a white person and no infliction of punishment, however trivial, should be permitted except by the award of some competent authority.[24]

Mistreatment of Aboriginals during 1836 by the members of Major Thomas Mitchell's third exploring expedition in New South Wales caused a similar declamation to be levelled at Governor Richard Bourke.[25] Such reiterations of the principle that Aboriginals and settlers were equal before the law may have soothed consciences in the Colonial Office, but it had very little real effect on relations between the races in the colonies. Stirling showed his opinion of the censure implied in Glenelg's dispatch by printing the dispatch without comment in the colonial *Government Gazette*, together with the earlier dispatch of 1831 which told settlers to protect themselves. His intention was obviously satiric. Stirling believed that the ultimate fate of the Aboriginal was extinction, but that in the meantime some form of protectorate was needed to pacify and settle the natives while nature ran its course.[26]

Most governors in the Australian colonies could not and did not give effect to the British policy that the Aboriginals were full British subjects. To have done so would have involved the overstretched colonial agencies for law enforcement in constant and thankless interference in the incessant and often bloody conflicts amongst the natives themselves. As British subjects under British sovereignty, Aboriginals should not have been allowed to settle their tribal and personal disputes by force. But the realities of the colonial situation forced governors to make unauthorized modifications in British policy in an attempt to compromise between firm instructions on the one hand and a situation in which such instructions were impossible of fulfilment on the other. This problem was resolved in New South Wales in a way which was also adopted in the other Australian colonies; the colonial authorities attempted merely to protect the lives of the native people, while all that was required from the Aboriginals was that they refrained from depredations against the lives and property of the settlers. How they acted towards one another when outside the areas of European administration was of no concern to the colonial government.[27] Thus Aboriginal law, which was not regarded as having any juridical authority in the Australian colonies, was granted a *de facto* recognition in the sense that Aboriginals generally were free to regulate their behaviour amongst themselves by their own laws except where such conduct would bring them into conflict with the persons or property of the white settlers. The only positive attempt to educate Australian Aboriginals into acceptance of the primacy of British law in regulating their own behaviour towards one another occurred between 1842 and 1853, when Charles La Trobe, the administrator of the Port Phillip district and later the lieutenant-governor of Victoria, experimented with a native police force in the Port Phillip area. He hoped that the native constables would keep order amongst their people, and at the same time that military discipline would hasten the detribalization and civilization of those involved and accustom them to British law. This attempt also failed, the native troopers soon becoming known as notorious drunkards both on and off duty, and the European officers as congenital incompetents.[28]

It was in 1835 that the Aboriginal inhabitants of the Port Phillip district had first become a matter of concern to the Colonial Office. In that year, the Port Phillip Bay Association was formed in Van Diemen's Land with the sole object of opening up that fertile and promising area of New South Wales for grazing and settlement. John Batman, as accredited representative of the Association, claimed to have entered into a treaty with the natives of Port Phillip Bay and to have purchased lands from them. In addition to imposing a new burden of administrative costs on the government at Sydney, settlement at Port Phillip raised again the question of ownership of waste lands in Australia and the Colonial Office was quick to take it up.

Glenelg informed Bourke in 1836 that although he felt the Aboriginals were entitled to protection,

> I yet believe that we should consult very ill for the real welfare of that helpless and unfortunate Race, by recognising in them any right to alienate to private adventurers the land of the Colony. It is indeed enough to observe, that such a concession would subvert the foundation on which all Proprietary Rights in New South Wales at present rest, and defeat a large part of the most important Regulations of the local Government.[29]

Colonial Office recognition of Batman's treaty could have had a catastrophic effect on the administration of land policy throughout Australia. It would have constituted a tacit acknowledgement by the British government that Australia's waste lands were not vested in the crown but belonged to the natives whose consent would therefore be needed if they were to continue to be sold. It would also be an admission that since the mid 1820s the British government had been selling what was not theirs to sell. For these reasons there was no question of the treaty being accepted. Natives in Australia were not reinvested with the ownership of their lands, and it is interesting to note in this context that in 1834 land in the new colony of South Australia had been disposed of by parliament with no reference to the aboriginal population.[30]

During these years, however, the House of Commons had secured the appointment of a select committee on Aboriginal Tribes (British settlements). This committee sat during 1836 and 1837 and considered what measures were necessary to secure the benefits mentioned in the address of 1834 for native inhabitants living in or around British settlements. Many humanitarians who had been involved in the anti-slavery campaign took an interest in the committee, which was under the chairmanship of T. Fowell Buxton, and they and their supporters dominated its proceedings. The committee's 1836 report deplored the fact that no notice had been taken of native territorial rights when New South Wales was first settled, and considerable concern was expressed over the rapid decline in Aboriginal numbers throughout the Australian settlements.[31] The reports published in 1836 and 1837 were mainly concerned with the situation in South Africa, but the committee seemed in no doubt that imperial support for christian missions to the natives would provide a viable solution to the aboriginal problem in Australia. In 1836, many of the group connected with the select committee were also involved in the formation of the Aborigines Protection Society, which for the rest of the nineteenth century acted as the conscience of the home government as well as of colonial societies in all matters pertaining to the christianizing and civilizing of native peoples. The final report of the select committee on Aboriginal tribes was presented to the House of Commons in June 1837, and recommended that since all lands in Australia had been expropriated without compensation to the natives, and because the British government was now selling such land, a moral obligation had been incurred to provide financial support for the maintenance of missionaries and protectors to look after the physical and spiritual welfare of the Aboriginals.[32] This was the origin of a system of Aboriginal protectorates which were established in the Australian colonies, and which lasted until the 1850s.

On 30 August 1837 James Stephen contacted the Treasury to secure approval for a scheme to appoint protectors of Aboriginals in various parts of New South Wales, Port Phillip, Van Diemen's Land[33] and South Australia. Stephen wrote that the settlement at Port Phillip and the new colony of South Australia had led the Colonial Office to fear 'the occurrence of those acts of violence which have, in too many instances, proved fatal to the Aboriginal Inhabitants where British Colonies have been planted'.[34] Treasury approbation was forthcoming, but protectorates were established only in the Port Phillip district of New South Wales, in South Australia, and in Western Australia. It was planned to expand the protectorate into northern New South Wales when this area became a separate colony, but this did not occur until after the protectorate system itself had been abolished.

The need for some form of protection for the Aboriginals could hardly be doubted. Notwithstanding the censure which the Colonial Office directed at Stirling in Western Australia, settlers in the colony continued to murder natives with impunity. In October, 1837 Dr L. Guistiniari, a colonist at Swan River, complained to the London Missionary Society of the sanguinary violence which characterized the general European settler's attitude towards the natives:

> It is a truth which is painful to relate, that in the 19th Century Englishmen and protestants, shall be so cruel and hunt after the aborigines [sic] like after a game, the innocent child is not spared; they are shot in the night time when peacibly [sic] asleep in their huts; when seeking food for their children, in one word the Monks of the Middle Age would blush if they would be accused of such cruelties which some of the settlers perpetrate.[35]

In 1838 the Port Phillip area was divided into four protectorate districts. A chief protector and four assistant protectors were appointed, with ultimate aim of encouraging the natives to give up their nomadic ways and to settle on reserves and learn farming. The plan eventually failed and the protectorate languished and died, largely as a result of severe reductions in the annual budget allocated by the colonial government. By 1842 both Governor George Gipps of New South Wales and C. J. La Trobe, the Port Phillip administrator, had condemned the system as unproductive.[36] Money to finance the protectorate was provided from the land revenues of New South Wales, and both Gipps and La Trobe felt that in a time of severe economic recession the £16 000 spent to that date could have been far more productively employed. The Colonial Office, however, did not favour disbanding the protectorates unless they were replaced by some other scheme of native welfare. Stanley, then colonial secretary, was extremely reluctant to accept colonial propositions that nothing could be done for the Aboriginals, that they were incapable of improvement, and that their speedy disappearance was inevitable.[37] Since Stanley was unfavourably disposed to leaving the natives unprotected, the colonial government allowed the protectorate to continue but starved it of funds. The money spent annually on the protectorate was cut back from an amount in excess of £7 000 in 1841 and 1842 to some £2 000 in 1843, and it remained in that vicinity until 1850.[38] The protectorate in South Australia was also rather ineffectual in the period under review, although in that colony, as in Western Australia, many of the native tribes lived far inland beyond the early frontier of settlement, and were thus left untouched by civilization until well into the second half of the nineteenth century. Nevertheless, the coastal tribes, together with those who lived along the overland stock route between New South Wales and South Australia, rapidly decayed as friction with the settlers and overlanders, as well as the debasing influence of government food depots and boarding schools, had their inexorable effects.[39]

The history of the protectorate in Western Australia followed a slightly different course. Two protectors arrived in the colony from Britain in January 1840. Their salaries were not drawn from the colony's land revenues, which were almost non-existent, but were added to the civil list for Western Australia and thus voted by the British parliament. Protectors' salaries, therefore, remained guaranteed throughout the 1840s and early 1850s, and Hasluck claims that they were at least partially successful during these years.[40] Progress was halted in 1854, however, when the burden of protectors' salaries together with other financial levies was transferred from the civil list to the colony's own revenues; and the office of protector disappeared when the colony's legislative council refused to vote salaries for officials whose sole responsibilities would be to ensure that natives were not mistreated.

During the 1840s, while the Colonial Office continued to advocate

the application of humane policies towards the Australian Aboriginals, the tide of British opinion appeared to ebb. Humanitarian attitudes no longer seemed to be as widespread as they had been in the
previous decade and there now developed a tendency to describe
Australian natives in derogatory terms similar to those used by William Dampier nearly a century and a half earlier. Such attitudes had
never ceased to exist, even amongst members of other government
departments. Sir John Barrow, for example, wrote the article on Australasia for a supplement to the sixth edition of the *Encyclopaedia
Britannica* (1815–24), and the article was incorporated into the seventh
edition in 1842. Barrow wrote that the only savage animal in Australia
was native man. Yet even statesmen with humanitarian leanings
appeared to be affected by the shifting climate of opinion. By 1844
Stanley had satisfied himself that the Australian Aboriginals were too
feeble a race to have proprietary rights over their lands, and he now felt
that all that justice required by way of recompense were the twin
benefits of civilization and christianity.[41]

In 1845 the writer Thomas McCombie informed readers of *Simmonds's Colonial Magazine* that the hapless Aboriginals were not
always of hideous appearance, and that when found in the wild they
were 'a fine noble-looking race of barbarians.' A certain degree of
eighteenth century enlightenment is still apparent in such a description, but McCombie went on to state that Aboriginal intellects were
'confined', and the languages resembled 'more the bubble-bubble of a
turkey-cock than the speech of a human being.' They were depicted as
treacherous and cruel to white men, and as a race 'upon which all
attempts at conciliation are thrown away; nothing but physical force
will keep them in subjection.'[42] This was a comfortable outlook for a
colonizing power, because by this time it was public knowledge that
many settlers in the Australian colonies ignored the home government's instructions to treat the natives with clemency and compassion,
and in fact followed a policy of active extermination. The brutalities
perpetrated by settlers against the local natives were a constant vexa-
tion to the Colonial Office; and the intransigence of colonial juries on
the few occasions when white men were brought to trial for such
activities appeared to fill colonial secretaries with a sense of frustration
and helpless despair.[43] The Aboriginal population was obviously
declining, and while this caused concern to humanitarians in the
Colonial Office, it tended to receive applause from important segments
of public opinion.[44] J. R. McCulloch did not express an unpopular
view when in 1847 he proclaimed that regret concerning the decline in
aboriginal numbers was 'hardly more reasonable than it would be to
complain of the drainage of marshes or of the disappearance of wild
animals.'[45]

Although the impersonal fact that the population of Australian natives was declining brought such open approval, Englishmen possessed little specific knowledge of the methods used by colonists to hasten such a trend. When the Reverend John Dunmore Lang and other experienced travellers began to provide detailed information on these affairs, some British readers became a little squeamish.[46] Lang described how settlers in the Moreton Bay district of New South Wales murdered Aboriginals by feeding them dampers (a type of bush pancake) laced with arsenic or mixed flour and arsenic together before leaving it where the natives could find it.[47] Such behaviour was far easier to countenance if one believed that settlers needed to keep Aboriginals in subjection by force, or that as a race natives were too depraved and degenerate to understand a rational appeal. Some British observers sought to find just such a theoretical justification for settler brutality and the result was a rampant cultural chauvinism.

> The savage, in his original state, is simply an animal superior to his own dog only in sharpness of intellect, but wholly inferior to his dog in fidelity and affection ... The truth is that civilization improves the features, the form, and the powers of the human frame. Men in society may be indolent, and throw away their advantages; but society is the place for men. Rousseau once made a noise by talking nonsense on this subject; but Rousseau *knew* that he was talking nonsense.[48]

During the 1840s educated Englishmen seemed to feel that some form of moral or ethical extenuation was necessary to explain the alienation of native lands in the colonies, and this resulted in two different approaches to the problem. One was the justification seen above, that primitive peoples were not really human beings at all, or else were so backward and inferior as to be virtually ineducable. On the other hand, there was the conviction enunciated by the Colonial Office that the benefits of christianity and civilization were adequate recompense for losses sustained by the natives in Australia.[49] In the public press, this latter view soon became charged with a feeling that because colonization brought christianity to pagan natives, the christian nations were duty-bound to colonize and civilize, and thereby to improve the moral character of native populations:

> When the moral and physical state of the people vanquished is, in consequence, raised higher in the scale of social existence, it becomes, then, a question whether the high ends of civilisation and emancipating mankind from ignorance and brutality does not outweigh the temporary evils which will attend their subjugation; whether the great good, in the aggregate, does not at least extenuate the means used in order to procure it.[50]

Official justification for the effects of empire upon native races was paternalist. Earl Grey was quite atypical when he flirted with the idea of forcing assimilation between settlers and Aborigines in New South Wales through a government-sponsored, inter-racial system of children's boarding schools;[51] and a recent writer has commented that xenophobia was the normal state of mind in Victorian times.[52] Consequently, Englishmen searched for a racialist doctrine which would legitimize feelings of cultural superiority by proving that 'the native' was permanently and genetically inferior.[53] Phillip Curtin has shown that the 1840s and 1850s were decades of great intellectual confusion in Britain with conflicting opinions concerning the primacy of physical or cultural criteria in determining racial differences.[54] The cultural arguments still held sway, but alongside these and growing progressively stronger developed a feeling that race and physical characteristics were the crucial mainsprings of human character and behaviour.[55]

Phrenology was the first serious attempt to provide a scientific foundation for this incipient racialism. It represented the union of a theory of localized brain functions with a primitive behaviouristic psychology and its underlying rationale was a belief that anatomical and physiological characteristics affected intellectual capacity. By the 1830s phrenology had become immensely popular in Britain,[56] and in 1842 a special committee of the British Association for the Advancement of Science drew up a questionnaire to be placed in the hands of intelligent travellers who might come into contact with non-European peoples. In the event that natives did appear the traveller was instructed to pay particular attention to their heads: 'The form of the head may be minutely and accurately described by employing the divisions and terms introduced by craniologists, and the corresponding development of moral and intellectual character should in conjunction be faithfully stated.'[57] Insofar as is affected attitudes towards the Aboriginals of Australia, the result of the phrenological fad was unfortunate, for scientific craniology reinforced existing cultural prejudices by appearing to prove that Aboriginals were scarcely human. Colonel Godfrey Mundy commented in 1846 that 'the Australian cranium is exceedingly ill shaped—the animal bumps largely preponderating over the intellectual';[58] scientists of international repute agreed.

> While, in countenance they present an extreme of the prognathous type hardly above that of the orang-outan, they possess at the same time the smallest brains of the whole of mankind; being according to Morton's measurements, seventeen cubic inches less than the brain of the teutonic race.[59]

In 1859 Charles Darwin published his *Origin of Species* and the social application of the evolutionary theories he propounded and popularized met the requirements for a scientific vindication of the findings of phrenology. Historians of Social Darwinism generally agree that the movement later identified by that name was already thriving well before Darwin published his book.[60]

Throughout the period studied here, British policy towards the Australian Aboriginals as expounded by the Colonial Office reflected both concern and goodwill. But official policy had little effect on colonial behaviour and settlers decimated Aboriginals with a comparatively free hand. Some of the dispatches from Downing Street reveal the chagrin and defeatism of officials who sympathized with the plight of the natives but were powerless to mitigate the behaviour of settlers on and beyond the frontiers of settlement. Colonial Office attitudes remained fairly constant throughout the period as did those of interested bodies like the Aborigines Protection Society and the various missionary societies. Other areas of British public opinion, however, tended to manifest distinctly unfavourable attitudes towards the natives of Australia, though the intensity of such views varied. Although a distinction needs to be observed, the evolutionary racialism of the later nineteenth century was firmly rooted in British cultural chauvinism during the 1830s and 1840s, and towards the end of this period a strain of nascent racialism can be discerned in British attitudes to a primitive people like the Aboriginals of Australia, which makes the ready acceptance of Social Darwinism in succeeding decades more intelligible.

7: Arcady the Brave 1828-50

Well-intentioned gloom concerning the probable future of Australia's Aboriginals did not run deep enough to affect the general consensus of overall optimism concerning British colonizing activities in Australia; and such cheerlessness was more than offset by sanguine expectations based upon the economic potential of the Australian colonies. The prospective economic role of the colonies was seen in terms of primary industry and of supplying raw materials for Britain's manufacturers. The 1820s were a decade of great pastoral expansion in Australia and antipodean exports of wool became increasingly consequential.[1] In 1821, the year when the first commercial export of wool was sent to England, the clip amounted to only 175 400 pounds. In 1830, 2 000 000 pounds of wool were sent to the United Kingdom, and exports steadily increased so that by 1850 Australia was sending an annual wool clip of just under 40 000 000 pounds to Britain, which at that time accounted for more than half of the mother country's entire import of wool.[2]

This is the background against which British attitudes towards land settlement in the Australian colonies should be viewed. In some respects opinion in Britain appeared to be out of touch with the economic realities of land utilization in Australia; during the first decade of the period under review there was an unrealistic preoccupation with agricultural development, and the influence of this notion continued to be felt throughout the 1840s when the majority of British observers and statesmen had recognized the suitability and economic supremacy of pastoral occupations. The discovery of gold in the 1850s added an entirely new dimension to British attitudes towards settlement and the structure of Australian society. For a short time the economic primacy of wool-growing was threatened as thousands from

120

Britain and the other Australian colonies deserted their jobs and joined in the rush to the goldfields.

As early as the 1820s some English commentators had realized that the future of the Australian colonies lay with sheep-farming,[3] but British views were dominated by those who thought of the colonies as agricultural settlements. Despite the growing importance of anti-podean wool to British industry, the Western Australian settlements of 1829 and 1840 were projected as agricultural colonies, as was South Australia in 1836. British statesmen and other interested observers during these years seemed incapable of discerning that Australian conditions were unsuitable for the development of a farm-based economy on the European model. The outstanding characteristic of the schemes for colonizing Western Australia and South Australia was an apparent lack of contact with reality, at least with Australian reality. They were based firmly enough on the British preconceptions and theories of the day, but the actual setting was something of a dream-world. In spite of a reasonably detailed knowledge of the coast, sites were selected in both cases with amazing nonchalance. Locations were picked for superficial appearance or on unreliable hearsay evidence; it was not the first time that tropical luxuriance was mistaken for fertility. In 1829, for example, one supporter discussed the proposed settlement in Western Australia, and commented that the land there was both 'picturesque and fertile', and the colony 'most inviting to the Agriculturist'.[4] On the other hand, Secretary to the Admiralty, John Barrow, warned against this single-minded absorption with farming. He pointed out that exports of wool from New South Wales and Van Diemen's Land had already reached substantial proportions, and that as a consequence of increased production to supply the profitable British market, the colonies on the eastern seaboard of Australia were growing rapidly in wealth and population.[5] Nevertheless, most Englishmen appeared unable to conceive of a settlement colony not consisting of small agricultural holdings, and this attitude towards the new colony was best illustrated by the *New Monthly Magazine and Literary Journal* which in 1829 assured its readers, quite erroneously, that the Swan River settlement was ideally suited for cultivation.[6]

Why were Britons so absorbed with tillage at this time? Admittedly, there had been little British experience with colonies depending for their economic vitality on nomadic animal husbandry, but inexperience with colonial sheep raising was not the only reason behind British preference for agriculture. Domestic conditions in Britain undoubtedly help to explain the perversity and resolution with which Englishmen generally tended to persevere in seeing the future of Australia associated with cultivation. Unemployment and the fear of

violent social unrest concentrated people's minds essentially on labourers and the working classes, so that when emigration was mentioned as a remedy or palliative, articulate, educated commentators,
drawn largely from the middle and upper classes, thought in terms of
the emigration of paupers and labourers. What could these do in the
colonies other than farm on their own account (as Horton argued) or
work as agricultural labourers as many of them already did in Britain?
There was no thought of factories or industrialization in Australia,
and how else were workers in the United Kingdom occupied but in
working on small farms? These familiar British circumstances restricted the vision of many Englishmen and reinforced their failure to
grasp the potentialities for pastoral development in Australia, as well
as the large-scale enterprise that sheep-farming there became, involving immense areas of land and substantial capital, in contrast to the
smaller scale of operations possible and prevalent at home.

There was a further element in British attitudes towards the utilization of Australia's waste lands which transcended practical considerations and predisposed many Englishmen to think highly of cultivation
and the agrarian life. The rapidity of nineteenth century industrial
growth contributed to an intellectual climate which reacted against the
prevailing tendencies of the age by idealizing an imagined past of rural
prosperity which had passed forever, and by yearning to return to a
golden age of individual self-sufficiency based on farming. The living
conditions of the industrial proletariat horrified many contemporaries,
and particularly the continuing momentum of population movement
from rural areas to the filth and squalor of industrial towns and cities.
In their denunciation of factories and machines, and aspiration for an
arcadian renewal, the romantic poets and the visionary William Blake
were as one. John Keats described the noise of the shuttles in the
spinning mills at Lancaster as 'that most disgusting of all noises',[7]
while William Blake cursed the 'dark Satanic Mills'[8] and the factory
machines which he claimed had displaced the rural occupations of
ploughman and shepherd,

> And in their stead intricate wheels invented, wheel without
> wheel,
> To perplex youth in their outgoings, and to bind to labours in
> Albion
> Of day and night the myriads of eternity that they may grind
> And polish brass and iron hour after hour, laborious task,
> Kept ignorant of its use that they might spend the days of
> wisdom
> In sorrowful drudgery to obtain a scanty pittance of bread,
> In ignorance to view a small portion and think that All,
> And call it Demonstration, blind to all the simple rules of life.[9]

Blake found comfort in mysticism, but it was to philosophical romanticism that many educated Englishmen turned when seeking emotional relief from the less pleasant aspects of industrial progress. The
message of William Wordsworth and the other romantic poets was that
social salvation could be found in the recreation of a lost age, in a
return to an Eden-like era of arcadian innocence in the midst of rural
surroundings.[10]

Although much of this veneration for the countryside predates the
growth of industrialism, the increasing utilization of the techniques of
mechanical mass-production in the years between Waterloo and the
Crimean War undoubtedly contributed to a British revival of neo-
physiocratic sentiment concerning the moral superiority of
agriculture. A recent scholar has pointed out that one of the dilemmas
of the early Victorian was that much of his literature, both for education and pleasure, originated in pre-industrial societies based on
property and agriculture.[11] Most of the Greek and Latin classics
reflected agricultural values, as did the continuing British habit of
measuring wealth in terms of land. Sentimentalism in favour of a
simpler life is a distinctly individual psychological phenomenon,
though it has been suggested that such an outlook had gained so wide
an acceptance in Britain during the first half of the nineteenth century
that it could very nearly be represented as a racial or national
characteristic.[12] Be that as it may, the idea that the ills of society could
be cured by a return to the land transcended class barriers and was
proposed by the working-class radical, William Cobbett, and the Tory,
Benjamin Disraeli.[13]

This romantic primitivism stood in opposition to the movement of
the age and infuriated more practical spirits like the historian Thomas
Macaulay who wrote in 1830:

> Here is wisdom. Here are the principles on which nations are to be
> governed. Rose-bushes and poor-rates, rather than steam-engines
> and independence. Mortality and cottages with weather-stains,
> rather than health and long life with edifices which time cannot
> mellow.[14]

Macaulay was a realist who knew that it was neither possible nor
desirable to reverse the tide of industrialization and return to the land
in Britain. But if the golden age could not be recovered in the United
Kingdom it might be realized in an isolated and unindustrialized
country like Australia. The cult of virgin lands could be aptly applied
in the antipodean colonies, which provided Britain with a psychological and emotional frontier of its own to match the attraction of the
American west.

The search for a colonial arcady was primitivism rather than uto-pianism, in that its inspiration came from the past, as it sought to re-establish a lost way of life in the New World. In so far as its philosophical postulates appeared to be realizable in Australia, the neo-physiocratic outlook became an influential conditioner of attitudes. Much of the social prejudice hitherto noted as characteristic of British middle- and upper-class attitudes towards colonial society in Australia becomes intelligible in this light. Many Britons had an idealized conception of the sort of backward-looking, traditionally hierarchical, yeoman society that they believed could and would be developed in Australia. Since this was at considerable variance with the egalitarian actuality on the frontier, a certain degree of disillusion with Australia was inevitable.

Moreover, as a corollary to the feeling that cultivating the soil represented a superior way of life, many Englishmen believed that pastoral occupations led inexorably to degeneration of character and brutishness. Australia was well known as a convict depository, and many of the shepherds and overseers on the isolated sheep farms were former exiles. The widespread dispersal of a morally corrupt popula-tion in the Australian bush was thought to militate against the adop-tion of the civilizing values enshrined in an agricultural ethos in which, of necessity, population was far more concentrated. The slaughter of Aboriginals on outback sheep stations lent weight to such views, and Archdeacon Broughton was not alone in fearing that the European population in Australia would relapse into heathen inhu-manity and savagery.[15] Wakefield had warned in 1829 that dispersal of the tainted colonial population in New South Wales would result in a people 'as wild as the inhabitants of the Pampas, or as gross, lethargic, and stupid as the boors of the Cape of Good Hope',[16] and other prominent observers agreed with him.[17] Lord Howick certainly rejected the notion that squatting could be regarded as in any way comparable to agriculture as a way of life for colonists, and seemed to be arguing in 1842 that cultivation offered a morally pre-eminent form of occupation in comparison with pastoral activity which encouraged the growth of a rude and immoral population.[18] He developed these ideas during 1845 and 1846, and maintained that because squatting caused the colonial population to spread thinly, it inhibited the expansion of churches and schools, and also rendered impracticable the ameliorative activities of ministers of religion. If colonists con-tinued to turn their energies to pastoral pursuits, he warned, the unavoidable result would be the establishment within a few genera-tions of 'a race approaching to barbarism'.[19]

Wakefield has often been described as a utilitarian,[20] but inasmuch as he dreamed of establishing an agricultural arcadia in Australia, he was in the mainstream of the romantic movement. Wakefield thought much and read voraciously about the colonization of Australia between 1827 and 1830 while he served a gaol sentence in Newgate prison, and his researches led him to formulate a body of colonizing theory which was destined to prove extremely influential in the decades to come. At that time Wakefield had no experience of Australian conditions, and he produced a work of fiction with English not colonial audiences in mind. He published a series of anonymous letters in the *Morning Chronicle,* beginning on 21 August 1829, which were ascribed to a young British settler in New South Wales. The letters colourfully depicted the vicissitudes which beset the new colonist in Australia, and indicated the divergence between the settler's early arcadian aspirations and colonial realities. Land, said Wakefield, was largely monopolized by the former convicts and the lower classes, and colonial society was consequently in a most depraved condition. Moreover, there existed an alarming degree of social mobility from the ranks of the colonial lower orders, as demonstrated by the rapid rise of the settler's family retainer who had been taken to the colony from England when the colonist departed for New South Wales:

> My own man, who had served me for eight years in England, and had often sworn that he would go the wide world over with me, seeing that I was the best of masters, never reached my new abode. He had saved about £150 in my service; and I had advised him to take the money out of a London Savings Bank, under an idea that he might obtain ten per cent for it at Sydney. He followed my advice. About a month after our arrival I missed him one morning. Before night I received a letter, by which he informed me that he had taken a grant of land near Hunter's River, and that he 'hoped we parted friends'. He is now one of the most consequential persons in the Colony, has grown enormously fat, feeds upon greasy dainties, drinks oceans of bottled porter and port wine, damns the Governor, and swears by all his gods, Jupiter, Jingo, and Old Harry, that this Colony must soon be independent.[21]

Wakefield's method for avoiding such unsettling social chaos in Australia was to recommend that the imperial government increase the price of colonial lands until they were placed beyond the reach of the lower classes. They could always be provided with farm cottages and small plots of land as tenants of the wealthy landowners,[22] and in this way labourers would be enabled to supplement their earnings as farm hands for the colonial lord of the manor.

Not surprisingly, Wakefield's theories proved persuasive to British readers who shared his prejudice in favour of an agricultural economy based on the English yeoman farmer, as well as his ignorance of conditions in the Australian colonies. The entire edifice of systematic colonization was based on unreality, and to this extent Wakefield and the contemporary utopian theorist Robert Owen had much in common. Both men shared the unusual good fortune in this period of influencing British public opinion to such an extent that attempts were made to put each theory into practice in a frontier environment. Owen represented an idealistic socialist whose ideas did not affect the development of the Australian colonies, though several private attempts were made to found settlements in America to implement his programme of agrarian communism and self-sufficiency.[23] Both Owen and Wakefield looked for a regeneration of man by returning him to the land in the newly developing countries of Australia and America, but Owen sought to make the lower classes independent, while Wakefield hoped to force them into dependence and subordination.

Systematic colonization, as outlined by Wakefield, was designed to re-create a past pattern of society and to perpetuate and reinforce British class distinctions in the colonies. Wakefield and his supporters shared a typically capitalist and middle-class outlook. They felt a strong antipathy towards the aristocratic element in British society, but they never sought to find common ground with, or showed sympathy towards, the working classes. As one of its prime concerns, systematic colonization was designed to ensure that land in the colonies was priced out of reach of emigrating British labourers. In this way, a pool of labour would be established and British workers precluded from owning land until they had worked as labourers for several years and saved the purchase money. Systematic colonization not only envisaged that labourers would remain workers for a considerable length of time, but also claimed that the ideal form of society in a new colony would be to produce a microcosm of traditional British society with its clearly defined class structure and lack of real social mobility for the lower orders. Colonial society in the eastern Australian colonies was criticized for being unbalanced, with a greatly preponderating working class most of whom 'came here to live, not to enjoy; to eat and drink, not to refine; to "settle"—that is, to roll in a gross plenty for the body, but to starve their minds'.[24] Wakefieldianism represented an appeal to the self-interest of Britain's professional and middle classes,[25] a philosophy for those to whom much had already been given. Not surprisingly, therefore, it received far more attention and debate in the public press than the less respectable Owenism.

Wakefield's theory of colonization appeared to be an empirical blueprint, but the intellectual foundations of his scheme lay in the romantic, neo-physiocratic view that in unindustrialized colonies arable land formed the main source of wealth and that agriculture was the surest of the wealth-producing occupations. Profitable opportunities for British financiers existed in Australia which possessed an almost unlimited extent of potentially valuable waste lands. Wakefield believed that a superabundance of accumulated capital in Britain kept interest rates so low that it encouraged commercial speculation in wildcat schemes and foreign ventures which promised a higher return than was normally obtainable at home.[26] He proposed that this idle capital be put to work in the colonies by using it to purchase farm lands which would rise in value as their productivity increased. This would be beneficial to the mother country as well as profitable to the individual capitalist: 'for such a country as England, a chief end of colonization is to obtain secure markets for the purchase of cheap corn; a steady supply of bread, liable to be increased with an increasing demand.'[27]

To many people inexperienced in the business of colonizing or unaware of actual conditions in Australia, Wakefield's analysis seemed persuasive and convincing. He satisfied the ageing Jeremy Bentham of the benefits and practical utility of his theory of systematic colonization and the old philosopher set to work to draft a constitution for a new province in Australia.[28] Some of Bentham's disciples joined with Wakefield and others to form various associations during the 1830s and 1840s designed to influence the land and emigration policies of the imperial government and to introduce the main principles of the theory into various parts of the empire. Wakefield was a skilful publicist and he had begun with the intention of rendering the Australian colonies attractive to the cupidity or business acumen of Britain's middle classes. He emphasized the considerable opportunities that awaited emigrants with capital, and concentrated attention on Britain's imperial duty and civilizing mission in fostering all that was best in English rural society and transplanting it in the colonies. Such propaganda could not have failed to affect British attitudes to the Australian colonies in the sense that it tended to dissociate emigration in the public mind from transportation and disgrace; it thereby encouraged a climate of opinion which helped to render emigration respectable for Britons from all ranks of society.

Scholars have differed over the precise degree to which Wakefieldian ideology influenced the Colonial Office, but they have generally agreed that such an influence existed, and that it did affect British colonial policy during the 1830s and 1840s.[29] With his dynamic personality, Howick exercised considerable authority under the vacillating leadership of the colonial secretary, Lord Goderich, between 1831 and 1833. Howick despised his chief and in 1833 maintained that he personally controlled colonial affairs because the secretary of state possessed a character so feeble as to render him 'unfit for his situation'.[30] Wakefield wrote to Howick in 1831 soliciting an interview to explain his views on imperial land policy in Australia.[31] Howick, perhaps because

of Wakefield's notoriety as a rake and convicted felon, politely declined
to grant the request though he did invite Wakefield to expand his ideas
and submit them in writing for the consideration of Lord Goderich
and the government.[32] Wakefield accepted this rebuff and decided
instead to publish his findings.[33]

By this time the Colonial Office had already initiated and completed
a reassessment of its attitudes towards land policy and settlement in
the Australian colonies, and many of Wakefield's ideas were acceptable because they fitted into the trend of official policy as it had
developed during the late 1820s.[34] This reappraisal resulted in a set of
instructions issued in 1831, which became known as the Ripon Regulations, and which were intended to rationalize British land and emigration policies in Australia and to ensure concentration of settlement
in compact agricultural communities.[35] That exports of wool from
New South Wales and Van Diemen's Land had already exceeded two
million pounds a year and were continuing to increase was treated as
a matter of little consequence, as was the fact that pastoral pursuits
already dominated many districts in the colonies. For the rest of the
decade British bureaucrats would attempt to force the development of
Australia into conformity with their agricultural preconceptions by
artificially concentrating settlement, and endeavouring to restrict the
pastoralists' freedom of access to colonial waste lands in a fruitless
effort to produce the 'hardy Peasantry' that the Ripon Regulations were
designed to encourage.[36] In 1834, for example, Lord Aberdeen
instructed Governor Bourke in New South Wales that under no circumstances should he authorize pastoralists to raise sheep beyond the
colony's official boundaries of settlement, since this would be contrary
to the spirit and intent of the land regulations specifically framed to
advance civilization by concentrating population.[37]

Imperial persistence in undertaking to establish an antipodean yeomanry did not exist in an intellectual vacuum, and some administrators at Downing Street were aware that conditions in Australia did
not favour agriculture and close-knit settlement:

> If however my information be accurate, the Eastern Shores of New
> Holland, at least on the Southern half of that great Region, so far as
> they have hitherto been explored, whether Coastwise or Inland
> present a physical impediment to the close concentration of the
> Inhabitants, with which it would be only futile to contend by human
> laws . . . Tillage can scarcely be pursued advantageously to any great
> extent; while the whole surface of the Country exhibits a range of
> sheep-walks which, though not naturally fertile, are yet, when
> occupied in large Masses, of almost unrivalled value for the pro-
> duction of the finest description of Wool.[38]

Nevertheless, imperial officials appeared to act in a most irrational manner and struggled to force colonial actuality to conform to misconceived imperial objectives. Even though he admitted that the Ripon Regulations could not successfully be applied in New South Wales, Glenelg continued to insist that the governor should ensure that the settlers observed them.[39]

The Ripon Regulations made waste lands in Australia available for purchase at auction with a minimum upset price of five shillings an acre. Revenue thus gained was earmarked to subsidize free pauper emigration to Australia. This represented an important change of emphasis in British policy, as an interlocking system of land sales and emigration had not hitherto been tried; but by and large the press ignored the event.[40] The *Times* seemed moderately favourable though the paper considered it nonsensical to apply a minimum price of five shillings in Van Diemen's Land and Western Australia, because land in both these colonies was worth considerably less than this figure.[41] Indeed, during 1833 a discussion on land grants in Western Australia, the *Times* adverted approvingly in Wakefield's 'Letter from Sydney'. 'This topic has been well treated in a little pamphlet published two or three years ago by a colonization society, and deserves to be well considered by the Government.'[42] Peter Burroughs maintains that the *Times* led an influential section of the press in 'bitter hostility' to Wakefield's theories,[43] but not until the following year, when the South Australian Association secured the passing of an act establishing the colony of South Australia and setting up a commission to organize the colonization along Wakefieldian lines,[44] did the press really begin to attack systematic colonization and the physiocratic ideology it sought to implement. An abstract theory which reflected in vague terms many of the romantic predispositions of the day could be tolerated and even admired; but an attempt to put the theory into effect removed debate from the realm of intellectual speculation to that of practical business. As this transformation occurred, so criticism became virulent and partisan.

The overtones of romantic conservatism in Wakefield's proposals, particularly those aspects of the South Australian scheme which anticipated the establishment of a sturdy colonial yeomanry and the imposition of an extraordinary check on upward social mobility from the ranks of the new peasantry, were treated with considerable scepticism or hostility by many English commentators. Not all philosophical radicals were supporters of systematic colonization, and one utilitarian publicist savagely attacked the plans published by the South Australian Association and dismissed them, together with the entire scheme for ensuring that capitalists would be provided with a permanent pool

of labour, as a poorly disguised attempt to subject the emigrant labourers to 'villeinage'. In this critic's opinion, one of the main inducements to emigration lay in the prospect of becoming an independent
proprietor: 'Men go to Colonies to better themselves. Here is a Colony
by Act of Parliament, where nobody shall better themselves.'[45] This
was not a lone point of view, and other writers claimed that the whole
scheme would be positively detrimental to the interests of emigrants
from the labouring classes. The *Courier*, for example, commented that
British workmen were not fools and that few would be willing 'to
emigrate to a colony where wages will be low and land bad and dear'.[46]

Other contemporaries made the further point that Wakefieldian
theories were entirely untested, and some opposed the South Australian Association because they were perturbed that an independent
business company should be granted such all-embracing authority by
the crown. If land was to be sold in South Australia and the proceeds
used to subsidize the free emigration of British labourers, then the
imperial government should conduct such affairs and be accountable
to parliament for its actions. The South Australian Association would
do nothing that could not be done better by the experienced functionaries in the Colonial Office who were at least honourably motivated
and responsible to the nation. The association, on the other hand, was
accountable only to its members who constituted a 'joint stock company mixed up of Utopian theorists, and perhaps—for we assert nothing offensive—of selfish and mercenary adventurers'.[47]

Robert Gouger, the association's secretary, wrote a letter of protest
to the editor of the *Times*, in which he complained of the harsh tone of
the paper's disapproval and denied that the South Australian Association was either a company or a joint-stock undertaking. Waste lands in
South Australia were vested in the crown and would be sold by the
imperial government, not by the association. The *Times* remained
unconvinced. What was the need for the association, it pointedly
enquired, if the crown was selling waste lands; and why was an act of
parliament necessary if the South Australian Association was not
going to possess supervisory and legal powers of unusual
dimensions?[48] The following day the paper returned to the attack and
denounced the South Australian scheme as 'a joint stock juggle for
getting British paupers scalped by bushmen in Southern Australia'.[49]
The *Times* was not alone in its criticisms of the scheme: the Whig
Courier described it as a 'quackish project', while the Tory *Standard*
contemptuously dismissed South Australia as a 'job'.[50]

Critics had been perspicacious in pointing out that the South Australian Association contained a strange assortment of idealistic
romanticists and hard-headed businessmen intent on profitable
investments and land speculation. Like all proposals to reconstitute

society, Wakefieldianism ran into difficulties when its adherents attempted to translate it into action. The inevitable conflict between the escapist fantasy of the original concept and the profit-minded approach of financiers and capitalists, whose support was vital if the blueprint for South Australia was ever to reach fruition, was never adequately resolved. Wakefield himself claimed that his theories had been so watered down in the interests of practicality and in order to conciliate and attract investment from financiers and businessmen that he withdrew his support.[51] Yet a sufficiently large deposit of theory was retained to render the South Australian scheme unworkable, and within four years of the first settlement in 1836 the colony was bankrupt.[52] A smaller Wakefieldian settlement at Australind in Western Australia was to suffer a similar fate between 1840 and 1844.[53] By 1840 more than 12 000 British emigrants had been attracted to South Australia and the colony could not be abandoned. The imperial government was therefore forced to take control and the settlement became a crown colony under the complete jurisdiction of the Colonial Office. The settlement at Australind never attracted many emigrants and by 1844 it had become a deserted hamlet. Arcady was not readily realizable in Australia.

Wakefield continued to develop and publicize his theory during the 1830s and 1840s, and the settlement of New Zealand in 1840 owed a great deal to his influence.[54] This programme of propaganda kept his ideas continually before the public,[55] and some notable conversions were made. In 1841, for example, the *Westminster Review* turned full circle and became an unequivocal supporter of Wakefield's ideas. The journal carried an article by Henry Chapman, legal advocate for the Wakefieldian New Zealand Company, in which the sale of colonial waste lands and the expenditure of the proceeds on the conveyance of labourers to the colonies were described as 'the two great principles of colonization'.[56] Similarly, John Barrow wrote an article which showed clear evidence of his conversion to Wakefieldian principles of colonization. He no longer believed that wool production should continue to expand at the expense of colonial agriculture, even though it was a substantially more remunerative occupation for the colonists. Barrow considered that the rate of expansion of British manufacturing could not keep pace with the accelerating level of wool production in Australia, and he feared that if a switch was not made to agriculture in the immediate future, the production of wool would reach market saturation point and the colonists would find themselves faced with a glut. In general Barrow accepted all the tenets of Wakefield's thesis, though he did confess to reservations concerning the idea of a fixed price for all colonial land irrespective of quality of location. Nevertheless, his discussion of Western Australia proved to be a resume of all the Wakefieldian arguments against that unfortunate colony. The original land grants had been too large, and no regard had been paid to the differing abilities of the grantees; there had been an insufficient supply of labour to work the huge grants, and no land fund existed to subsidize the emigration of extra workers from Britain; consequently the settlement had languished and dispersed.[57] The recantation of former opponents like the *Westminster* and *Quarterly Reviews* gives some indication of the extent to which Wakefieldian dialectic had percolated amongst the middle and upper classes in Britain since 1829. It was no longer possible for Englishmen to discuss settlement colonies without revealing their debt to Wakefield's glib and facile theories.

Although the barrage of Wakefieldian propaganda throughout the 1830s slowly won converts from amongst his former assailants, who began to express concern over the extent of Australia's reliance on the production of wool, Wakefield himself commenced to move belatedly in the other direction. He came to recognize that it was impractical to expect Australia to develop as a predominantly agricultural country when the squatting interests were so entrenched and produced so much wealth. He finally came to realize that, 'the prosperity of New South Wales, for example, is wholly dependent on the use of vast tracts of natural pasturage'.[58] Wakefield attempted to overcome this obstacle to cultivation by proposing a two-tiered system of land administration under which clearly defined boundaries would be set for agricultural settlement within the limits of which land would be highly priced. Beyond these 'counties' all land would be classified as pasturage available without charge to those large capitalists who had become the chief wool growers in the colonies.[59] Squatting in Australia required a prohibitive capital outlay which effectively placed it beyond the reach of labourers or small capitalists who would be forced to turn to subsistence agriculture if they wished to set up for themselves in the colonies. Thus it was essential that agricultural land be priced out of their reach, thereby providing a work force for the pastoral industry.[60] This design constituted an impracticable attempt to compromise between the realities of land utilization in Australia and the ideal of establishing a landed yeomanry. Wakefield had failed to resolve the underlying conflict between concentration and sheep-farming.

The British tendency to view Australia as an emotional, as well as an economic, frontier and to romanticize colonial primary production received further stimulus with the appearance in 1844 of a new periodical, *Simmonds's Colonial Magazine and Foreign Miscellany*. This journal devoted itself exclusively to imperial affairs and at first seemed likely to provide a forum for informed debate. The preface to the first issue boasted that the magazine's library contained more works of reference and information pertaining to the colonies than any other such establishment in the world.[61] Unfortunately, the magazine did not fulfil this promise, and its treatment of the Australian colonies was overly romantic and quite uncritical. The journal described the founding and subsequent development of New South Wales, for example, without once mentioning convicts, prisons, or gaolers.[62] The same issue was equally enthusiastic about the prospects and prosperity of Van Diemen's Land, South Australia, New South Wales and Western Australia; yet at this time Western Australia was moribund, Governor George Grey had instituted a regime of great austerity in South Australia, and both New South Wales and Van Diemen's Land were in the grip of a severe depression.

Englishmen who claimed to know the antipodes seemed every bit as ignorant of the true state of affairs there as were the colonial reformers and other speculative armchair critics. Systematic colonization had become the rallying cry of Wakefieldian theorists, and was often used as a convenient label to describe Wakefield's distinctive principles of colonization.[63] Some measure of his success as a propagandist can be gauged from the extent to which his specialized vocabulary came to be adopted by literate Englishmen to describe other arrangements. In 1845, for example, *Simmonds's Colonial Magazine* proposed its own 'systematic plan of colonization' which consisted of two nostrums between which the imperial government could choose and thereby systematize its colonial administration. Firstly, the government could vote a sum of money to be used for emigration—in other words a return to the earlier system operated by Wilmot Horton. Secondly, emigration could be facilitated by free grants of land in the colonies—also a return to an earlier pattern of settlement abandoned in 1831 in favour of the Ripon Regulations.[64] The journal's use of the term systematic colonization, with all its popularly accepted Wakefieldian connotations, to describe British colonizing practices prior to 1829 illustrates the extent to which general usage had robbed the expression of its distinctive meaning. The overall looseness and imprecision of Wakefield's formulations undoubtedly encouraged this erosion of semantic content; this shift provides a singular example of the movement and influence of contemporary ideas, and of the process known as fractional distillation, whereby various parts of a complex of ideas break away and become absorbed into contemporary consciousness in an almost subliminal manner. A similar perversion of Wakefieldian terminology occurred in 1848, when *Fraser's Magazine* advocated that waste lands in Australia be given away free to British capitalists who would ship indentured labourers from the mother country to work their holdings. This plan also was described as a scheme for systematic colonization.[65]

At first sight, these blueprints appear to have little in common with Wakefieldian notions of systematic colonization. But the differences all relate to techniques, and the three systems share a common outlook in regarding the establishment of agricultural settlements as the *sine qua non* of antipodean colonization. The goal was still unrealistic—an Australia filled with yeomen farmers. Yet the same year, the essayist George Groly informed the readers of *Blackwood's Magazine* that Australia was capable through agriculture 'of supplying the wants of double the population of Europe'.[66] Only the previous year he had proclaimed that although admirably suited for rearing sheep and cattle, the soil of Australia was infertile for agriculture.[67]

Arcadian sentiment transcended class barriers and received support from the working classes, though naturally they stressed the independence of the anticipated yeomanry in Australia, whereas middle- and upper-class Wakefieldians emphasized the dependency of agricultural labourers on their masters if they ever hoped to save enough money to purchase land to support themselves. In 1838, the *Operative* attacked the extensive aristocratic ownership of land in Britain, and accused the upper classes of depriving the true owners, the British people, of their patrimony.[68] Some of Wakefield's supporters pandered to these opinions in an effort to popularize their point of view and gain working-class support for systematic colonization. In 1839, during a parliamentary degate on colonial waste lands, Henry George Ward claimed that 'What are termed the waste lands are emphatically public lands, the inheritance—the patrimony of every poor man in England, Ireland, and Scotland, who pays allegiance to the Crown—and as such I claim them'.[69] That same year the *Operative* printed a letter from John Stephen which advocated emigration to South Australia, where lands could be obtained relatively easily, and which warned labourers that they had no chance of returning to the land if they remained in Britain.[70] The writer Samuel Sidney, who had demanded the lands of Australia as farms for 'my labouring fellow-countrymen',[71] for all his opposition to the techniques and capitalist orientation of Wakefieldian colonization, shared Wakefield's dream of establishing an agrarian colonial economy. Both propagandists were equally affected by arcadian ideals though they differed markedly in other areas of their theories. Yet Sidney had no other choice: independence for the working classes in a rural environment could come only from agriculture. Labourers lacked the capital for sheep farming. In 1852, the working-class periodical *The Operative* carried an article which indicated that the lower orders in Britain continued to view land as a necessary prerequisite of independence and liberty. In a reaction against the wage slavery of industrialism, the journal maintained that the real strength and stamina of a country was to be found in its peasantry, and that the simplicity of rural life bred both virtue and courage, as well as a love of liberty which made 'true genuine sons of the earth' invincible.[72] Samuel Sidney believed that Australia had the potentiality to become a working man's paradise,

> an El Dorado and an Arcadia combined, where the hardest and the easiest, best-paid employments are to be found, where every striving man who rears a race of industrious children, may sit under the shadow of his own vine and his own fig-tree—not without work, but with little care—living on his own land, looking down to the valleys to his herds—towards the hills to his flocks, amid the humming of bees, which know no winters.[73]

Wakefield would have found nothing objectionable in such a tableau save the lowly origins of Sidney's colonist.

If, as Peter Burroughs claims, the Australian Lands Sales Act which passed through parliament in 1842 constituted the high-water mark of Wakefieldian influence on imperial policies affecting waste lands and their disposal in Australia,[74] it also marked an approximate turning point in popular attitudes. Although the attempt to re-establish the golden age of agricultural cultivation continued right through the period under review, some Englishmen had begun to realize that Australia's providential destiny lay with the pastoral industry. The corollary of this more realistic assessment of Australian potential was the recognition that concentrated agricultural settlement did not suit Australian conditions; 'sheep-walks and concentration are not very easily reconcilable'.[75]

In these circumstances, the prime importance of agriculture as a major conditioner of British attitudes towards the potential productivity of Australian waste lands was coming to an end. Some Englishmen had realized that sheep-farming in Australia required substantial capital, thus placing it outside the range of possibilities for emigrant labourers. The attraction of social exclusiveness was thereby added to the lure of large and comparatively quick returns earned by capital invested in the pastoral industry, and this development helps to account for the growing interest shown in the pastoral side of Australian development by middle and upper class Englishmen during the late 1830s and 1840s. The money to finance the pastoral boom years between 1836 and 1841 came from the United Kingdom, but capital outlay was no guarantee that investors knew much about the country in which they hoped to make financial gains.[76] Funds for Australian speculations during this period usually came from large British trading banks and smaller joint-stock loan and mortgage companies which were encouraged by the high rate of profit on investments in the booming Australian economy. David S. Macmillan has pointed out that small Scottish loan companies were floated around 1839 and 1840 in the confident expectation of earning annual profits on their Australian operations of 40 per cent or higher.[77] Many of the people providing the financial backing for these companies were lower middle class and had been attracted by the prospective high returns. They knew little of Australian conditions or of the activities of their companies' agents in the colonies who invested the funds entrusted to them by shareholders in the mother country.[78] Consequently, although the flow of British capital preceded and sustained the pastoral boom, British attitudes did not begin to shift discernibly in favour of sheep-farming until the early 1840s when the boom was almost over.

Naturally this change of emphasis received a philosophical gloss, and became a separate, though complementary, facet of nineteenth-century romanticism, embracing the sentimental glorification of nature and the purgatorial properties of the simple life. The middle classes in Britain found much that was attractive in the life of an Australian squatter. British society in its upper levels remained fairly exclusive, and social movement into the higher gradations could take several generations. Although the 1832 Reform Bill had admitted the middle classes to a share in the government of the country, it was difficult for them to rise socially into the ranks of the landed gentry and aristocracy:

> Money placed in land could not, of course, always purchase automatic and instantaneous acceptance. Established county society often scorned newcomers as vulgar aspirants, and it might take two generations for humble origins to be forgiven, in the course of which it might become congenial or politic to sever connection with the business on which the fortune was founded.[79]

Australian squatting presented an escape from social group pressures into a more individualistic world where few artificial social barriers hindered a free man with capital from rising as high in society as his abilities, money, and connections would take him.

The crass materialism which activated Australian squatters as a class[80] could be camouflaged by stressing the romantic doctrine that man was by nature good, and could rediscover the best in himself by returning to a way of life as close to Nature as possible. Under this reasoning the Australian bush began to take on a mystical and religious symbolism for some British authors, and the natural scenery encountered by a squatter was thought to possess some form of morally regenerating influence: 'Inanimate nature is universally lovely amidst these wildernesses, and a cheerful unprejudiced eye may often observe strong assimilation going forward, in the human character, to the faultless still-life around, which God has retained under His own more immediate control'.[81] In the Australian pastoral industry man was more than just a parasite on the physical and spiritual restorative powers of Nature; he was living by the ideal 'natural law' propounded by the European physiocrats, modifying and making use of Nature without destroying it,[82] and thus being an entrepreneur in the very best sense. In this way the colonial squatter fulfilled the Victorian ideals of self-help and economic advance, and at the same time was able to experience the sentimental spirituality of realizing through the harmony of his way of life that Man was a part of Nature in his own right. Bulwer Lytton's lyrical evocation of night in the Australian bush exemplifies this quasi-religious involvement of the solitary squatter with his surroundings.

> Night in Australia! How impossible to describe its beauty! Heaven seems, in that new world, so much nearer to earth! Every star stands out so bright and particular, as if fresh from the time when the Maker willed it. And the moon like a large silvery sun,—the least object on which it shines so distinct and so still. Now and then a sound breaks the silence, but a sound so much in harmony with the solitude that it only deepens its charms ... and the flowers hang noiseless over your head as you ride through a grove of the giant gum-trees. Now the air is literally charged with the odors, and the sense of fragrance grows almost painful in its pleasure.[83]

For the English writer the Australian pastoral industry appeared to offer a means of escape to a simpler and nobler way of life, a return to nature which provided a release for the human spirit constrained by the industrialism and social restrictions of life in Britain.

The financial success of Australian squatters greatly interested the British public, and many an advocate of emigration utilized stories of their incredible rise to riches as a means of encouraging Britons to settle in the antipodean colonies. In 1839, Patrick Matthew surveyed the various areas of the world available for settlement by would-be emigrants from Britain, and concluded that the small capitalist with a taste for country life and the desire to acquire a fortune need only embark for Australia. If upon arrival he outlayed his capital in purchasing a few hundred thousand fine-woolled sheep, several bullocks to carry his baggage, and engaged one or more assistant shepherds he was well on the way to wealthy independence. All he now required for the realization of his dreams would be to start with his whole retinue for the wilderness where vast areas of pasture land cost nothing. 'In this patriarchal way' wrote Matthew, 'our colonist can, it is said, nearly double his flock every season; and at the end of eight or ten years will have at least a hundred times the number of sheep he commenced with'.[84]

Matthew demonstrated another common British misconception

concerning pastoral life in Australia when he informed his readers that
the pasture lands were so extensive that a squatter need not limit his
flocks to prevent over-cropping, for 'when one valley fails of herbage,
he can resort to another'.[85] Bulwer Lytton similarly wrote of galloping
a horse 'over those green rolling plains' of Australia,[86] and Samuel
Sidney described an exploring party, which included his brother John,
riding during a season of severe drought 'along plains which, as far as
the eye could reach, were covered with rich grass, higher than the
necks of their horses'.[87] The reality of course was very different, but
the harsh truth of squatting life was not allowed to interfere with
fantasies of middle-class Englishmen making easy money at the
antipodes. So widespread was the British tendency to romanticize the
pastoral industry in Australia that even a ruinous drought and the
collapse of colonial money-markets, such as that of the early 1840s,
(although providing an instructive warning for many) stimulated some
to hail such tribulations as a golden opportunity to embrace the
squatting life at a discount. In 1839, George Crawley advised his
family in Britain that the drought in New South Wales had opened up
splendid business opportunities because 'people are obliged to sell
their sheep cattle and land at a great disadvantage'.[88] Crawley followed
his own advice and speculated widely in land and stock almost ruining
himself as a consequence, so that by 1842 he was seriously contemplating re-emigration to South America.[89] The *Economist* advised its
readers during 1843 and 1844 that small capitalists could make a quick
killing or a profitable long-term investment by becoming squatters.
The paper declared that £500 would purchase land and livestock which
would have fetched £5000 before the drought;[90] and later, that a few
hundred pounds of capital invested immediately in Australia would
realize between 2 and 500 per cent profit within three or four years.[91]
Such ideas were based on British experience and reflected British
rather than Australian values. Land was regarded in Victorian
England as possessing an intrinsic worth of its own, and Englishmen
found it extremely difficult to adjust to the antipodean situation where
land was abundant and only appreciated if it could be put to use. Utility
constituted the main standard of value on the frontier and at a time of
drought and economic depression there was little financial return to be
expected from land or stock. Thomas Peel of Swan River was by no
means the last Englishman to go bankrupt for failure to realize that in
Australia land in itself was worthless, no matter what value might have
been placed upon similar holdings in the closely settled and more
compact United Kingdom.

Although the social value of land in Australia was usually considerably lower than in the United Kingdom, British judgements on the
worth of colonial land continued to reflect an English scale of values.

Most Britons believed that ownership of land somehow conferred social legitimacy on money gained in trade, or commerce and industry.[92] Possession of land was regarded as a most powerful bulwark against democratic tendencies,[93] and many Englishmen felt that pioneering colonial environments were by nature dangerously predisposed towards egalitarianism.[94] Thus the appeal of Wakefieldianism to some Englishmen is partially explicable, for that great propagandist was attempting to export to Britain's overseas territories time-honoured English concepts of property and the social valuation placed on its ownership.

This conviction that social institutions in Australia could be used to shape the character of the emerging society was common in Britain, though English churchmen implied that the imperial government's emphasis on land was only part of the remedy and that the Church of England in the colonies should again be raised to the pre-eminent position it enjoyed between 1826 and 1829,[95] since it alone could avert the rise of barbarism and republicanism in Australia.[96] Archdeacon Broughton believed that the church was the repository of civilized values, and that it was the main barrier between a robber republic of ex-convicts on the one hand and Roman Catholic despotism on the other.[97] Clergymen in Australia knew that squatters systematically murdered Aboriginals, and they feared the rising political and social influence of pastoral barbarism.[98]

If the productivity and profitability of a squatter's land was romanticized in Britain, so also was the social background and status of the squatter himself. Britons were inaccurately informed that the pastoralists often came from the upper ranks of British society, and the explorer George Grey viewed them as aristocrats: 'The Overlanders are generally descended from good families, have received a liberal education, (Etonians and Oxonians are to be found amongst them) and even at their first start in the colonies, were possessed of what is considered an independence'.[99] To Grey, these adventurers formed scions of an ancient stock who could find no outlet for their enterprise and restlessness in Britain, and he found amongst them a degree of sophistication and polish that he had not expected to encounter in such a mode of life. 'In the distant desert', wrote Grey, 'you unexpectedly stumble on a finished gentleman'.[1] This opinion was not an isolated one, and Grey's idealized squatters were similarly depicted by an Englishman visiting his squatter son during 1843: 'Graduates of Oxford, Cambridge, Edinburgh, and Dublin, are scattered through the bush; and one may see Cicero and Euripides lying cheek by jowl with sheep-shears, bullock-whips, and constables' fetters'.[2]

The way of life of such young bloods also won applause for its manly vigour, simplicity, and an element of wild and reckless excitement. According to Bulwer Lytton, squatters possessed 'a health which an antediluvian might have envied', and 'nerves so seasoned with horse-breaking, cattle-driving, fighting with wild blacks' that they were rendered quite impervious to fear.[3] Except for an annual trip to Sydney to dispose of their wool-clip and purchase supplies, the squatters' amusements were restricted to kangaroo hunting with the occasional variation of a hurdle race or a steeplechase.[4] This was a way of life which commended itself to many Englishmen, and Christopher Hodgson was voicing a wider approval when he commented that he could 'never wish for a happier life than a squatter's'.[5]

Such fulsome eulogies of squatting society and the pastoral life did not go unopposed, however, and in 1845 the novelist Thomas McCombie attacked the squatting interests in Australia for their ungentlemanly pursuit of wealth and advancement. He refuted George Grey's claim that the Australian pastoralists were representatives of aristocratic families in Britain, and denied that social position in England was at all respected by squatting society in Australia. In short, McCombie found squatters to be mercenary boors; 'there exists in the Colonies but one aristocracy, and that is of wealth: rank and talent are nothing in the scales. The Colonists worship no God but Plutus: Rank is not of much account; talent is respected abstractedly, but it commands almost no respect for individuals'.[6]

As was previously noted, the imperial authorities were also doubtful that a thinly spread pastoral society would encourage the advance of civilization in Australia, and Earl Grey seemed to fear that isolated squatter society carried within it the seeds of a colonial relapse into savagery.[7] Grey was concerned over the effects of squatting on the future tone and values of Australian society, but Charles Dickens implied that the age of the pastoralist as barbarian had already arrived. Abel Magwitch of *Great Expectations* made his fortune as a squatter. He was first sent to Australia, however, as a convict, and he comments on his return to England that other convicts also found prosperity in the same occupation: 'I've done wonderful well. There's others went out alonger me as has done well, too, but no man has done nigh as well as me. I'm famous for it'.[8] The romantic notion of nature as a character-regenerating agent is implicitly denied by Dickens, and Magwitch's isolation only fuels the inner fires of his determination to revenge himself on society by making Pip a gentleman:

> When I was a hired-out shepherd in a solitary hut, not seeing no faces but faces of sheep till I half-forgot wot men's and women's faces was like, I see yourn . . . 'Lord strike me dead', I says each time—and I goes out in the open air to say it under the open heavens—'but wot, if I gets liberty and money, I'll make that boy a gentleman!' And I done it.[9]

Magwitch had become a pastoralist and a man of property in Australia but his essential ferocity was unaltered, and he died in a British prison after committing murder. Abel Magwitch the squatter represented the dark side of Bulwer Lytton's Pisistratus Caxton.

The unoccupied lands of Australia meant many things to different Englishmen in the period under review, but whether they hoped to establish peasant agriculture or an aristocracy of squatters at the antipodes, an element of romantic idealism formed a common factor behind such anticipations. Scholars have claimed that the success of Wakefieldian dialectic in achieving so remarkable a degree of popularity against heavy odds during the 1830s and 1840s can be attributed to Wakefield's own enthusiastic and forceful personality combined with his extraordinary powers of persuasion.[10] Undoubtedly these assertions contain a grain of truth, but they ignore the fact that Wakefield systematized for many Englishmen feelings and emotions antagonistic to industrial materialism which were already current and widely accepted in their abstract and intellectual form. In so far as he advocated a moral and physical renewal in the wilderness, Wakefield was preaching to the already converted. It was one of the ironies of Australian development that the conflict in Britain between Wakefieldians and the followers of Samuel Sidney should be based on the fanciful and visionary theories of two writers of fiction, neither of whom had personal experience of Australia, but both of whom tapped and synthesized a predominant feeling of their times, that there was more to life than industrialization and that the good life could be rediscovered in the vast waste lands of Australia.

8: El Dorado 1851–55

In the event, these attitudes were soon destined to become irrelevant. During 1850 and 1851, huge auriferous deposits were discovered in New South Wales and the new colony of Victoria, and British emigrants accordingly began to flock to Australia to seek their fortunes. Arcady quickly gave way to El Dorado, and the change was reflected in a widespread public renewal of British interest in Australia.

Initial British reaction to the gold discoveries in Australia was cautious and not particularly enthusiastic, though some Englishmen apparently felt that private individuals should be precluded from ownership of gold discovered on crown-lands, and that the entire advantages from the recent gold strikes should be retained by the imperial government and devoted to the liquidation of the National Debt.[1] The *Economist* proclaimed that gold strikes in Australia were a doubtful advantage either to the mother country or the colonies themselves; 'The pursuit of mining and especially of gold digging, is essentially a lottery, in which the prizes are very alluring, but the blanks are very numerous.' The paper feared that British industry would be disrupted by a diminution in Australian production of wool, and expressed concern over the probable effect of gold on Australian character. It foresaw a danger that speculation would supplant steady industry, and a spirit of gambling would take the place of stoic and patient endurance amongst the lower orders.[2] British workers also initially expressed similar reservations. In 1851, *The Operative* was uneasy over the effects to be expected from the gold discoveries, particularly the impetus to economic individualism which would endanger working-class solidarity by filling the heads of the labouring classes with dreams of quick wealth, with

142

> Nothing nobler—nothing higher,
> Than the unappeased desire—
> The quenchless thirst for Gold.[3]

The *Economist* had raised an important issue when it feared that one of the main effects of gold in Australia would be the dislocation of a major segment of British industry, and the following year the paper pointed out that an acute shortage of labour existed in the colonies and that the production of wool was seriously threatened.[4] The *Times* reported that same month that the Yorkshire woollen industry had sent a deputation to the prime minister which had stressed the need for a large emigration to reach Australia before the shearing season.[5] The newspaper disagreed with the deputation's argument that an increased British emigration would save the pastoral industry. There was nothing to guarantee that if the imperial government did sent out more emigrants they would prefer sheep-tending to chancing their arms at the goldfields. What was needed was an incentive sufficiently strong to attract and retain emigrant labourers in the pastoral industry. The *Times* advocated that all emigrants be offered a free grant of land as soon as they arrived in Australia; this might induce those with more sober personalities and family commitments to choose the sureness of land in preference to the gamble for gold. It might also be possible, the paper estimated, to provide a floating, though temporary, labour force in Australia by raising the licence fee to prospect for and mine gold to a level at which most emigrants would be forced to work for a time in order to save he money. Unsuccessful miners would periodically be compelled to return to pastoral work, and newly-arrived emigrants would be further encouraged to accept the offer of a free farm.[6]

Nevertheless, the demands of the Yorkshire deputation were supported by other organs of the press, which reiterated the standard generalization that Britain relied heavily on supplies of raw materials from Australia. If unemployment and ruin were to be avoided at home then a new colonial work force had to be found.[7] In this instance, however, the imperial government had no need to encourage emigration. A great enthusiasm for travel to Australia during 1852 seemed more than likely to satisfy colonial labour requirements. Indeed, by June 1852 Sir John Pakington, the new colonial secretary, was complaining that the demand for private emigration to Australia had become so great that the authorities were finding it increasingly difficult to obtain ships for the conveyance of assisted emigrants.[8]

Some British commentators predicted that the gold discoveries in Australia would have an even greater impact on the mother country than the expected reduction in the volume of wool exported. They feared that price levels would rise in proportion to the overall increase in the total amount of gold in circulation. This depreciation of currency would have a significant effect on long-term contracts, payable in fixed amounts of money irrespective of its change in value, and on landlords and people with fixed incomes who would be brought into conflict with one another.[9] Archibald Alison maintained that a pernicious inflation would be caused by the unlooked-for growth in the supplies of gold,[10] while John Lalor held that the Australian gold discoveries were an unmitigated calamity. Lalor believed that the transmission of newly-mined gold to Britain would lower interest rates and foster speculation in the mother country which already enjoyed an uncomfortable superabundance of capital. Wages and prices would spiral upwards, as supplies of wool from the colonies diminished altogether and colonists pursued the chimera of immediate wealth and neglected their pastoral pursuits. Lalor affirmed that a connection existed between the production of wool in Australia and the level of wages in the United Kingdom: 'To multitudes of the manufacturing population wool is as necessary as bread. Without the wool there is no way of getting the bread.'[11] Lalor also feared that the entire system of Britain's industrial relations would be adversely affected by the gold discoveries because untold wealth would be placed in the hands of people ill-equipped to handle it responsibly. Such *nouveau riche* would tend to demand luxury goods and British industry would be disrupted as production schedules and targets were recklessly abandoned in the rush to meet the demands of a wealthy new market:

> Meanwhile, the production of gold instead of wool, while it will be a doubtful advantage to the goldfinders, will be a certain loss to the majority of mankind; for its effect must mainly be to cause a new distribution of all the other products of human labour in favour of the discoverers. Neither they nor any others want the gold for its own sake, but only as a means of procuring commodities; and though the new demand will, of course, stimulate and increase production, its chief effect must be to disorder the industrial relations already in existence.[12]

Commentators said repeatedly that long-term wealth could never come to Australia from gold-digging and that it was 'her sheep-farms and her fertility to which she must look for a future of real abundance and prosperity.[13] The same point was wryly made by *Punch* in 1852 when it stated that 'The only drawback on all this prosperity is the awkward fact, that the gold cannot be eaten.'[14]

British industrial production was affected in other ways by the gold discoveries in Australia, and not all the effects were bad. The journalist, D. T. Coulton, took a far more optimistic view of the situation than did Alison or Lalor when he pointed out that the large influx of population to Australia had caused the prices of all commodities in the colonies there to rise, and thus 'a field is opened for the industry of the mother country, which, it is obvious, will not be neglected.'[15] Other observers took a similar line and drew the attention of their readers to the high wage rates paid in the colonies in order to keep labourers from withdrawing to the diggings. Such critics called for a steady encouragement to be given to emigration to Australia; 'Every labourer despatched to Australia will become a better customer for our manufactures than he ever was before;' it was more profitable to send him shirts and knives in exchange for wool and gold than to maintain him at home in return for his labour in the fields.[16] Trade figures for these years show that the optimists were closer to the truth in their estimates. Great Britain's exports to Australia rose from under three million pounds value in 1851 to fourteen and a half million pounds in 1853.[17]

Some Englishmen, however, were so convinced that monetary values would be eroded by the depreciation of currency that statistics would not have persuaded them that the real value of Britain's exports had risen to a level comparable with monetary value. In 1853, Professor Hancock advised the twenty-second meeting of the British Association for the Advancement of Science that the great increase in the world's supplies of gold from California and Australia must produce a fall in the value of the precious metal which would cause disastrous confusion in all trading and other international monetary matters. As a remedy, Hancock suggested that Britain should switch from gold to a silver standard of value.[18] *Punch* reacted in characteristic fashion by warning that currency would become so depreciated that 'we should not be astonished at finding some eccentric ticket-of-leave man sending over, in a fit of liberality, a remittance in payment of the National Debt.'[19]

Professor Hancock was a protagonist in an economic debate which had begun in England as early as 1819, but which the gold discoveries in Australia again raised to public prominence. Britain had been on the gold standard since 1816, which meant that the value of its currency was based on a given weight of gold of a given fineness, that the Bank of England was obliged by law to buy and sell gold at fixed prices, and that the movement of gold into and out of the country was free of all restriction.[20] Hancock and other British economists were concerned that gold itself would be depreciated by the rapid flow from the new mines in Australia; consequently they agitated for a silver standard that would be more likely than gold to ensure a stable pound.[21] Australia's seemingly unlimited capacity to produce gold raised the spectre of international currency depreciation. If gold dropped in value while silver remained steady then British currency would be devalued *vis à vis* the currency of countries on a silver standard like Holland and

Belgium, or a bimetallist standard like France and the United States of America. Thus Australian gold caused disquietude amongst some economists and encouraged a movement for a complete reorientation of British currency before impending devaluation generated a swing in the terms of trade against Britain and in favour of her international competitors. The imperial government, however, remained unsympathetic to those who favoured a change in the existing standard, and determined to discourage any discussion which raised the slightest doubt about the value of gold. In 1853, W. E. Gladstone, then Chancellor of the Exchequer, smartly rejected Henry Drummond's request for a parliamentary inquiry into the altered value of the gold standard by replying that the government 'have no intention, under present circumstances, and as at present advised, of appointing any Committee to inquire into this subject.'[22]

In contrast to the gloomy forebodings of those who favoured a silver standard, other Britons suggested that Australia could be a divine instrument to advance the interests of society and the furtherance of God's plan for the world. The evangelical Earl of Shaftesbury thought that the gold discoveries in Australia had been supernaturally inspired in order to force mankind into fulfilling the commandment to replenish the earth.[23] In a similar vein, D. T. Coulton reminded readers of the *Quarterly Review* that 'All objects and events are under the control of infinite power, and in servitude to the designs of infinite wisdom and goodness.' Thus there could be no doubt that 'the treasures of Australia have been opened under the special Providence of God.'[24]

If some Englishmen found balm and comfort in the belief that Britain enjoyed a form of divine protection from the ravages of currency depreciation and inflation precipitated by the Australian gold strikes, others based their optimism on more mundane economic theory. In 1852, the *Economist* denounced the doom-criers as unduly alarmist. Although the chance discovery of huge nuggets of gold which instantaneously enriched their finders attracted considerable publicity, these finds were the exception not the rule. Most of the gold unearthed had to be earned with back-breaking labour and many miners were unsuccessful. The paper argued that a ready market could be found for all the gold discovered in Australia and California, and even if future supplies did eventually produce an excess

> Theory, in accordance with the short experience of the last two years, teaches us that there is little reason to justify the apprehensions of a great fall in the value of gold; but if it did take place, coincident as it would be with the fallen value of almost all the other products of labour, it would not be a subject for regret. It would be an additional reward for industry and an additional stimulus to

peaceful exertion, and should be hailed rather by rejoicing than apprehensions.[25]

The following year, William Newmarch presented a similar view to the twenty-third meeting of the British Association for the Advancement of Science when he claimed that gold had been propitious to both Britain and Australia. The Australian colonies would develop even more quickly than in the past because of the new discoveries which had created an abundance of colonial capital and lowered interest rates. 'In our own country', he wrote, 'it has quickened and extended trade; and exerted an influence which thus far is beneficial wherever it has been felt.'[26] That same year William Westgarth's reports from the colony of Victoria were published in Edinburgh, and with first-hand knowledge he laid to rest one of the major concerns which had troubled Englishmen since 1851. Westgarth believed that no serious reduction would occur in the supplies of wool from Australia, since population was pouring into the colony and the pastoralists had found that they could make do with smaller numbers of herdsmen than they had hitherto thought possible.[27] Indeed, in Port Phillip during 1851 some squatters staffed their holdings entirely with Aboriginals and the experiment had succeeded reasonably well.[28] Trade figures for the years between 1850 and 1855 show that the volume of Australian wool exported to Britain continued to increase during the years of gold discoveries.[29]

Other facets of Britain's economy also prospered as a result of the Australian gold strikes, and one of the most notable areas of resurgence occurred in shipping and shipbuilding. Sir John Pakington had complained in 1852 that the demand for ships had progressed to such an extent that it was almost impossible to find vessels for the Australia run.[30] Dickens described the incredible scenes which took place daily in the ship-chandlers' offices, where 'Legions of banker's clerks, merchants' lads, embryo secretaries, and incipient cashiers . . . beg of hard-hearted ship-brokers to grant them the favour of a berth in their last-advertised . . . emigrant ship.'[31] Merchantmen were diverted from the Indian trade to cope with the rush, while numerous orders for new ships were placed with the shipbuilders of Nova Scotia and the United States, who specialized in the construction of huge clippers capable of carrying the crowds of British adventurers waiting to make their fortunes in Australia.[32] British shipbuilding also shared in this boom, and G. B. Johnson in 1853 depicted the revitalizing effect of the Australian gold discoveries on what had been a declining industry;

We ceased to hear of shipping lying idle in the docks of our leading seaports. We ceased to hear of our seamen entering into the service of rival countries. Our building-yards, both at home and in the

American colonies, became scenes of unprecedented activity; and every branch of industry connected directly or indirectly with shipping, was placed in a prosperous condition . . . Australia has saved the British shipowner from ruin.[33]

Johnson was not exaggerating, and a modern historian of British shipping has commented that 'The new Australian trade, more than any other, formed and moulded the whole business of professional deep-sea ship-owning as we know it today'.[34]

If the shipping interests regarded the rush to Australia as a beneficial stimulus, other portions of the British community regarded it as a mixed blessing. During this period there occurred a series of strikes and wage claims which indicated to the satisfaction of the *Times* that emigration of labourers to Australia was running at such a high rate that it endangered the basis of the social pyramid.[35] But even the *Times* was forced to admit that an influx of new blood to fill the vacancies caused by emigration would be an invigorating experience for many large business establishments.[36] A contributor to *Fraser's Magazine* predicted that the great emigration to Australia would cause an improvement in the condition of the labouring classes at home,[37] and *The Operative* recognized the importance of Australia's goldfields as an integral part of the British class struggle when it anticipated that a general social levelling would result in Britain from their discovery. *The Operative* was satisfied that one inexorable consequence of the Australian gold strikes would be a fall in British interest rates, which in turn would ensure that the upper classes who lived on interest earned by accumulated capital would earn less. Wages, on the other hand, would rise, and therein lay 'the solution of that "vexed question", as between capital and labour, which has been the stumbling block of ethical and social philosophers in modern times.'[38]

The type of emigrant attracted to Australia by the gold discoveries also provoked varied comment in Britain. As already noted, some Englishmen felt that the gold-seekers were socially as well as economically the 'bottom of the barrel' and comprised the scum of the lower classes.[39] It was not only British emigrants who caused this disquiet, however, and a significant emigration to Australia from the United States of America contributed to British feelings of uneasiness. The *Morning Chronicle* informed its readers that Australia was attracting 'a dangerous class of adventurers' from the United States, and advocated both British and Chinese emigration to the antipodes because 'It is desirable to occupy the ground, as far as possible, before American adventurers turn their attention to the California of the South.'[40] Many contemporary Englishmen believed that the American presence exacerbated the ever-present danger of republicanism. The

Spectator affirmed that one pronounced effect of the gold discoveries had been the encouragement of a spirit of republican independence and democracy amongst the population of the Australian colonies.[41] The imperial government appeared similarly uneasy. The lieutenant-governor of Victoria, Charles La Trobe, was instructed to exercise vigilance following reports from the British consul at Philadelphia that many Americans, who travelled to Australia ostensibly to join in the search for gold, were really revolutionaries dedicated to fomenting republican rebellion in Britain's antipodean colonies.[42]

Fears of deleterious American influence or of republicanism did little to depress the enthusiasm of Britain's working classes who had overcome their early distrust and seemed delighted to take advantage of opportunities to emigrate to the diggings at the antipodes; the superior drawing power of gold over peasant farming is evident from the emigration figures. In 1850, only fourteen thousand British emigrants travelled to Australia, whereas in 1852 there were more than eighty-six thousand.[43] In the majority of cases the lure of wealth undoubtedly motivated emigration to Australia during the early 1850s, as Britain's lower orders seized their opportunities with optimistic enthusiasm. Australia's gold raised the morale and self-esteem of emigrants from the unprivileged ranks of British society who no longer saw themselves as exiles but as pioneers.

> Here's off, here's off to the diggings of gold,
> Australia's our home where wealth is untold;
> Up, up, with your picks, take your shovel in hand.
> Here's off, here's off to a happier land.
> We dread not the voyage, though distant and long,
> We've a compass to steer by, our arms they are strong.
> And ne'er into misery unheeded we'll fall
> While Melbourne's rich gold fields are open to all.[44]

The short-term effects of this working-class exodus to Australia appalled Wakefield, who foresaw the development of an unacceptably egalitarian society on the goldfields, which with a few exceptions would consist of 'a sort of navvies rolling in money without a master . . . The law of person or property is the revolver or the bowie-knife. It is a monstrous Socialism, under which all enjoyment and power is monopolized by the proletaires.' Wakefield's solution to this problem took the form of a proposal that the imperial government recruit a work force of submissive Chinese labourers for Australia.[45] Samuel Sidney continued to cling tenaciously to his ideal of peasant proprietorship, and hoped that a few of the emigrants might forego the dream of rapid affluence on the diggings and concentrate on supplying the necessities of life to such a lucrative market—to make their fortunes 'by the gold-diggers, but not by gold-diggings.'[46]   The march of events, however, had overtaken these agricultural theorists, though they continued to reflect a wider British concern over the moral character and the socially levelling tendencies of the new mining industry. The *Economist* had raised these questions as early as 1851, when it averred that, 'Hazard and speculation supplant steady industry; a spirit of gambling takes the place of patient endurance; and, in the search for gold, real wealth and solid character are alike sacrificed.'[47] During these years, many Englishmen deplored the social chaos caused by the discovery of gold and were openly resentful that diggers from the lower classes could suddenly acquire fabulous wealth. William Westgarth felt that the 'accustomed relations and gradations of society have been too suddenly upset. The increase and the misuse of means have kept pace together.'[48] William Shaw was outraged by the 'swagger and effrontery' of lower-class miners in Sydney who delighted in making ostentatious display of their new-found prosperity.[49] It was not only the successful miners who contracted the infectious egalitarianism; colonial tradesmen and merchants were reputed to be every bit as independent as the diggers. Perhaps abundance had made them casual, but they generally adopted a 'take it or leave it' tone with their customers, and gave no change below a sixpence.[50] William Dobie described how the established patterns of deference for social superiors were distorted by the widespread availability of ready money amongst the colonial lower classes. He illustrated his argument by recounting the fate of a squatter who had queried the price of some small article in a shop and received the following retort from the shopkeeper for his pains: 'You can keep your *lousy* eighteenpence; I don't make my living by the patronage of *bloody* squatters.'[51]

Gold had provided a strong stimulus to the social fluidity that had already existed in Australia, but more than a hint of envy could be discerned in much of the criticism levelled in England at frontier egalitarianism. The economic success of working-class emigrants was not a subject calculated to warm the hearts of British observers from the higher ranks of society at home who would have preferred the relative fruitfulness of gold-digging to be dependent on social status rather than physical strength and luck. 'In no part of the world' protested one critic, 'are the smiles of Fortune so capricious as here—masters become servants, and servants masters; the poor become rich and the rich often become poor from over-speculation and reckless expenditure.'[52] The *Times* similarly lamented that 'the vested interests of the colony suffer by their unequal competition with the enormous wealth which the working classes are dividing among themselves.' The paper called for the dispatch of British troops to

Australia, the raising of mining licence fees to a level which would place them beyond the reach of newly-arrived labourers, and the use of the army to collect licence fees and evict unlicenced miners from the diggings. 'It depends upon our Government whether the boundless treasures of Australia shall be employed in debauching and corrupting the lower orders . . . and in ruining those who have invested capital under the protection of our Government.'[53] The *Economist* lectured colonists in a similar tone on the moral problems caused by the easy availability of riches and suggested that wealth without hard labour was an inferior product. 'Wealth, as the rule, is only to be obtained by continuous and skilful industry, and the little, and perhaps only apparent exception of the gold-finding, will give permanent prosperity merely as it stimulates to continuous exertion.'[54] Even the fact that much of the new wealth was spent on purchasing British goods did not dissuade such critics from accusing the colonists of selfishness and extravagance which were attributed to the high wage rates that pastoralists had to pay in order to keep their workers away from the diggings. 'With such wages', the *Economist* commented critically, 'every person is a large consumer, and the consumption of such a community must be quite enormous compared to the old stinted and frugal communities of Europe.'[55]

The moral dangers of speculative mining and easy riches were said to be compounded in Australia by the presence of convicts, ex-convicts, and a criminally tainted population.[56] Earl Grey was in a minority when he perversely argued that the gold discoveries had rendered the continuation of transportation to eastern Australia essential because free labour could not be kept away from the goldfields. He denied that criminals would actively desire transportation to Van Diemen's Land and claimed that those who wished to reach the mines of Australia could do so far more easily than via the sufferings and privations of convict discipline.[57] In this assumption, however, Grey was incorrect. During 1852, the convicts under sentence of transportation in the hulks at Woolwich had mutinied, and insolently asserted that the imperial government had 'broken faith' with them by not carrying out their sentences.[58]

Most British writers tended to lump the lower orders in the colonies together with the convicts and to denigrate the colonial working classes as immoral and depraved. F. Lancelott was very much a lone voice in 1852 when he commented on the good behaviour he had witnessed at the Bathurst diggings in New South Wales. He reported few cases of drunkenness and no fighting; the sabbath was said to be carefully observed and the laws respected; and 'the highly commendable morality and good conduct of the miners generally, strikingly contrasted with the savage violence, the Lynch law, and the brute force said to be dominant at California.'[59] On the other hand, the *Times* described the colonial lower orders as consisting of the most desperate and incorrigible of Britain's criminal population and called for the dispatch of British troops to protect life and property from 'the invasion of a lawless mob.'[60] John Sherer related to his readers how the mere proximity of such people tended to deprave, and stated that after a short stay at the goldfields even the most upright Englishmen became a little lax in their morals.[61]

If the lure of gold caused the moral debilitation of honourable men, the diggings also acted as a magnet for some of the more vicious ex-convicts from Van Diemen's Land. A recent scholar has noted how as 1852 progressed the degree of violence on the Victorian diggings increased.[62] Mrs Charles Clacy imaginatively depicted night on the goldfields in a way which would have reinforced all the existing British prejudices towards the type of society that was emerging at the antipodes.

'But night here at the diggings is the characteristic time: murder here—murder there—revolvers cracking—blunderbusses bombing—rifles going off—balls whistling—one man groaning with a broken leg—another shouting because he couldn't find the way to his hole, and a third equally vociferous because he has tumbled into one—this man swearing—another praying—a party of bacchanals chanting various ditties to different time and tune, or rather minus both.'[63]

Another writer who became a police magistrate at the Ballarat diggings in Victoria commented in similar vein on the disorders which came to his attention. He described the miners as forming a carcass upon which all the old convicts, or 'Van-demonian vultures' preyed. Every type and variety of crime was rife on the goldfields so that no London police office could experience a greater range of crime than appeared upon the charge-sheets of the police at Ballarat.[64]

Few features of colonial life at this time appear to have struck British visitors so forcibly as this prevalence of crime and disregard for the law, and the natural temptation was to link these characteristics with the presence of convicts. Writers agreed that the combination of low or unrestricted electoral franchises and great wealth would be socially disastrous in a country where the population 'is of a very mixed character, not very amenable nor much attached to any particular kind of law, and very much given to follow their own inclinations, and to regard their own will as their only law.'[65] The *Times* had referred to the goldfield population as 'a lawless mob,'[66] and visitors to the diggings were often appalled by the state in which they found society; extravagance and profligacy, drunkenness and robbery seemed to be the prevailing standards of behaviour.

Many of these criticisms were not new. The convict antecedents of Australian settlement had made similar evaluations of colonial society popular amongst Englishmen during the 1830s and 1840s. Gold, however, dramatized the Australian frontier in a way that squatting and pastoral development had never done. Lawlessness was endemic to a frontier environment, but lawlessness accompanied by the rapid accumulation of riches on the part of the lower orders of society excited a fascinated though censorious interest amongst Britain's middle and upper classes, while it simultaneously caused a massive emigration from the lower levels of the social pyramid. The gold boom ensured that Australia was far better known to Englishmen by 1855 than had been the case five years earlier, but its reputation had not gained by the greater exposure. Not a few British writers remained profoundly disturbed at the altered direction imparted by the gold discoveries to the pattern of Australian development, and they also feared the disturbing social and economic effects that Australia's gold might produce in Britain. The disquieting degree to which the United Kingdom had come to rely on her Australian colonies for raw material to supply English woollen manufacturers became a subject of serious debate, as did the unforeseen ability of Australia's gold exports to effect the stability of Britain's wage- and price-levels and to endanger the international standing of the British pound. Commentators were concerned to discover that developments in the colonies could cause inflation in England, and thereby theoretically had the power to bring about an overall reduction of human welfare in Britain. The *Economist* expressed the general tenor of British uneasiness in 1852, when it commented wistfully; 'It would clearly have been more convenient and more profitable if our imports of other commodities had been greater, and of gold less.'[67]

9: The Land of Contrarieties

In addition to touching upon the more mundane aspects of colonial development, British attitudes towards the Australian colonies in the period under review included a striation of opinions of a more extravagant nature. Many of these more fanciful notions represented a somewhat pale reflection of the suppositions of ancient and medieval geographers who believed that everything in the southern hemisphere was inverted and governed by different laws from those pertaining to the northern hemisphere. The ancients had claimed that monsters dwelt in those regions, and the distinctive, unusual flora and fauna of Australia seemed to lend weight to this long-standing view.[1] The belief that the laws of nature were also reversed at the antipodes was similarly sanctified by age, and this too played a part in influencing British attitudes during the first half of the nineteenth century.[2] Initial British astonishment at animals like the kangaroo and platypus had strengthened the view that Australia was a land of strange contradictions and eccentricities. The concept of antipodal inversion arose from British reflections upon the unusual plants and animals discovered during the early years of Australian settlement; but as the agricultural and pastoral potentialities of the country began to receive attention in England, the idea of reversal was also expressed in these contexts, and it tinged British attitudes to many aspects of Australian development right through to the 1850s.

Contrarieties abounded at the antipodes. In 1830, Robert Dawson commented that in Australia it was the poorer soils which carried the most trees, up to three times as many as were found in richer soils. This improbable state of affairs was inexplicable in an era which knew nothing about soil chemistry, trace elements and the like; but Dawson ascribed it to antipodal inversion with the remark that this 'like most other things in this strange country, is, I believe, nearly the reverse of what we find in England.'[3] In the same vein, the traveller Holman noted four years later that in New South Wales 'nature has provided principles of fertility, exactly the reverse of those which observation has discovered to regulate the vegetable world of Europe.'[4] It was not just a peculiarity of soil and climate that concerned Britons, but also a sense of strangeness that Britain could be in any way reliant upon the produce of such an outlandish and abnormal country. The *Leeds Mercury*, in 1832, found it most unsettling that Britain should import more wool from Australia than from Spain, a traditional supplier of fine merino wool: 'There is something so topsy turvy and revolutionary in these changes, that we think Lord Eldon ought to watch them with much anxiety.'[5]

As already noted, many British observers felt that convict and emancipist affluence in Australia constituted a bizarre reversal of natural law,[6] and Archbishop Whately informed the House of Lords that in New South Wales 'a new standard of opinion had been set up which makes vice virtue and virtue vice.'[7] Charles Rowcroft also believed that natural laws were reversed in Australia, and in 1843 he published a popular anthology entitled *Tales of the Colonies*, which by 1845 had passed through three editions. In this work Rowcroft described Australian cherries which had the stone on the outside of the fruit like a coconut shell, and maintained into the bargain that antipodal rivers flowed uphill.[8]

Imaginative invention of this type was common from the days of the first settlement at Botany Bay in 1788,[9] but the discovery of Australia's goldfields in the early 1850s caught the attention of British satirists who found in the concept of inversion a useful method of rationalizing in a humorous way the strange twists of fortune and of explaining the social disorientation and mobility of the gold-diggings. The idea of Australia as an eccentric contradictory environment had become so widespread in Britain by 1853 that the *Globe* newspaper could comment that 'Nobody is surprised at anything in Australia. It is a land of adventure, where matters are exactly reversed, and a day is looked upon as lost which is not signalized by some half-dozen freaks of Fortune.'[10] Other writers felt the same; it was widely believed that gold-seekers would see strange sights as they made their way to the diggings, like pears and cherries growing together on the same tree, with the pears attached and hanging by the wrong end.[11]

All these feakish antipodal contradictions were gathered together during the 1850s by the anonymous author of *The Land of Contrarieties* and together with many other imaginative inventions assembled into a long satirical poem in mock-heroic rhyming couplets.[12] The verse covers a full range of animal inconsistencies from the platypus,

> There beasts have mallards' bills and legs,
> Have spurs like cocks, like hens lay eggs.

to the emu

> And birds, although they cannot fly,
> In swiftness with the greyhound vie.

It also iound amusement in the distinctive flora of the country where grass was said to grow upon tree trunks, and the foliage to hang vertically rather than horizontally. European plants taken to the antipodes underwent a fundamental change of nature and apple trees no longer bore fruit but produced apple cider inside their trunks. An even more elemental metamorphosis took place in European animals shipped to Australia, as evidenced by the transformation in imported sheep which were said to become carnivorous:

> There the voracious ewe-sheep crams
> Her paunch with flesh of tender lambs.

The inversion of moral values was also described in terms which echoed Whately and reflected little credit on the colonial populace,

> There every servant gets his place
> By character of foul disgrace
> There vice is virtue, virtue vice,
> And all that's vile is voted nice.

The poem ends by revealing that Australia has been the object of this critical attention.

> Now of what place can such strange tales
> Be told with truth, but New South Wales?

The Land of Contrarieties was an obvious attempt at poetic whimsy, but even handbooks for the instruction of prospective settlers reproduced such fanciful notions,[13] and Samuel Butler's geography textbook for schools admitted that the whole continent was remarkable and contained many sigularities.[14]

If these whimsical fantasies represented Australia as distinctive, another nineteenth-century stream of British literary consciousness depicted the little-known country in European or African terms. With a little poetical licence the unfamiliar took on the attributes of the hackneyed commonplace. The evangelical clergyman James Montgomery was so stimulated on reading the journals of Australian exploration which had been published by Matthew Flinders in 1814 that he wrote a poem which imaginatively depicted the creation and development of some small islands discovered by Flinders in a lagoon on Kangaroo Island, just off the coast of what later become the colony of South Australia. According to Montgomery's poem, which appeared in 1827, these islands were the productions of coral worms, and in the course of their evolution came to be populated by lions, leopards, antelope, jackals, and crocodiles. A 'fierce ungovernable savage' race of natives also appeared, who delighted in sacrificing any excess population to these wild beasts. The natives were described in terms which were probably derived from the Red Indians of North America, and were said to use the sling and the bow and arrow as their main weapons.[15] Montgomery's description had nothing in common with reality; he was merely making use of an antipodal setting to establish a stylized theatrical scenario in which one of these fierce cannibals he had invented would beg 'the unknown God' to send teachers capable of revealing the deity and his laws to his unenlightened brothers.[16]

Other English writers tended to depict Australia as an antipodean Europe. In 1837 Lady Mary Fox published a fictitious account of an exploring expedition into the interior of Australia, which announced in the first paragraph the 'wonderful discovery' of a civilized European nation living in the interior of New Holland. The terrain through which the expedition passed was typically European, including a chain of lakes which ended in a beautiful green and fertile land.[17] This inclination to picture the Australian landscape in English terms permeated Henry Haistwell Hardy's lyrical homage to Australian potential in 1843, and led him to describe green pastures, forests and 'spreading meres', and to glory in the hope of future greatness:

> And may not here—at earth's remotest bound—
> A second Britain rear her loft head . . .,[18]

These writers probably misrepresented Australian scenery in an unconscious effort to make their literary productions intelligible to domestic English audiences; but literature was not the only area in which Australian nature could be distorted. A recent scholar has revealed that British landscape artists who had actually visited the antipodean colonies were guilty of a similar falsification, and that they made comprehensive alterations to their original sketches of Australian scenes in order to bring their paintings into line with the accepted precepts of picturesque composition of the day. Eucalypt trees tended to take on the characteristics of the English oak, and during the first fifty years of Australian settlement the faithful imitation of Australia's individualistic trees and vegetation was thought to constitute an offence to good taste.[19]

Despite the many strange eccentricities of Australia and the wistfulness of British commentators who regretted that it was not more like home, Britons generally seem to have felt that in settling New Holland they had achieved something worthwhile.[20] In the years between 1828 and 1855, however, considerable debate raged amongst Englishmen concerning the exact nature of this laudable accomplishment, and some observers maintained that the Australian colonies were sufficiently individualistic to constitute a distinct category of empire all their own. This was particularly true of the convict colonies, and an element of antipodean particularism had begun to appear in British attitudes during the 1820s when the advent of free colonists began to conflict with the penal motive which underlay the original conception of settlement. In 1822, Earl Bathurst, then secretary of state for war and colonies, had written that the great error into which Lachlan Macquarie—the recently recalled Governor of New South Wales—had fallen,

> was to consider the Settlement as a Colony, and not as a place of Punishment and Reform ... I am aware that it has made such advances as a Colony, that it has grown to have the Interest, and has a claim therefore to the Protection of a Colony—but this must be a secondary consideration.[21]

Bathurst was by no means the only Englishman who took this line. In 1828 the Reverend Sydney Smith expressed doubts concerning the advantages of colonies and formal empire to Britain. Smith proclaimed empire in the old sense of governing another country to be unprofitable; and obviously felt that this represented a not uncommon view when he commented that, 'Fifty years ago, it would have been necessary to prove by argument that it is not necessary to govern a country in order to derive the greatest possible advantage from the only really profitable relations, those of commerce.' If utility was to be measured in commercial terms, however, the settlements in New South Wales and Van Diemen's Land remained unprofitable, but Smith explained that Australia was 'removed by distance beyond the *natural* sphere of European connexion; its future commerce must be Asiatic.'[22] The stress on *'natural'* indicates that in Smith's opinion Britain had created an artificial environment and connection when it sent convicts to the antipodes, and this placed Australia outside the area of discussion when normal empire was under consideration. True to his preoccupation with fiscal advantage, Smith advocated an increased British emigration to South America in preference to the British colonies of settlement. He claimed that if 50 000 Britons were to settle in South America, they would impose their tastes and appetites on the entire local population, thereby providing the mother country with a huge new market. Conversely, an emigration of 50 000 to North America or Australia increased Britain's overseas market by only 50 000 units.[23]

The protracted existence of convict transportation led some British commentators into a continued estimation of Australia as an unusual imperial appendage. In 1838, Lord Brougham wrote an article for the *Edinburgh Review* in which he predicted the ultimate absorption of Canada by the United States of America—an eventuality which he represented as putting 'an end to our remaining empire'.[24]Clearly in this context Brougham was differentiating between settlement colonies and territories like India which had been gained by conquest from indigenous native races. The 'colonial empire' might disappear with Canada, but India, the Cape, and the Australian colonies, to name but a few, would still be attached to Britain. Brougham did not appear to regard the Australian dependencies as colonies of settlement analogous to Canada, yet they certainly were not foreign-populated territories in the same way as India or the Cape. In that same year, *Blackwood's Magazine* carried a joint article by George Groly and John Wilson which distinguished between 'colonies' and 'conquests', but placed New South Wales squarely with the settlement colonies, thereby refusing to allow that the presence of convicts altered the status of a settlement in any way.[25] These writers defined a colony as the establishment by a nation of a community of its people in a new land, and then proceeded to describe New South Wales as the most successful of all British colonies.[26] Far from being persuaded by the Canadian rebellions that empire represented an onerous and profitless hegemony, Groly and Wilson struck a note which was to recur in British commentary throughout the 1840s—namely, that Britain had a special dispensation from divine providence to colonize the world:

> Without entering into those higher considerations which seem to connect this striking peculiarity [that is, success in colonizing] with national virtue, it may be fairly observed that, of all European countries, England is the one whose intercourse is capable of conferring the largest share of moral and physical advantages upon those, her remote and struggling offspring.[27]

During the 1840s, confidence in the spiritual rectitude and moral status of Britain's imperial ventures helped to impart an aura of enthusiastic optimism to Englishmen's opinions regarding the future of the Australian colonies. The country had demonstrated its capacity to produce wealth through the pastoral industry, and convicts were no longer transported to New South Wales. It became fashionable to depict Australia as an embryo empire in its own right. Arthur Hodgson described Australia as 'one of the proudest monuments of the christian civilization of our country ... the centre of a new Empire in the Southern Hemisphere, from which all the blessings of Britain will radiate to millions yet unborn.'[28] Bulwer Lytton similarly perceived the influence of 'the All-beneficent Father' in the rise of Australia, 'offering bread to the famished, hope to the desperate; in very truth enabling the "New World to redress the balance of the Old".'[29] George Groly predicted the development of an Anglo-Saxon empire in Australia which would quickly extend its dominion over the indolent inhabitants of South East Asia,[30] and he foresaw such a state transferring the benefits of English civilization—laws, habits, industrial activity, and national freedom—'to the richest, but the most abject countries of the globe; an imperial England at the Antipodes, securing, invigorating, and crowning all its benefits by its religion.'[31] The rising tide of Britain's chauvinistic confidence, however, was expressed in its most arrogant and extreme form in an article written by the poet Aubrey de Vere in 1850, in which be called for a vigorous policy of colonization throughout the world that would provide Britain with an ever-increasing free-trade market secure from hostile tariffs, while at the same time fulfilling a divine civilizing destiny:

> Colonization is reserved especially for those nations which have approved themselves worthy of transmitting their names and institutions entwined with the future hopes of man. It is through the noblest nations that nature extends the race ... It is not for nothing ·hat to England has been committed the sway of an empire on which the sun never sets, ... It is a noble work to plant the foot of England and extend her sceptre by the banks of streams unnamed, and over regions yet unknown,—and to conquer, not by the tyrannous subjugation of inferior races, but by the victories of mind over brute matter and blind mechanic obstacles.[32]

Imperial chauvinism did not exist in a vacuum, and De Vere's passing reference to tariffs is a reminder that throughout the period under review a powerful and vociferous free-trade lobby was engaged in criticizing the empire as an anachronism which placed an unnecessary financial burden on Britain. Led by Richard Cobden and John Bright, the free-traders argued that political suzerainty over areas of European settlement overseas was not a prerequisite for commercially profitable trading relations.[33] This view was not new and it had enjoyed the support of the *Times* during 1831, though the newspaper, like Cobden and Bright, did not advocate that the colonies be simply cast adrift, since moral obligations to the colonists, as well as British prestige had to be considered. The imperial authorities could not 'scuttle a colony' because some foreign rival might take it over.[34] Britain was thus often forced into what could be termed pre-emptive imperialism, in that she retained or even extended her formal empire in order to exclude other powers. Small military stations were originally introduced into Van Diemen's Land and Western Australia in 1803 and 1826 respectively, to anticipate and forestall an expected

French initiative in these areas; a similarly preclusive motive was partly responsible for the annexation of New Zealand in 1840.[35]

Attacks on empire by free-traders forced supporters of colonization on to the defensive and caused proponents of settlement and political dominion to seek theoretical justifications for empire. Hubristic cultural chauvinism formed a common response, but there were others. Alfred Mallalieu, a London journalist, maintained that free-traders oversimplified complex issues, and charged that they suffered from *'moneymania'*, a disease in which the leading characteristics were allegedly the endurance of mental hallucinations under which the person afflicted attempted 'to reduce all argument into arithmetical quantities.'[36] Nor should free-trade arithmetic be applied to Australia, he felt, because New South Wales, Van Diemen's Land, and Norfolk Island were never settled with the intention of commercial profit; they had been prisons first and foremost, and economic profitability had never been anticipated.[37]

It was the social critic and industrialist W. R. Greg, however, who took Cobdenite arguments against colonies and turned them against the free-traders. He held that colonies were intrinsically valuable and formed important adjuncts to free-trade. Greg convinced himself that British colonies would never raise tariff barriers against the mother country, and that the constitutional connection with Britain would ensure a continuing desire for British goods; 'are not our own colonies the last markets from which we shall be driven by the increasing numbers and developing energies of rival producers? Are they not both our safest, our most permanent, and, per head, our largest customers?'[38] The empire could become the nucleus of a far-flung free-trade union and trading bloc, and for these reasons he believed colonies provided the most favourable conditions to secure Britain's economic growth. This theory contained profound implications for the colonies and reveals something of the mentality which underlay the attitudes of the influential pro-imperial lobby during this period. The conceptual basis on which proponents of an imperial *zollverein* rested their case was a conviction that only thereby could Britain's commerce be made secure and goods interchanged freely on an extensive scale. Britain's potential capacity for large-scale mechanized production could best be exploited under these circumstances, and would lead to large economies of scale as the less efficient producers in the colonies were forced to compete or go under. In a sense, this outlook amounted to economic Darwinism, in that those most fitted to survive did so, although Darwin's theories did not become widely known until late in the 1850s. No idea of trusteeship was involved here, no concern that the economic potential of the colonies might be best served if colonial manufacturers were not forced to compete with the highly industrialized and heavily capitalized industries in Britain. The attitude in this case was exploitive; colonies were seen as suppliers of raw materials and buyers of finished products *ad infinitum.*

British exploitation of Australia is a continuing theme throughout the years convered by this study and the welfare of the antipodean colonies was often at risk, as British bureaucrats wilfully resisted colonial initiative and obstinately attempted to administer the colonies in a fashion which best suited their circumscribed view of the world and their preconceptions of British advantage. The exploitive mentality seemed most common in observers from the middle and upper echelons of English society, and unlike the lower classes, who came eventually to see Australia as a promised land, Britons from the higher levels of society entertained mixed feelings about the colonies. For many such people, Australia was a place in which to gain wealth. That accomplished, they would leave. As in Bulwer Lytton's *The Caxtons,* Charles Read's *Gold,* or the real-life case of Robert Lowe, the heroes made their fortunes and then returned to the United Kingdom to live in a style befitting a gentleman. The social status and cultural life they desired was unobtainable in the colonies, where a demeaning contact with convict servants or newly-rich parvenus, who had come out as labourers or tradesmen, could not be avoided. Australia was for them a mere stepping-stone, a way-station on the road to wealth and retirement in Britain. Not surprisingly, during the 1840s such temporary colonists often supported moves to reintroduce convict transportation into New South Wales, or to import native coolies as labourers.[39] Other middle-class observers in Britain, like Wakefield and the colonial reformers, saw Australia in terms of a new home for members of their own class and envisaged permanent settlement. People who thought in this way generally opposed attempts to resume transportation to New South Wales and supported the campaign to abolish the convict system in Van Diemen's Land. The tone of colonial society was momentous to them and they were interested in advancing civilized values even if this meant denying the antipodean colonies access to cheap supplies of convict or native labour.

The focus and emphasis of British attitudes to Australia altered perceptibly between 1828 and 1855. In the first decade of the period under review the prevailing tendency was to view Australia as a prison-farm and a home for Britain's paupers who would cultivate small peasant holdings and develop a subsistence agriculture. At this time colonial society was depicted by English critics as morally tainted, socially inferior, and unacceptably egalitarian. As a consequence, the settlers were totally unfitted for a measure of self-government or the grant of an elective franchise. By the late 1830s the rapid growth of the pastoral industry had begun to draw attention to

Australia's utility as an important supplier of wool for British manufacturers. Wool formed the antipodean colonies' major export staple and the country's capacity to produce it seemed virtually unlimited. During the 1840s British ideas of agricultural settlement gave place to a recognition of the primacy of squatting. Meanwhile, incomes from sheep-farming grew progressively larger as the colonial economies recovered from a severe depression in the early years of the decade, and the flow of free emigration from Britain picked up and continued to gather momentum. Furthermore, after 1840, convicts were no longer sent to New South Wales in large numbers and the relative predominance of emancipated felons in the demographic balance of colonial society rapidly declined.

Alterations in the structure of society in New South Wales together with the establishment of free colonies in South and Western Australia helped to render colonists more respectable in British eyes, and this in turn made possible the grant of limited self-government to the senior colony in 1842, though many Englishmen still believed that Australian settlers were predisposed to democratic republicanism. Following upon the Canadian rebellions in 1837, the imperial authorities came to realize that unpopular policies could not be enforced in settlement colonies without recourse to a politically and economically unacceptable level of force. In Australia Britain decided to allow a constitutional advance before colonists took it for themselves. Consequently, in 1850 representative government, similar to that in New South Wales, was conferred upon the colonies of Victoria, Van Diemen's Land, and South Australia, though some British commentators were doubtful of the wisdom in granting such concessions to immature societies. The discovery of gold during the 1850s and the detrimental effect of abundance on traditional patterns of class deference in the colonies reinforced British misgivings concerning the rawness and democratic precocity of such frontier environments. Largely as a result of colonial agitation and defiance during these years, all transportation of convicts to eastern Australia ceased in 1852, and since the colonists had demonstrated their capacity to produce simultaneously both gold and wool, British authorities resolved to grant full responsible government. Cabinet government presupposed the existence of political parties, and Australia's embryo political groupings, unlike those in Canada, were insufficiently developed to cope with a ministerial system. In this instance the mother country forced the pace of colonial growth. The inevitable result of such a policy in democratically-inclined colonial communities only confirmed the presentiments of conservative British critics, and by 1859 four Australian colonies possessed manhood suffrage and the secret ballot.[40]

A further dimension to British attitudes towards Australia existed, however, and one must remember that the country constituted an emotional as well as a physical frontier for nineteenth-century Englishmen. In a sense Australia performed a similar psychological function—though on a smaller scale—to that which A. J. P. Taylor has assigned to empires in the closing decades of the nineteenth century. Taylor has put forward the persuasive thesis that a general European war was averted in the years between 1871 and 1914 because the rival powers were able to work out their competitiveness on a non-European stage, in far-off corners of the world where there existed little danger of touching off a European conflagration which none of them really desired. Empire, in this view, enabled international tensions to be released in a way which did not endanger the stability of the balance of powers in Europe.[41] In much the same way during the first half of the nineteenth century, Australia provided a venue where Britain's domestic tensions could be released and where Englishmen at home could pursue the divisive class rivalries inherent in British society without endangering the social fabric of the mother country. Parliamentary radicals could, by implication, attack Britain's aristocracy and the House of Lords by denying that such appurtenances were in any way relevant to the constitutional apparatus of self-governing colonies. By transferring these domestic, political and social conflicts to a colonial context, they were robbed of much of their emotional impact and Englishmen could discuss the issues in an atmosphere uninfluenced by the feeling that to argue against the British constitution was somehow treasonable and disloyal. In a similar way, the repressed fear of democracy shared by many of Britain's middle and upper classes could take the respectably conventionalized form of envy and distrust at the affluence and social mobility enjoyed by emancipated convicts and the labouring classes in Australia. Emigration to the antipodean colonies was seen as a social safety-valve for the mother country, but many Englishmen in the upper levels of society felt that some immigrant labourers in the colonies became well-to-do in an almost indecently short time after their arrival.

If commentators from the upper ranks of British society found such affluence distasteful, it was only a precursor to the perturbations they were destined to feel during the 1850s when Britain's reciprocal economic relations with and reliance upon her Australian colonies were fully demonstrated. The Australia-wide depression in the early years of the 1840s had been reflected in widespread distress in the Leeds district, the main centre of the woollen industry. In 1842, at least 20 000 people were living on incomes averaging only 11d. per week.[42] But the colonial depression only directly affected this one area of Britain which relied heavily on imports of wool from Australia. In the 1850s, on the other hand, observers feared that the entire British economy would feel the effects of Australia's gold discoveries which would interfere with British production patterns, devalue the currency, lower interest rates, and perhaps even cause a swing in the terms of international trade against Britain. British debate over these possibilities, together with varying appraisals of the degree to which the goldfields would provide a beneficial stimulus to industrial production, was conducted at a sophisticated level of economic reasoning quite different from earlier treatment of the Australian colonies, which had tended to be based upon ignorance and wishful thinking. This may have been caused by the unexpected appearance of Australian gold, or it could have been the result of a rapid British awakening to the unpleasant fact that their country was economically vulnerable and that vital areas of its economic life were no longer subject to direct control. Whatever the reason, the impact of Australia's gold on British attitudes towards Australia and things Australian was dramatic.

In the light of all this active attention to the Australian colonies and the obvious interest engendered by Britain's dependencies in Australia throughout the period of this study, it is hard to credit the traditional interpretation of these years as a period of rampant anti-imperialist sentiment. C. A. Bodelsen and Robert Livingstone Schuyler have put forward the theory that Britain became disillusioned with empire following the loss of the thirteen American colonies in 1783, and for the next eighty years or more continued to view her remaining colonies as a useless and wasteful burden. Empire involved the mother country in great expenditure for imperial defence and caused international ill-feeling and the danger of wars. Such risks were undertaken for the protection of settlements which, like America, would probably separate as soon as they became mature and useful communities. According to these writers, the years between 1828 and 1855 fell within a wider period in which Britons in general were either indifferent or hostile to the empire.[43]

While this interpretation has found favour with many historians of empire,[44] most historians of Australia implicitly deny its relevance to their own area of interest. After all, New South Wales was first settled only five years after 1783 and this event seemingly provides ample evidence that Englishmen quickly recovered from any residual anti-imperial sentiment caused by recognition of American independence. Whether Britain sought the antipodes for a distant prison,[45] a secure source of flax and naval stores,[46] a military base for operations off the South American coast,[47] or a trading entrepôt for Asiatic commerce,[48] the colonization and continued spread of settlement in Australia during the first half of the nineteenth century certainly does not strengthen the case for anti-imperialism. Except for a very brief period in the 1850s, when British statesmen were in advance of the ruling cliques which controlled the Australian legislative councils, colonial demands for autonomy and self-government were resisted, and colonists were informed that imperial advantage took precedence over colonial welfare. Curiosity existed at a sufficiently intense level during these years in Britain to produce several concrete proposals for new methods of conducting emigration, for improving the convict system, for administering the waste lands and improving colonial society, as well as for a constitutional union or association of Britain and her colonies—hardly evidence of anti-imperialism. Ignorance of the realities in Australia did not mean indifference, nor was it synonymous with antipathy towards colonies.

What does emerge from a study of British attitudes towards the Australian colonies during these years is a clear tendency for British thinking to be compartmentalized. Aboriginal affairs, for example, formed a major topic in which many Englishmen claimed to find colonial behaviour reprehensible. Imperial trusteeship afforded this declining people little practical protection from the rapacity of settlers who pushed them off their tribal lands and opened up the countryside for wool-growing. Britain's need for Australian wool was allowed to override considerations of Aboriginal welfare, yet Englishmen never appeared to realize that a remedy for colonial ill-treatment of the natives lay ready at hand.

France became Britain's major competitor in the manufacture of woollen goods during this period.[49] She was not a prospective customer for Australian wool since she possessed her own extensive merino flocks and had erected a high tariff to protect them from rival producers like Australia, New Zealand and South America.[50] If Britain, therefore, patronized its traditional though more expensive sources of wool in Germany and Spain, or turned to the alternative supplies in South America, the result would be a decline in the demand for Australian wool and a reduction in the stimulus to Australian squatters to continue land-grabbing at the expense of the Aboriginals. Despite unavailing humanitarian anguish in the mother country, the interests of native tribes in Australia were subordinated to laissez-faire economics in the United Kingdom, not so much because British businessmen were especially perfidious, but because English statesmen could not recognize that British demand for Australian wool formed a major cause of colonial mistreatment of the Aboriginals.

The flexibility and convenience of thematic thinking when Australian affairs were under consideration fostered a wide range of attitudes, because it enabled a single commentator to express legitimately the entire gamut of opinion from disdainful superiority to enthusiastic appreciation, depending on the aspect of antipodean development under discussion. The attitudes of the third Earl Grey provide a good example of this process, and most Englishmen appeared to be equally susceptible to this form of mental compartmentalization.

Nor were the contradictions engendered by this approach necessarily as straightforward or mutually exclusive as they would at first appear to have been. The seemingly disparate attitudes towards the many-faceted development of the Australian colonies were not without pattern. Convictism, constitutional advance, emigration, squatting, and the gold discoveries constituted the main strands of colonial evolution in Australia, and although they produced contradictory attitudes amongst British observers and commentators, each attitude could logically be justified within the limitations of its conceptual frame of reference. A recent scholar has noted that British society during the Victorian era was intellectually eclectic, tolerating and encompassing 'all the diversity, and much of the perversity, of which the human mind is capable'.[51] British attitudes towards the Australian colonies reflected this complexity. British envy and social jealousy concerning the affluence of the colonial lower orders represented a negative response to that rapidity of colonial economic progress which encouraged British emigration and investment. The refusal of the eastern Australian colonists in the 1850s to submit any longer to British exploitation regarding convict transportation, or the endless reiteration of colonial complaints over the slow pace of constitutional advance during the 1840s, antagonized some British statesmen and commentators; but this forceful aggressiveness formed the obverse side of that same vitality and dynamism Britons had discerned and admired, and which they confidently expected would result in the emergence of a new imperial power in South East Asia.

When reviewing British attitudes towards Australia in the years between 1828 and 1855, one should remember that despite all the manifold shortcomings Englishmen discerned or imagined they had discerned in antipodean colonial society, Britons in general retained a curious optimism and enthusiasm concerning the future prospects of these dependencies. Nor were such expectations without sound foundations. With the single exception of Western Australia, all the Australian colonies had become economically viable and politically independent by 1855, and many contemporary Britons believed that the colonies stood on the threshold of a remarkable destiny. Colonel Mundy echoed the opinions of many of his fellow-countrymen during the 1850s when he concluded the final volume of his Australian reminiscences with the following tribute:

Whether or not it may be my destiny to revisit the Colony, it is impossible for me to foresee; — but, so long as I live, I shall watch her progress with interest and solicitude; and, while predicting for her a prosperous future, I shall be disappointed if she achieve not a brilliant one.[52]

Appendix

THE LAND OF CONTRARIETIES (Anon. 1850s)

'There is a land in distant seas
Full of all contrarieties.
There beasts have mallards' bills and legs,
Have spurs like cocks, like hens lay eggs.
There quadrupeds go on two feet,
And yet few quadrupeds so fleet:
And birds, although they cannot fly,
In swiftness with the greyhound vie.
With equal wonder you may see
The foxes fly from tree to tree;
And what they value most—so wary—
These foxes in their pockets carry.
There parrots walk upon the ground,
And grass upon the trees is found.
On other trees another wonder,
Leaves without upper side or under.
There apple-trees no fruit produce,
But from their trunks pour cid'rous juice.
The pears you'll scarce with hatchet cut;
Stones are outside the cherries put;
Swans are not white, but black as soot.
There the voracious ewe-sheep crams
Her paunch with flesh of tender lambs.
There neither herb, nor root, nor fruit
Will any christian palate suit,

169

Unless in desp'rate need you'd fill ye
With root of fern and stalk of lily.
Instead of bread, and beef, and broth,
Men feast on many a roasted moth,
And find their most delicious food
In grubs picked out of rotten wood.
There birds construct them shady bowers,
Deck'd with bright feathers, shells, and flowers;
To these the cocks and hens resort,
Run to and fro, and gaily sport.
Others a hot-bed join to make,
To hatch the eggs which they forsake.
There missiles to far distance sent
Come whizzing back with force unspent.
There courting swains their passion prove
By knocking down the girls they love.
There every servant gets his place
By character of foul disgrace.
There vice is virtue, virtue vice,
And all that's vile is voted nice.
The sun, when you to face him turn ye,
From right to left performs his journey.
The North winds scorch; but when the breeze is
Full from the South, why then it freezes.
Now of what place can such strange tales
Be told with truth, but New South Wales?'

Abbreviations

B.E.M.	*Blackwood's Edinburgh Magazine*
E.R.	*Edinburgh Review*
F.M.	*Fraser's Magazine for Town and Country*
G.N.C.T.U.	Grand National Consolidated Trades Union
H.R.A.	*Historical Records of Australia*
H.W.	*Household Words*
L.M.S.	London Missionary Society
N.M.M.	*New Monthly Magazine and Literary Journal*
Q.R.	*Quarterly Review*
R.N.	Royal Navy
S.C.M.	*Simmond's Colonial Magazine and Foreign Miscellany*
S.P.G.	Society for the Propagation of the Gospel
W.R.	*Westminster Review*

Notes
Introduction

[1] Bodelson, *Studies in Mid-Victorian Imperialism*; Schuyler, *The Fall of the Old Colonial System*; Fieldhouse, *The Colonial Empires*, pp. 177-80.

[2] Gallagher and Robinson, 'The Imperialism of Free Trade', pp. 1-15; Galbraith, 'Myths of the "Little England" Era', pp. 34-48; Semmel, 'The Philosophic Radicals and Colonialism', pp. 513-25; MacDonagh, 'The Anti-Imperialism of Free Trade', pp. 489-501; Winch, 'Classical Economics and the Case for Colonization', pp. 387-99. These important articles have been reprinted in a single anthology, see Shaw (ed.), *Great Britain and the Colonies 1815-1865*.

[3] Shaw, *The Story of Australia*; R. Ward, *The Australian Legend*; Crowley, *Australia's Western Third*; Crawford, *Australia*.

[4] Fitzpatrick, *British Imperialism and Australia 1783-1833*; Fitzpatrick, *The British Empire in Australia 1834-1939*; J. M. Ward, *Empire in the Antipodes*.

[5] Clark, *A History of Australia*, Vols. 1-3.

[6] Pike, *Paradise of Dissent*; J. M. Ward, *Earl Grey and the Australian Colonies 1846-1857*; Shaw, *Convicts and the Colonies*; Burroughs, *Britain and Australia 1831-1855*; Macmillan, *Scotland and Australia 1788-1850*; Eddy, *Britain and the Australian Colonies 1818-1831*.

[7] 'British Attitudes to the Colonies, c. 1820-1850', pp. 71-95.

1:   Convictism I 1828-40

[1] For evidence that Norfolk Island's main function between the 1830s and the 1850s was to serve British interests as conceived by the Colonial and Home Offices, see Hoare, *Norfolk Island*; chs 1, 2.

[2] Shaw, *Convicts and the Colonies*, chs 7, 8.

[3] Ibid., p. 152.

[4] Whately, *Thoughts on Secondary Punishments in a Letter to Earl Grey*, pp. 3, 126-7.

[5] *The Liberal Awakening 1815-1830* (New York, 1926), p. 106.

[6] Peel to Reverend Sydney Smith, 24 March 1826, in Arthur Aspinall and E. Anthony Smith (eds.), *English Historical Documents 1783-1832*, vol. XI (London, 1959), p. 388.

[7] *Times*, 14 January, 29 May 1828; *Courier*, 29 May 1828.

[8] 'Emigration', *Edinburgh Review*, vol. 47, no. 93, (1828), p. 206.

[9] Ibid., pp. 206-14.

[10] *Gentleman's Magazine*, vol. 98, pt. 1 (1828), p. 212.

[11] See Chapter 7 below.

[12] Vol. 99, pt. 2 (1829), special supplement.

[13] Vol. 1, no. 6 (1830), p. 727.

[14] Anderson, *Farewell to Old England*, pp. 72-3.

[15] Ibid., pp. 91-2.

[16] Report of the Select Committee on Transportation, *Parliamentary Papers* 1838 (669) XXII, p. 40.

[17] Shaw, *Convicts and the Colonies*, p. 261.

[18] Ibid., p. 274.

[19] Ibid., p. 255. *See also* W. D. Forsyth, *Governor Arthur's Convict System*, p. 104.

[20] Report of the Select Committee on Transportation, op. cit., pp. 5-8.

[21] Stanley to Bourke, 21 August 1833, CO 202/30.

[22] Howick to S.M. Phillips, 25 March 1831, CO 202/26.

[23] Ibid.

[24] Hay to Spring Rice, 29 December 1831, CO 202/28.

[25] Stanley to Bourke, 21 August 1833, CO 202/30; and Stanley to Arthur, 26 August 1833, CO 408/9.

[26] Reports of the Select Committee of Secondary Punishment, *Parliamentary Papers* 1831 (276) VII; and 1831-2 (547) VII.

[27] Howick's Journal, 1 March 1834, Grey Papers, University of Durham.

[28] Bourke to Stanley, 15 January 1834, CO 201/238; Bourke to Glenelg, 18 December 1835, CO 201/248.

[29] Arthur to Stanley, 24 January, 4 February 1834; Arthur to Hay, 30 January 1834, CO 280/46. Arthur to Stanley, 1 March, 4 April 1834, CO 280/47. Arthur to Hay, 10 May 1834, CO 280/48.

[30] Charles Darwin, 29 January 1836, in *Journal of Researches into the Geology and Natural History of the Various Countries visited during the Voyage of H.M.S. Beagle round the World*, pp. 428-9.

[31] Forsyth, *Governor Arthur's Convict System*, pp. 97-8.

[32] Whately, *Thoughts on Secondary Punishments*, p. 77.

[33] For more detailed discussion of Wakefield's theories see chapter 7 below.

[34] New South Wales, *Q.R.*, vol. 53 (1835), p. 9.

[35] *An Historical and Statistical Account of New South Wales, both as a Penal Settlement and as a British Colony.*

[36] Vol. 1, no. 1 (1835), p. 46.

[37] 'What is our External Policy and Condition', *Blackwood's Edinburgh Magazine*, vol. 34, no. 248 (1836), p. 789.

[38] Arthur to Hay, 25 July 1832, CO 280/34; Arthur to Goderich, 1 July 1833, CO 280/42. See also Arthur, *Defence of Transportation in Reply to the Archbishop of Dublin*, passim.

[39] *Thoughts on Convict Management* (Hobart, 1839).

[40] Burroughs, *Britain and Australia*, p. 334.

[41] Bourke to Aberdeen, 12 July 1835, CO 201/246; Arthur to Glenelg, 2 October 1835, CO 280/59.

[42] Spring Rice to Bourke, 15 November 1834, CO 202/32; Glenelg to Bourke, 10 July 1835, CO 202/32.

[43] In addition, Wakefield himself was a constant attendant at the early meetings of the committee, both as a witness and as an unofficial advisor to the chairman. See Sweetman, *Australian Constitutional Development*, p. 133.

[44] Report of the Select Committee on Transportation, *Parliamentary Papers*, 1837-8 (669) XXII.

[45] Maconochie's report was enclosed in Franklin to Glenelg, 7 October 1837, CO 280/80.

[46] Glenelg to Bourke, 26 May 1837, CO 202/34; and Glenelg to Franklin, 30 May 1837, CO 408/12.

[47] See Fox (ed.), *Account of an Expedition to the Interior of New Holland*.

48 Paper submitted by Lord Howick to the Select Committee on Transportation, 31 May 1838. Colonial Papers—Transportation, Grey Papers.

49 *Empire in the Antipodes*, p. 40.

50 Paper by Lord Howick on transportation, 23 November 1838. Colonial Papers—Transportation, Grey Papers.

51 Draft Memorandum on Convict Transportation, 2 January 1839, PRO 30/22 folio 3C, Russell Papers.

52 See Hutt to Stanley, 28 April 1845, CO 18/39; Fitzroy to Grey, 21 March 1849, CO 201/411, and 18 December 1850, CO 201/433; G. Fife Angas to Grey, 4 July 1849, CO 13/66.

53 George Crawley to George Henry Gibbs, 15 October 1839. Family Letters, vol. xvi (1833-40), Gibbs Papers, Guildhall Library. See also John Waugh (ed.), *Three Years Practical Experience as a Settler in New South Wales* (Edinburgh, 1838), cited in Macmillan, *Scotland and Australia*, pp. 311-12; Fitzpatrick, *The British Empire in Australia*, pp. 40-1; Butlin, *Australia and New Zealand Bank*, p. 20.

54 'The Australian Colonies', *Quarterly Review*, vol. 68 (1841), pp. 93-4.

55 W. Molesworth in *Mirror of Parliament*, vol. III, 5 May 1840, p. 2812. Wakefield, *A Letter from Sydney, the Principal Town of Australasia*, pp. 82-90.

56 'Mitchell's Second and Third Expeditions', B.E.M., vol. 45, no. 279 (1839), pp. 113-14.

57 Roe, *Quest for Authority in Eastern Australia 1835-1851*, p. 53; Melbourne, *Early Constitutional Development in Australia*, p. 227.

58 Arthur to Spring Rice, 20 April 1835, CO 280/56. See also Melbourne, op. cit., pp. 229-30.

59 Robson, *The Convict Settlers of Australia*, p. 92.

60 *Examiner*, 10 May 1840; *Globe*, 28 April 1840; *Leeds Mercury*, 9 May 1840; *Spectator*, 16 May 1840.

61 *Mirror of Parliament*, vol. III, 5 May 1840, p. 2797.

62 Roe, op. cit., p. 25.

63 *Mirror of Parliament*, vol. III, 5 May 1840, p. 2817.

64 Ibid., vol. IV, 19 May 1840, p. 3134.

65 *Mirror of Parliament*, vol. III, 5 May 1840, pp. 2800-1.

66 Ibid., p. 2820.

67 Ibid., p. 2821.

68 Ibid., p. 2822.

69 Ibid, Mahon was supported in a half-hearted manner by Charles Buller who was opposed to transportation and assignment, and would have preferred to see the whole system discontinued. If the government was determined to keep transporting convicts to Van Diemen's Land, however, then Buller felt that assignment was 'the only rational way' of organizing the continuation. Ibid., p. 2825.

70 Forsyth, *Governor Arthur's Convict System*, pp. 167-8.

71 Williams, *Capitalism and Slavery*, pp. 181, 183-90. Comments that a vigorous propaganda campaign from British humanitarians had succeeded in raising anti-slavery sentiments to the status of a popular religion in England during the 1830s. Consequently when opponents of convict assignment equated the system with slavery they tapped a reservoir of illogical emotionalism of quite overwhelming proportions.

2: *Convictism II 1840–55*

1 For example, the revenues from sales of waste land in Van Diemen's Land

came to £58 427 in 1841. By 1845, the income from this source had declined to £1609.

2 Stanley to Gipps, 27 July 1844, CO 202/48; Gladstone to Fitzroy, 30 April 1846, CO 202/50; Grey to Fitzroy, 3 September 1847, CO 202/51; 7 March and 3 September 1848, CO 202/54. Both Lord Stanley and Earl Grey specifically referred to this decision in 1840 as a mistake. For Stanley see *Hansard*, 3rd Series, vol. LXXXIV, 3 March 1846, cols. 483-4; for Grey see his *The Colonial Policy of Lord John Russell's Administration*, vol.2, p. 4.

3 Gladstone to Fitzroy, 7 May 1846, CO 202/50; Grey to Fitzroy, 15 November 1846, CO 202/51.

4 Grey, op. cit., vol. 2, pp. 16, 66-8.

5 Governor George Gipps had informed the Colonial Office in December 1840 that opposition to the dismemberment of New South Wales had united colonists of all political divisions within the colony. See Gipps to Russell, 19 December 1840, CO 201/300.

6 *Hansard*, 3rd series, vol. XC, 5 March 1847, cols. 898-921.

7 Ibid., vol. XCIII, 3 June 1847, cols. 89-90.

8 *Hansard*, 3rd series, vol. LXXXIV, 3 March 1846, cols. 483-8.

9 *Globe*, 6 March and 27 May 1846.

10 *Spectator*, 6 September 1845.

11 *The Bushranger of Van Diemen's Land*, p. 1.

12 *Times*, 12 January, 6 March 1847. See also *Spectator*, 27 February 1847.

13 *A Voice from the Far Interior of Australia*, pp. 60-1.

14 'What is to be done with our Criminals' *Edinburgh Review*, vol. 86, no. 173 (1847), pp. 221-38.

15 Fitzroy to Gladstone, 6 November 1846, CO 201/369; Fitzroy to Grey, 9 January 1847, CO 201/379; and 1 and 24 February 1847, CO 201/380.

16 Denison to Grey, 20 August 1847, CO 280/211.

17 Shaw, *Convicts and the Colonies*, pp. 327-34.

18 Fitzgerald to Grey, 3 March 1849, CO 18/50.

19 The settlers' memorial was enclosed in Clarke to Stanley, 2 January 1847, CO 18/44; and Grey's affirmation in principle in Grey to Fitzgerald, 5 August 1848, CO 397/9.

20 Grey to Fitzgerald, 12 July 1849, CO 397/9.

21 Denison to Grey, 20 August 1847, CO 280/211; see also Grey's minute on Fitzroy to Grey, 10 April 1848, CO 201/396.

22 Denison to Grey, 31 December 1847, CO 280/216; Fitzroy to Grey, 1 May 1849, CO 201/413.

23 Grey to Russell, 1 November 1849, PRO 30/22, folio 8B, Russell Papers, London.

24 Grey to Fitzroy, 18 November 1849, CO 202/56.

25 Russell to Grey, 20 November 1849, Colonial Affairs (various), Grey Papers.

26 Grey to Fitzroy, 16 November 1849, CO 202/56.

27 Grey to Fitzroy, 18 November 1849, CO 202/56. See also Grey, *Colonial Policy*, vol. 2, pp. 48-50.

28 'The Transportation Question', *B.E.M.*, vol. 66, no. 409, (1849), pp. 526-35.

29 Grey to Denison, 22 April and 30 May 1849, CO 408/32.

30 *Hansard*, 3rd series, vol. CIX, 14 March 1850, col. 871.

31 Fitzroy to Grey, 19 June 1851, CO 201/441.

32 Grey to Denison, 24 January 1852, CO 408/37. See also Grey, op. cit., vol. 2, pp. 55-6.

33 *Spectator*, 21 August 1852; *Morning Chronicle*, 28 December 1852.

34 *Transportation not Necessary*, p. 60.

[35] Quennell (ed.), *Mayhew's London*, pp. 368, 546. See also Anderson, *Farewell to Old England.* p. 9.

[36] *The Operative*, pt. 3, no. 11 (1851), pp. 161-2. It should be noted at this point, that in the period under review there were two working-class publications with this title. One was a newspaper published during the 1830s which will be cited hereafter simply as *Operative*, and the other was the periodical published during the 1850s which will be cited as *The Operative.*

[37] Grey's contemporaries commented that his stubborn and obstinate nature was one of the reasons for his unpopularity with cabinet colleagues. See Charles Greville's comments during 1838, 1845, in L. Strachey and R. Fulford (eds.), *The Greville Memoirs 1814-1860*, 8 vols London, 1938, vol. IV, p. 20; vol. V, p. 259; vol. VI, p. 198. For Lord John Russell's attitude see Ward, *Earl Grey and the Australian Colonies*, p. 165.

[38] Grey to Fitzroy, 7 December 1851, CO 202/60. See also Grey, *Colonial Policy*, vol. 2, p. 87.

[39] *Times*, 17 August, 1 and 6 October 1852.

[40] Confidential report by Colonel Jebb, 1 November 1852, correspondence, Grey Papers.

[41] *Hansard*, 3rd series, vol. CXXIII, 11 November 1852, col. 21; Pakington to Fitzroy, 9 December 1852, CO 202/60; Pakington to Denison, 14 December 1852, CO 408/37.

[42] *Empire in the Antipodes*, p. 49.

[43] See R. M. Hartwell, 'The Pastoral Ascendancy 1820-50', in Greenwood (ed.), *Australia: A Social and Political History*, p. 87.

[44] *Hansard*, 3rd series, vol. CXXIX, 9 August 1853, col. 1536. Stanley (now Lord Derby) had put forward a similar argument in the House of Lords three months earlier. See ibid., vol. CXXVII, 10 May 1853, col. 49.

[45] Ibid., vol. CXXIX, (9 August 1853), col. 1536.

[46] Ibid., vol. CXXVII, 10 May 1853, col. 23.

[47] *Hansard*, 3rd series, vol. CXXVII, 10 May 1853, cols. 49, 68.

[48] 'The Management and Disposal of our Criminal Population' *Edinburgh Review*, vol. 100, no. 204 (1854), pp. 284-9. See also similar opinions in *Globe*, 30 July 1849.

[49] Mundy, *Our Antipodes*, vol. 3, p. 161.

[50] In 1850 Earl Grey estimated that there were 48 000 ex-convicts in New South Wales and Van Diemen's Land; see Grey, op. cit., vol. 2, p. 76.

[51] 'New South Wales', *Edinburgh Review*, no. 93 (1828) p. 92.

[52] Ibid., pp. 95-6. This was a point of view which also appeared in 'Cunningham's New South Wales', *Quarterly Review*, vol. 37 (1828), p. 6.

[53] *Globe*, 29 June 1832.

[54] 'What is our External Policy and Condition', *Blackwood's Edinburgh Magazine*, vol. 39, no. 248 (1836), p. 789.

[55] 'Life in the Penal Colonies' W. R., vol. 27, no. 53 (1837), p. 93.

[56] Arnold to Sir John Franklin (newly appointed lieutenant-governor of Van Diemen's Land), 20 July 1836; in Stanley, *The Life and Correspondence of Thomas Arnold*, p. 386.

[57] 'The British Colonization of New Zealand', *B.E.M.*, vol. 42, no. 266 (1837), p. 793.

[58] 'New South Wales', *B.E.M.*, vol. 44, no. 277 (1838), pp. 690-2.

[59] *Expedition to the Interior of New Holland*, p. 30.

[60] *Operative*, 25 November 1838.

[61] Anderson, *Farewell to Old England*, pp. 129-30. Similar sentiments were expressed in prose by Whately, *Thoughts on Secondary Punishments*, p. 82.

[62] Murray to Darling, 30 August 1828, CO 202/21.

[63] Glenelg to Bourke, 30 November 1835, CO 202/32.

[64] Report of the Select Committee on Secondary Punishments, *Parliamentary Papers* 1831 (276) VII, p. 143; Whately, op. cit., p. 151.

[65] James Stephen to W. F. Strangways, 28 September 1836, CO 202/35.

[66] James Stephen to W. F. Strangways, 31 October 1836, CO 202/35.

[67] 'New South Wales', *Quarterly Review*, vol. 62 (1838), p. 475.

[68] Ibid., p. 482.

[69] Dixon, *The Condition and Capabilities of Van Diemen's Land as a Place of Emigration*, pp. 52-3, 81. See also the numerous pejorative references already mentioned above which likened New South Wales' pastoralists to slave owners.

[70] 'Wanderings in New South Wales', *Q.R.*, vol. 53 (1835), pp. 9-10.

[71] *New Monthly Magazine and Humorist*, vol. 62 (1841), p. 50.

[72] *Mirror of Parliament*, vol. 111, 5 May 1840, pp. 2806, 2812.

[73] *Globe*, 28 April 1840; *Leeds Mercury*, 9 May 1840.

[74] Globe, 28 April 1840. See also Sidney, *A Voice from the Far Interior of Australia*, p. 55.

[75] Stanley to Gipps, 17 May 1845, CO 202/50.

[76] Grey to Fitzroy, 11 August 1848, CO 202/54.

[77] Grey's minute on Fitzroy to Grey, 21 March 1849, CO 201/411.

[78] 'The Bushman; or Life in a New Country', *F. M.*, vol. 37, no. 219 (1848), p. 356.

[79] *Hansard*, 3rd series, vol. XIII, 28 June 1832, cols. 1105-15.

[80] *Hansard*, 3rd series, vol. LXXXIV, 3 March 1846, col. 498.

[81] Minute of a conversation between Lord Grey and S. King at the Colonial Office 1852. Colonial Papers—Transportation, Grey Papers.

[82] See chapter 8 below.

[83] Yarborough to W. H. Daubeney, 1849. Daubeney Papers 6110 (IV/4/8), Lincolnshire Archives Office. Letter summary from National Registry of Archives, London.

[84] 'Colonial Reform', *Fraser's Magazine for Town and Country*, vol. 41, no. 243 (1850), p. 373.

[85] 'Gold and Emigration', ibid., vol. 46, no. 272 (1852), p. 130.

[86] *Australia in Western Imaginative Prose Writings* (Chapel Hill, 1967), p. 66.

[87] Engels to Karl Marx, 23 September 1851, in Mayer (ed.) *Marx, Engels and Australia*, p. 104.

[88] 'New South Wales', *Edinburgh Review*, vol. 47, no. 93 (1828) p. 89.

[89] Vol. 98, pt. 1 (1828), p. 212.

[90] 'Emigration and the United States', *F. M.*, vol. 16, no. 95 (1837), p. 563.

[91] New series, vol. 10 (1838), p. 359

[92] 'Mitchell's Second and Third Expeditions', *Blackwood's Edinburgh Magazine*, vol. 45, no. 279 (1839), p. 113.

[93] 'What is to be done with our Criminals', *Edinburgh Review*, vol. 86, no. 173 (1847), p. 255.

[94] Vol. 18 (1849), p. 160.

3: *Constitutional Advance I 1828–49*

[1] Macmillan, *Scotland and Australia*, p. 53.

[2] Bigge's formal Reports were three in number and were published as Parliamentary Papers during 1822 and 1823. These have been exhaustively studied in John Douglas Ritchie, *Punishment and Profit: the Reports of*

Commissioner John Bigge on the Colonies of New South Wales and Van Diemen's Land 1822-23 (Melbourne, 1970).

[3] 4 George IV, c. 96 (1823). Constitutional and judicial developments in Australia during the 1820s are discussed in considerable detail in Eddy, *Britain and the Australian Colonies.*

[4] See, for example, Glenelg to Franklin, 9 May 1838, CO 408/14. Sir John Franklin's unhappy experiences in Van Diemen's Land are described at length in Fitzpatrick, *Sir John Franklin in Tasmania 1837-1843*; and also in his own autobiographical pamphlet, *Narrative of Some Passages in the History of Van Diemen's Land* (London, 1845).

[5] John Macarthur Jnr. to Horton, 11 July 1826, CO 201/179.

[6] *Journals of the House of Commons* vol. 83 (1828), p. 247; see also Darling to Bathurst, 31 January 1827, CO 201/181.

[7] p. 68.

[8] See chapter 2 below.

[9] *Times*, 11 September 1828.

[10] Cunningham, *Two Years in New South Wales*, vol. 2, p. 247; [Sydney Smith], 'New South Wales', *Edinburgh Review*, vol. 47, no. 93 (1828), p. 97; [John Barrow], 'New South Wales', *Quarterly Review*, vol. 39 (1829), p. 342.

[11] Cunningham, op. cit., p. 248; [Smith], op. cit., p. 97; [Barrow], op. cit., p. 342.

[12] Darling to Hay, 9 February 1827, CO 201/181.

[13] *Times*, 28 May 1830.

[14] Cunningham, op. cit., vol. 2, p. 352; Wilson, *Narrative of a Voyage Round the World*, p. 189; [Horace Twiss], 'New South Wales', *Quarterly Review*, vol. 62 (1838), p. 483.

[15] *Hansard*, 2nd series, vol. XIX, 20 April 1828, col. 1461. The Whig *Courier*, 29 January 1832, made the same point; 'we must trust to a Free Press to restrain the eccentricities which are apt to attach to the conduct of all Governors in distant colonies'. The act of 1828 specifically recognized that in New South Wales the press acted in a representative capacity, and it contained a provision which required that all bills proposed by the governor for presentation to the legislative council were to be advertised in the newspapers eight clear days before the council considered them.

[16] Draft Minute, June 1831, CO 201/225.

[17] *Hansard*, 3rd series, vol. XIII, 28 June 1832, col. 1090.

[18] Notes on Lytton Bulwer's Motion on New South Wales, September 1831. Colonial Papers—New South Wales, Grey Papers.

[19] See Draft Minute of Instructions for Major General Bourke, June 1831, CO 201/225. Support for a jury system in New South Wales was widespread, see *Globe*, 29 June 1832; *Courier*, 29 June 1832; *Morning Chronicle*, 28 and 29 June 1832; *Times*, 29 June 1832; *Examiner*, 1 July 1832.

[20] *Hansard*, 3rd series, vol. XIII, 28 June 1832, col. 1106.

[21] Although only New South Wales and Van Diemen's Land were convict colonies at this time, British attitudes regarding Australia as a whole usually seem to have been established on an evaluation of circumstances in the two older colonies. Western Australia was impoverished with a tiny and almost static population, and South Australia was not founded until 1836 and had within four years dissolved into bankruptcy amidst an orgy of land speculation.

[22] James Mudie, *The Felonry of New South Wales* (London, 1837); and James Macarthur, *New South Wales: Its Present State and Future Prospects* (London, 1837).

[23] [Twiss], 'New South Wales', *Quarterly Review*, vol. 62 (1838), p. 491; *Metropolitan Magazine*, vol. 20, no. 78 (1837), pp. 1-2.

[24] *Hansard*, 3rd series, vol. XXV, 23 and 29 July 1834, cols. 429-32, 700-6.

[25] 4 and 5 William IV, c. 95, sec. XXIII.

[26] Bourke to Stanley, 25 December 1833, CO 201/233.

[27] *Hansard*, 3rd series, vol. XXIX, 3 July 1835, col. 227.

[28] Bourke to Glenelg, 26 December 1835, CO 201/248.

[29] Forbes to Stephen, 13 October 1836, CO 201/257. In 1839 Governor George Gipps, Bourke's successor in New South Wales, echoed Forbes's claim that indirect representation through municipal institutions was unsuited to the needs of the colony, and that the colonists desired representation through members elected directly to the legislative council. See Gipps to Glenelg, 1 January 1839, CO 201/284.

[30] Abstract of a Paper on the Government of New South Wales by Charles Buller, February 1838. Colonial Papers—New South Wales, Grey Papers.

[31] Melbourne, *Early Constitutional Development in Australia*, pp. 247-8.

[32] Notes on Buller's Abstract, Colonial Papers—New South Wales, Grey Papers.

[33] Sinclair, *A History of New Zealand*, p. 86.

[34] Notes on Buller's Abstract, loc. cit.

[35] Sir Henry Taylor to E. D. Fairfield, 26 March 1871, CO 7/143. Reprinted in Higham, 'Sir Henry Taylor and the Establishment of Crown Colony Government in the West Indies', pp. 92-6.

[36] Melbourne, *Early Constitutional Development in Australia*, pp. 247-8.

[37] The bill was ordered to be printed on 6 July 1840. *Parliamentary Papers*, 1840 (445) 111, p. 207.

[38] *Hansard*, 3rd series, vol. LV, 14 July 1840, cols. 451 and 556.

[39] Although convict transportation to New South Wales ceased in 1840, convicts already serving sentences there remained.

[40] 'Comparative Prospects of our New Colonies', *Westminster Review*, vol. 35, no. 1 (1841), p. 143.

[41] 'The Australian Colonies', *Quarterly Review*, vol. 68 (1841), p. 106.

[42] Russell to Franklin, 31 August 1840, CO 408/19.

[43] Stanley to Franklin, 6 July 1842, CO 408/21.

[44] *Hansard*, 3rd series, vol. LXIII, 26 May 1842, col. 880.

[45] Stanley to Gipps, 5 September 1842, CO 202/45.

[46] *Hansard*, 3rd series, vol. LXII, 28 April 1842, col. 1178.

[47] Burroughs, *Britain and Australia*, p. 373.

[48] British attitudes to crown-lands are discussed in some detail in chapter 7 below.

[49] Second Report of the Select Committee on South Australia, *Parliamentary Papers*, 1841 (394) IV.

[50] 5 and 6 Vic., c. 61. See also Stanley to Grey, 6 September 1842, CO 396/2.

[51] Grey to Stanley, 2 July 1843, CO 13/33; and Stanley to Grey, 8 February 1845, CO 396/6.

[52] Pike, *Paradise of Dissent*, p. 397.

[53] See Burroughs, op. cit., appendix 111.

[54] Crowley, *Australia's Western Third*, p. 53.

[55] Stirling to Glenelg, 15 October 1835, CO 18/15.

[56] Gipps to Stanley, 28 October 1843, CO 201/335; and 3 November 1843, CO 201/336.

[57] Stanley to Gipps, 29 March 1844, CO 202/48.

[58] Hutt to Stanley, 15 August 1845, CO 18/39; see also Townsley, *The Struggle for Self-Government in Tasmania 1842-1856*, p. 84.

[59] Melbourne, op. cit., pp. 298-9.

[60] Stanley to Gipps, 16 March 1845, CO 202/50.

[61] Stanley to Gipps, 20 August 1845, CO 202/50.

[62] Stanley to Gipps, 20 August 1845, CO 202/50.

[63] For Russell's attitude during the Canadian crisis, see Burroughs, *The Canadian Crisis and British Colonial Policy 1828-1841*, pp. 110-11, passim.

[64] Grey to Fitzroy, 31 July 1847, CO 201/375.

[65] Melbourne, op. cit., pp. 351-2 comments that Grey's contemplated intentions were 'untried theories'. See also Ward, *Earl Grey and the Australian Colonies*, p. 45.

[66] Howick to Spring Rice, 2 April 1832, Mc. 13374, folio 1, Monteagle Papers, National Library, Dublin.

[67] 'Free Institutions in Australia', *Simmond's Colonial Magazine*, vol. 11 (1847), p. 330; see also 'Editor's Note Book', *ibid.*, vol. 15 (1848), p. 424. Criticism in England also came from Archibald Cunninghame a representative of the New South Wales' squatting interests; see Cunninghame to Grey, 31 October 1847, CO 201/390.

[68] 'Life in a New Country', *Fraser's Magazine for Town and Country*, vol. 37, no. 219 (1848), p. 356.

[69] Ibid., p. 575.

[70] Sweetman, *Australian Constitutional Development*, pp. 218-19.

[71] Fitzroy to Grey, 11 August 1848, CO 201/399.

[72] Grey to Fitzroy, 31 July 1848, CO 202/54.

[73] See Ward, *Earl Grey and the Australian Colonies*, p. 18, and Cell, *British Colonial Administration in the Mid-Nineteenth Century*, p. 118.

[74] Grey to Fitzroy, 31 July 1848, CO 202/54.

[75] *Times*, 25 January 1849.

[76] Cell, op. cit., pp. 88-9, and Clark, *A Short History of Australia*, p. 107. The influence of de Tocqueville on the British intelligentsia has been described by David Paul Crook, *American Democracy in British Politics 1815-1850* (Oxford, 1965), pp. 166-98.

[77] Roebuck, *The Colonies of England*; Thring, *The Supremacy of Great Britain not inconsistent with Self-Government for the Colonies*. See also Sir William Molesworth in *Hansard*, 3rd series, vol. CX, 13 May 1850, col. 1182.

[78] James Stephen was appointed secretary to the committee on Grey's recommendation, and he and Grey dominated its proceedings. See Ward, *Earl Grey and the Australian Colonies*, p. 97; and Melbourne, *Early Constitutional Development*, p. 369.

[79] Draft of report in CO 201/438; and printed version in *Parliamentary Papers* 1849, (1074) XXXV.

[80] Draft report by Sir James Stephen on Australian Legislatures, 21 February 1849. Colonial Papers—Australia, Grey Papers.

[81] Herman Merivale's observations on a draft report on Australian Legislatures by Sir James Stephen, 23 March 1849. Colonial Papers—Australia, Grey Papers.

[82] Ibid. It may be relevant to note that salaries for members of parliament was a perennial demand from Chartists and other domestic political radicals during these years in Britain.

[83] Ibid.

[84] *Parliamentary Papers*, 1849 (375), 1.

[85] *Times*, 18 and 20 April 1849; 'Transportation and Convict Colonies', *Simmonds's Colonial Magazine*, vol. 18 (1849), pp. 160-4.

[86] *Morning Chronicle*, 4 July, 19 July 1849; and *Standard*, 3 July 1849.

4:   *Constitutional Advance II 1850–55*

[1] Young and Handcock (eds.) *English Historical Documents 1833-1874*, pp. 22, 27.

[2] Burroughs, *British Attitudes Towards Canada 1822-1849*, p. 3.

[3] *Examiner*, 21 July 1849.

[4] *Times*, 26 May 1849.

[5] Ward, *Earl Grey and the Australian Colonies*, pp. 30-2.

[6] *Times*, 6 June 1849. Similar sentiments of approval were also expressed in 'Colonies and Constitutions', *New Monthly Magazine and Humorist*, vol. 86 (1849), p. 192.

[7] *Spectator*, 9 June and 25 August 1849.

[8] The theories of Samuel Sidney will be discussed in chapters 5 and 7 below.

[9] 'Introduction', *Sidney's Emigrants' Journal and Traveller's Magazine*, no. 1 (August 1849), pp. IV-V.

[10] Cell, *British Colonial Administration*, p. 98. See also Hamburger, *Intellectuals in Politics*, passim.

[11] *Hansard*, 3rd series, vol. CVIII, 12 February, 1840, col. 576.

[12] A popular convention to assess colonial opinion had been suggested in Canada during the late 1830s and rejected by the imperial government as dangerously democratic. See Burroughs, *The Canadian Crisis and British Colonial Policy*, pp. 61-2.

[13] *Hansard*, 3rd series, vol. CVIII, 12 February, 1850, cols. 573-4. Molesworth's attempts during the debates over this bill to demarcate exact spheres of influence between imperial and colonial concerns brought him censure from unsympathetic newspapers. The *Globe* claimed that such fine distinctions were beyond the reach of the human intellect while the *Economist* disclaimed any faith in the ability 'of the Charing Cross school of colonial reformers to extemporise constitutions for the colonies'. See *Globe*, 7 May 1850; and *Economist*, 6 April 1850. Molesworth did win support, however, from *Leed's Mercury*, 16 February 1850 and *Simmonds's Colonial Magazine*, vol. 18 (1850), pp. 238 and 324.

[14] ibid., cols. 585-6.

[15] *Times*, 20 February 1850; Examiner, 16 February and 20 April 1850; *Spectator*, 23 February 1850; *Morning Chronicle*, 14 June 1850; *Globe*, 19 February 1850.

[16] *Standard*, 20 April and 7 May 1850.

[17] This was part of a wider contemporary debate in Britain concerning the role and functions of upper houses in England and the United States of America. Crook, *American Democracy in British Politics*, pp. 142-52.

[18] *Hansard*, 3rd series, vol. CVIII, 12 February 1850, cols. 585-6, 592.

[19] *Hansard*, 3rd series, vol. CVIII, 12 February 1850, cols. 590-1.

[20] *Times*, 4 February 1850. See also *Standard*, 1 June 1850.

[21] *Hansard*, 3rd series, vol. CVIII, 12 February 1850, col. 606. See also Adderley, *Some Reflections on the Speech of the Right Honourable Lord John Russell on Colonial Policy*, p. 27.

[22] Ibid., col. 597. Gladstone was supported by his parliamentary colleagues, ibid., cols. 608-11.

[23] *Gladstone and Britain's Imperial Policy*, pp. 27-34.

[24] *Hansard*, 3rd series, vol. CVIII, 12 February 1850, col. 599. See also Roebuck's view ibid., cols. 588-91. Gladstone's argument that a nominated upper house was the precursor of a British party in the colonies also appeared in 'The Australian Constitution', *Simmonds's Colonial Magazine*, vol. 18 (1850), p. 238.

[25] Ibid., 12 and 18 February 1840, cols. 610, 977-8. See also ibid., vol. CIX, 22 March 1850, cols. 1262, 1267.

[26] Ibid., 12 and 18 February 1850, cols. 590 and 712-13. See also *Simmonds's Colonial Magazine*, vol. 18 (1850), pp. 238, 324 which reiterated these arguments.

[27] Ibid., vol. CIX 22 March 1850, col. 1269. This was a point of view also propounded by the *Globe*, 19 February 1850.

[28] 'The Colonial Reform Party', *New Monthly Magazine and Humorist*, vol. 88 (1850), p. 218. See also *Morning Chronicle*, 3 June 1850; *Globe*, 19 February 1850; *Manchester Courier*, 16 February 1850; *Leeds Mercury*, 16 February 1850. See also Spencer Walpole's statement to the House of Commons, 'they should grant to the colonies, as nearly as possible, their own form of government. They ought to combine, so far as they could, the conservative caution of the House of Lords with the vigorous activity of the House of Commons ... They ought to bring the constitution of the colonies into the closest harmony with that constitution which had worked so well in the parent State'. *Hansard*, 3rd series, vol. CIX, 22 March 1850, col. 1280.

[29] *Hansard*, 3rd series, vol. CX, 25 April 1850, col. 800.

[30] Ibid., vol. CXI, 14 June 1850, col. 1224.

[31] Ibid., vol. CVIII, 12 February 1850, col. 555 and vol. CX, 19 April 1850, col. 568.

[32] Ibid., vol. CX, 25 April 1850, col. 802.

[33] Ibid., vol. CVIII, 18 February 1850, col. 1014.

[34] Ibid., vol. CX (25 April 1850), cols. 800, 803-4.

[35] Ibid., vol. CX, 13 May 1850, col. 1326.

[36] See for example *Morning Chronicle*, 14 June 1850 and *Spectator*, 23 February 1850.

[37] 'Colonial Reform', *F.M.*, vol. 41, no. 243 (1850), pp. 377-8.

[38] Ward, *Earl Grey and the Australian Colonies*, pp. 194-5; Sweetman, *Australian Constitutional Development*, pp. 225-7.

[39] *Hansard*, 3rd series, vol. CXI, 6 May 1850, cols. 1217-20, 1224-5.

[40] Ibid., vol. CXII, 28 June 1850, cols. 601-3.

[41] 'Colonial Reform', op. cit., p. 375.

[42] Ibid.

[43] *Hansard*, 3rd series, vol. CX, 6 May 1850, col. 1164.

[44] Ibid., vol. CXI, 11 June 1850, col. 1048.

[45] 13 and 14 Vic., cap. 59, secs. 11, 12.

[46] *Times*, 16 August 1853.

[47] Grey to Fitzroy, 30 August 1850, CO 202/58.

[48] Fitzroy to Grey, 18 June 1851, CO 201/441; 15 January 1852, CO 201/450.

[49] Grey to Fitzroy, 23 January 1852, CI 202/60.

[50] This was the antithesis of imperial trusteeship which sought the overall well-being of the empire. See, for example, Grey's views on Australian waste lands being held in trust for the benefit of all British subjects 'not merely the few thousands who may at this moment inhabit a particular Colony'; in his *Colonial Policy*, vol. 1, p. 319.

[51] 'Influence of Last Election on Colonial Affairs', *Colonial and Asiatic Review*, vol. 1 (1852), p. 231.

[52] Knight, *Illiberal Liberal: Robert Lowe in New South Wales 1842-1850*, p. 253 comments that from 1850 to 1867 Lowe contributed three leading articles a week to the *Times*.

[53] *Times*, 17 May 1852.

[54] Ibid., 22 May 1852.

[55] *Morning Chronicle*, 19 June 1852.

[56] *Examiner*, 30 October 1852.

[57] Fitzroy to Pakington, 20 August 1852, CO 201/453.

[58] *Times*, 21 June 1852. It should also be noted, that dire prognostications concerning the possibility of rebellion in Australia although based on Britain's eighteenth century experience in America, were probably reinforced by the fact that Britain's domestic radicals used the same vocabulary in pressing their demands for political change during the first half of the nineteenth century as did settlers in the colonies. Taxation without representation, for example, was a charge continually levelled at parliament by working-class extremists in Britain when agitating for democracy and universal male suffrage. There was a clear threat of violence from such radicals during the period under review here, and British distaste for similar claims couched in identical terminology and emanating from a tainted population in Australia, could not fail to have been affected by the domestic situation. This perhaps helps in some measure to explain the existence of an outlook characterized by pessimistic fatalism regarding the future of Britain's links with the Australian colonies like that enunciated by the *Times* above. For a discussion of the utilization of the taxation without representation slogan by British working-class agitators during these years see Rosenblatt, *The Chartist Movement in Its Social and Economic Aspects*, pp. 30, 32.

[59] Cell, *British Colonial Administration*, pp. 127, 134.

[60] Pakington to Fitzroy, 15 December 1852, CO 202/60.

[61] *Times*, 24 December 1852.

[62] Newcastle to Fitzroy, 4 August 1853, CO 202/63.

[63] Ward, *Empire in the Antipodes*, p. 83.

[64] Pakington to Denison, 14 December 1852, CO 408/37; Newcastle to Denison, 22 February 1853, CO 408/37.

[65] Cell, op. cit., p. 144.

[66] Denison to Newcastle, 25 August 1853, CO 280/308.

[67] *Times*, 16 August 1853.

[68] Young felt so strongly in favour of nominated upper houses that he withheld from the colonists Newcastle's dispatch which removed British insistence on a second house, and failed to report to the Colonial Office the wave of dissent and uproar in South Australia over the necessity, under Pakington's terms of reference, to have a bicameral legislature. See Pike, *Paradise of Dissent*, p. 468.

[69] *Times*, 31 October 1853. In fact, the Colonial Office agreed, and the draft constitution was returned to South Australia in 1855 with instructions that fresh elections were to be held and then the constitution was to be resubmitted to the legislative council for further discussion and amendment. Russell to MacDonnell, 4 May 1855, CO 396/12.

[70] *Times*, 31 October 1853. Shaw, *The Land of Promise*, p. 14 found the concept of a New South Wales' aristocracy to be hilarious. He described such a development as '*baronius paradoxus*'.

[71] Grey to Fitzroy, 23 February 1852, CO 202/60.

[72] *Times*, 21 April 1854.

[73] The most important alteration was the exclusion from the bills of sections

which sought to distinguish by definition between areas of imperial and local concern. Also excluded were several sections which would have diminished the authority of the Crown and to which the Queen was constitutionally unable to consent.

74 *Hansard*, 3rd series, vol. CXXXVIII, 17 May 1855, col. 728.

75 Ibid., vol. CXXXIX, 10 July 1855, cols. 653-6.

76 Ibid., vol. CXXXVIII, 17 May 1855, col. 723. Lowe's views won support from other parliamentarians, ibid., cols. 732-5; 1957-59; 2005-6.

77 Ibid., vol. CXXXVIII, 14 June 1855, cols. 1989-90.

78 Ibid., vol. CXXXVIII, 17 May 1855, cols. 727-33. Other government supporters stressed the danger of opposing constitutional settlements devised by the colonists themselves. See ibid., cols. 735-6; 1982-4; 2006-12.

79 *Times*, 8 September, 1855.

80 *Globe*, 18 May 1855.

81 *Leeds Mercury*, 3 July 1855.

82 Grey, *Colonial Policy*, vol. 2, pp. 87, 111.

83 *Hansard*, 3rd series, vol. VI, 16 August 1831, cols. 111-15, and 141-2.

84 Russell to Grey, 19 August 1849, PRO 30/22, folio 8A, Russell Papers.

85 Ibid.

86 Ward, *Earl Grey and the Australian Colonies*, p. 165.

87 Grey to Russell, 23 August 1849, PRO 30/22, folio 8A, Russell Papers.

88 Peter Burroughs, *The Colonial Reformers and Canada 1830-1849* (Toronto, 1969), p. 182.

89 *Colonial Gazette*, 25 September 1839; William Westgarth, 'The Administration of the Colonies', *Simmonds's Colonial Magazine*, vol. 7 (1846), pp. 268-9; Wakefield, *A View of the Art of Colonization*, pp. 309-12; 'Our Colonial Empire', *Westminster Review*, vol. 2 (1852), p. 417. James Stephen also felt that such a council which he described as 'A Board of Colonial Commissioners' would perform a most useful function in an advisory capacity. See his Memorandum on the Colonial Office, 4 October 1839, PRO 30/22, folio 3C, Russell Papers.

90 Cell, *British Colonial Administration*, p. 24 has noted that the Colonial Office usually did not control events but drifted with them.

91 Ibid., pp. 42, 46. See also Knaplund, *Gladstone and Britain's Imperial Policy*, p. 21.

5:   Emigration 1828–55

1 Burroughs, *Britain and Australia*, appendix 11.

2 The effect of this process of change on attitudes towards Australia is discussed in Chapter 7 below.

3 Rostow, *British Economy of the Nineteenth Century*, pp. 120-1.

4 £50 000 in 1819 to send settlers to South Africa; £68 790 to send families from southern Ireland to Canada and the Cape; to finance emigration from Ireland to Canada £15 000 in 1823, £30 000 in 1825, and £10 000 in 1827. For full details of these experiments see Johnston, *British Emigration Policy 1815-1830: 'Shovelling Out Paupers'*, pp. 32-56, 69-90.

5 Burroughs, *The Colonial Reformers and Canada*, p. 51.

6 Helm, *Modern British History*, pp. 23-4. By 1816, for example it was necessary to raise more than £31 million annually to meet the interest charge on the National Debt, as against less than £10 million in 1793.

7 Carrothers, *Emigration from the British Isles*, p. 73. See also Draft Report of Commissioners for Emigration as submitted in February 1832, but not as

finally adopted by the Commission; Colonial Papers—Emigration, Grey Papers.

8 Macmillan, *Scotland and Australia*, p. 254.

9 Cobbett, *The Emigrant's Guide in Ten Letters addressed to the Tax-Payers of England*, pp. 39-40. A recent scholar has shown that there was a further dimension to the reluctance of British paupers to emigrate to Australia during the 1820s, and this was the fact that they were already involved in a major social upheaval and movement of population from the rural areas to the industrial cities which in many cases amounted to a psychological if not a physical emigration. See Macmillan, op. cit., pp. 16-17.

10 *Cobbett's Two-penny Trash; or Politics for the Poor*, vol. 1 (March 1831).

11 Ibid., July 1831.

12 Burroughs, *Britain and Australia*, p. 121.

13 Ibid.

14 *Cobbett's Two-Penny Trash*, op. cit.

15 *The Emigrants' Guide*, p. 40.

16 MacDonagh, *A Pattern of Government Growth 1800-60*, p. 25.

17 *Home Colonies*, p. 28.

18 'Mr Wilmot Horton and Emigration', *Blackwood's Edinburgh Magazine*, vol. 23, no. 135 (1828), p. 191.

19 Ibid. Support for home colonies was widespread, and even in Ireland—the home of absentee landlordism—the conservative Dublin newspaper the *Evening Packet*, 26 September 1829, saw such a plan as the ultimate solution to the wretchedness of pauperism. Lord Howick who was soon to become under-secretary at the Colonial Office had found such a point of view very persuasive. He confided to his diary in January 1830 his opinion 'that this plan affords a better prospect than any yet suggested of improving the condition of the poor and diminishing the burden of maintaining them'. Howick's Journal, 2 January 1830, Grey Papers.

20 *Operative*, 3 February 1839.

21 Ray Boston, *British Chartists in America 1839-1900* (Manchester, 1971), p. 18.

22 Burroughs, *Britain and Australia*, appendix 11. On North American emigration see S. C. Johnson, *A History of Emigration from the United Kingdom to North America, 1763-1912* (London, 1913); W. S. Shepperson, *British Emigration to North America* (Minneapolis 1957); and Helen I. Cowan, *British Emigration to British North America* (Toronto, 1961).

23 'New South Wales', *Edinburgh Review*, vol. 47, no. 93 (1828), p. 99.

24 'Emigration', *Edinburgh Review*, vol. 47, no. 93 (1828), pp. 206-14. This outlook was shared by other commentators, see 'Emigration to Australasia', *Gentleman's Magazine*, vol. 98, pt. 1 (1828), p. 212.

25 Ibid., p. 209. For a full discussion of Horton's schemes see Johnston, *British Emigration Policy*, pp. 57-68.

26 *Standard*, 5 June 1829.

27 *Courier*, 5 June 1829.

28 *Times*, 22 August 1826.

29 'New Colony on Swan River', *Q.R.*, vol. 39 (1829), p. 316.

30 *Court Journal*, 1 August 1829.

31 'The Picture of Australia', *Gentleman's Magazine*, vol. 99 pt. 2 (1829), p. 437; 'Swan River Settlement', *New Monthly Magazine and Literary Journal* vol. 25 (1829), p. 501.

32 'Emigration and Mr Wilmot Horton', *N.M.M.*, vol. 26 (1829), pp. 50-3.

33 Wakefield, *A Letter from Sydney, passim*.

[34] Goderich to Bourke, 28 September 1831, CO 202/27.

[35] Howick to Stewart, 7 October 1831, CO 202/28.

[36] Burroughs, *Britain and Australia*, p. 49.

[37] 'Causes and Remedies of Pauperism in the United Kingdom', *Q.R.*, vol. 43 (1830), p. 266. Proposals to provide an emigration fund by levying some sort of tax on Australian colonists appear to have been prominent about this time; another was suggested by the *Gentleman's Magazine*, vol. 99, pt. 2 (1829), special supplement.

[38] 'Causes and Cure of Disturbances and Pauperism', *E. R.*, vol. 53, no. 105 (1831), p. 53.

[39] 'Emigration—Letters from Canada', *Q.R.*, vol. 54 (1835), p. 424.

[40] *Courier*, 1, 4, 8 and 23 July 1834; *Times*, 2, 3 and 26 July 1834; *Standard*, 30 July 1834; [John Crawfurd], 'New South Australian Colony', *Westminster Review*, vol. 21, no. 42 (1834), p. 441.

[41] *Spectator*, 12, 19 July 1834; *Examiner*, 29 June 1834; 6 July 1834; *Morning Chronicle*, 9, 31 July 1834.

[42] 'Emigration and the United States', *Fraser's Magazine for Town and Country*, vol. 16, no. 95 (1837), pp. 562-3.

[43] Arthur to Goderich, 8 September 1832, CO 280/35; Arthur to Hay, 9 October 1832, CO 280/36; Bourke to Stanley, 21 January 1834, 20 March 1834, CO 201/238. The Reverend John Dunmore Lang was later to claim that this female immigration had turned the colony of New South Wales into 'a sink of prostitution'. See Lang, *Historical and Statistical Account of New South Wales*, vol. 2, p. 433.

[44] Madgwick, *Immigration into Eastern Australia 1788-1851*, p. 111.

[45] *Hansard*, 3rd series, vol. L111, 5 May 1840, cols. 1251-76.

[46] See London Emigration Committee's advertisement in Ingleton, *True Patriots All*, p. 155.

[47] Howick believed government participation in emigration would subvert private initiative. See Howick's paper of January 1832, Emigration file no. 5, Grey Papers. The activities of the emigration commission are outlined in Fred H. Hitchins, *The Colonial Land and Emigration Commission* (Philadelphia, 1931), pp. 10-14.

[48] Spring Rice to Bourke, 12 September 1834, CO 202/32.

[49] MacDonagh, *A Pattern of Government Growth*, pp. 18, 147.

[50] *MacMillan*, Scotland and Australia, p. 77.

[51] Carrothers, *Emigration from the British Isles*, p. 223.

[52] Pelling, *A History of British Trade Unionism*, p. 49; S. and B. Webb, *The History of Trade Unionism 1666-1920*, pp. 201-2. Sometimes emigration was the result of an unsuccessful strike. In 1852, for example, after the failure of a prolonged industrial dispute involving the Amalgamated Society of Engineers, Thomas Hughes and other middle-class liberals who had founded the movement for Christian Socialism and supported trade unionism, raised funds to enable thirty of the men to emigrate to Australia. See Mack and Armytage, *Thomas Hughes*, p. 66.

[53] *A Treatise on the Circumstances which determine the Rate of Wages and the Condition of the Labouring Classes*, pp. 84-5.

[54] Wilson, *Carlyle at His Zenith 1848-53*, p. 225.

[55] Ibid., p. 224.

[56] *A Letter from Sydney*, pp. 170-1; and *England and America*, pp. 233-45.

[57] T. F. Elliot to J. S. Mill, 4 December 1837, CO 386/21; see also similar sentiments in Stanley to Gipps, 29 September 1843, CO 202/48.

[58] Grey to Fitzroy, 11 December 1847, CO 202/54.

59 Glenelg to Bourke, 29 March 1837, CO 202/34; see also James Stephen to F. Strangways, 17 August 1837, CO 202/36.

60 Hodder, *George Fife Angas*, pp. 174-5.

61 Land and Emigration Commissioners to R. Vernon Smith, 16 December 1840, CO 386/58. See also the complaints of British workmen already in New South Wales, Abbott, 'The Emigration to Valparaiso in 1843'. *Labour History*, no. 19 (1970), p. 2.

62 Land and Emigration Commissioners to James Stephen, 5 January 1841, CO 386/58. See also 'New South Wales, Colonial Immigration—The Bounty System and its Frauds', *Fraser's Magazine for Town and Country*, vol. 28, no. 166 (1843), p. 441. For full details of the bounty and government systems see Madgwick, *Immigration into Eastern Australia*, pp. 130-68.

63 Russell to Gipps, 7 October 1840, CO 202/43.

64 'New South Wales,' *Q.R.*, vol. 62 (1838), p. 501.

65 *Times*, 12 September 1838.

66 'Mitchell's Second and Third Expeditions', *Blackwood's Edinburgh Magazine*, vol. 45, no. 279 (1839), pp. 113-16.

67 'The Colony of Western Australia', *New Monthly Magazine and Humorist*, vol. 57 (1839), p. 429.

68 Hartwell, 'The Pastoral Ascendency 1820-1850', in Greenwood (ed.), *Australia*, pp. 70-2.

69 *Operative*, 3 February 1839.

70 *Operative*, 10 February 1839.

71 'New Theory of Colonization', *E.R.*, vol. 71, no. 144 (1840), pp. 517-24.

72 Butlin, *Foundations of the Australian Monetary System 1788-1851*, ch. 10.

73 Fitzpatrick, *The British Empire in Australia*, pp. 71-4.

74 Hartwell, op. cit., p. 84.

75 *Hansard*, 3rd series, vol. LIV, 22 June 1840, col. 1379. See also Stanley's speech, *Hansard*, 3rd series, vol. LXVIII, 6 April 1843, col. 546.

76 *Spectator*, 16 May 1840, accused the British Government of robbing New South Wales; *Times*, 16 June 1840; *Courier*, 4 June 1840; *Morning Chronicle*, 23 June 1840; *Examiner*, 15 March 1840.

77 Grey to Russell, 4 July 1841, CO 13/20.

78 *Hansard*, 3rd series, vol. LX, 4 Febuary 1842, col. 82.

79 'Colonization—The Only Cure for National Distress—Mr. Charles Buller's Speech', *F.M.*, vol. 27, no. 162 (1843), p. 740.

80 *Hansard*, 3rd series, vol. LXVIII, 6 April 1843, cols. 484-599.

81 Ibid., cols. 484-531.

82 *Courier*, 5 February 1842. Other papers in favour of Buller's motion were *Morning Chronicle*, 11 July 1842, 7 April 1843; *Standard*, 7 April 1843. Strongest opposition came from the *Globe*, 7 and 8 April 1843, which argued that Britain had no business assuming responsibility for those who chose to seek their fortunes in British dependencies.

83 Abbott, 'The Emigration to Valparaiso', *Labour History*, no. 19 (1970), p. 9. See also the fifth annual report of the colonial lands and emigration commissioners, *Parliamentary Papers*, 1845 (617) XXVII, which states that during 1844-45, 674 British labourers re-emigrated from New South Wales and Van Diemen's Land to South America.

84 Stanley to Grey, 31 December 1841, CO 396/2.

85 Grey, *Speech on Emigration to Australia and Reply on the Same Subject to Lord Monteagle*, p. 22.

86 Grey to Young, 21 July 1848, CO 396/7.

[87] 'The Emigrant Ship', *Illustrated London News*, 13 April 1844, reprinted in Ingleton, *True Patriots All*, p. 230.

[88] Lansbury, *Arcady in Australia*, p. 62.

[89] *Sidney's Australian Handbook*, preface.

[90] *Settlers and Convicts: or Recollections of Sixteen Years Labour in the Australian Backwoods*, p. 233.

[91] Caroline Chisholm to Lord Monteagle, 6 October 1848, MS. 13 400, Monteagle Papers.

[92] Margaret Kiddle, 'The Meeting of Caroline Chisholm and Charles Dickens', *Historical Studies, Australia and New Zealand*, vol. 3, no. 12 (1949), p. 296.

[93] Kiddle, 'Caroline Chisholm and Charles Dickens', Ibid., vol. 3, no. 10 (1945), p. 86.

[94] 'A Bundle of Emigrants' Letters', *H.W.*, 30 March 1850.

[95] Grey to Charles Dickens, 11 April 1852, Colonial Affairs (Various), Grey Papers.

[96] Lang attacked Mrs Chisholm in a series of articles written for the *British Banner* 1848-9. See Kiddle, 'Caroline Chisholm and Charles Dickens', loc. cit., pp. 80-1.

[97] See file on 'Godley Scheme for Emigration 1846-47', MS. 13 400, Monteagle Papers. Lord John Russell also favoured a British loan for Irish emigration, see folio on 'Remarks on Emigration Poor Law and Ireland 18 December', Emigration, Grey Papers. See also support from Wilkinson, *A letter to the Right Honourable Lord Ashley on the Necessity of an Extended Government Plan of Emigration to the Australian Colonies* passim.; and Fletcher, *Letter to the Right Honourable Earl Grey on the Subject of Emigration*, passim.

[98] Cited by D. Simpson, 'Charles Dickens and the Empire', *Royal Commonwealth Society Library Notes*, new series, no. 162 (June 1970), p. 5.

[99] *Colonial Policy*, vol. 1, pp. 329-30.

[1] Ibid., p. 332.

[2] 'Remarks on Emigration Poor Law and Ireland, 18 December 1848', Emigration, Grey Papers.

[3] *Colonial Policy*, vol. 1, p. 240.

[4] *The Journal of an Expedition into Tropical Australia in Search of a Route from Sydney to the Gulf of Carpentaria.*

[5] *Times*, 20 and 24 May, 1848, 4 July 1849.

[6] 'What is to be done with Our Criminals', *Edinburgh Review*, vol. 86, no. 173 (1847), p. 272.

[7] 'Colonization', *Blackwood's Edinburgh Magazine*, vol. 64, no. 393 (1848), p. 66.

[8] 'The Question of General Emigration', *N.M.M.*, vol. 83 (1848), p. 525.

[9] 'The Emigrant's Song to his Wife', *New Monthly Magazine and Humorist*, vol. 84 (1848), p. 23.

[10] PatriciaThomson, *The Victorian Heroine*, ch. 5. See also Laver, *The Age of Optimism*, p. 103.

[11] Charles Dickens, *David Copperfield* (London, 1848), ch. 51.

[12] Ibid., ch. 47.

[13] Lansbury, *Arcady in Australia*, p. 107.

[14] The other three roads to respectability were, finding work, opening small shops or lodging houses, and marriage; see *The Other Victorians*, p. 6.

[15] Vol. 1, pp. 192-3.

[16] Simpson, 'Charles Dickens and the Empire', *Royal Commonwealth Society Library Notes*, op. cit., p. 5.

[17] Pt. 15, ch. 1.

[18] Ibid., pt. 13, ch. 4.

[19] Ibid., pt. 17, ch. 1.

[20] Grey to Fitzroy, 7 July 1848, CO 202/54. Private benefactors provided extensive loans to labourers and their families for emigration to Australia. This was particularly the case in Ireland where some landlords assisted their tenants to emigrate. In October 1846 Earl Grey had suggested that relief of Irish distress by emigration to Australia could be significantly increased if Irish landlords were to supplement the colonial emigration funds by loans of £8 to £10 per family of emigrants. Grey to Monteagle, 16 October 1846, Monteagle Papers, MS. 13 400. Lord and Lady Monteagle certainly appear to have advanced a great deal of money in this way to enable their tenants to emigrate. See MS. 13 400, Monteagle Papers, passim.

[21] In 1850 the population of the northern and southern portions of New South Wales was: New South Wales, 189 341; Port Phillip 76 162. Five years later the populations had risen to New South Wales 277 579, Victoria 364 324. T. A. Coghlan, *A Comparative Account of the Seven Colonies of Australasia* (Sydney, 1891) pp. 21-2.

[22] In 1853 *Gold* was produced at the famous theatre in Drury Lane: *The Gold Regions of Australia* at the Victoria Theatre; and *The Emigrant's Progress* at the Strand Theatre; see Lansbury, *Arcady in Australia*, pp. 109-10.

[23] 'Gold Discoveries', *Q.R.*, vol. 91 (1852), pp. 524-6.

[24] Ibid., p. 526.

[25] 'The Celestials at Home and Abroad', *Blackwood's Edinburgh Magazine*, vol. 72, no. 441 (1852), p. 100.

[26] Pakington to Fitzroy, 17 July 1852, CO 202/60.

[27] 'Gold and Emigration', *F.M.*, vol. 46, no. 272 (1852), pp. 127-38.

[28] Ibid., p. 129.

[29] 'The Colonists' Notebook', *Colonial Magazine and East India Review*, vol. 23 (1852), p. 169.

[30] 'On Emigration to Australia', Ibid., p. 550.

[31] No. 77 (1852), pp. 474-9.

[32] Engels to Marx, 23 September 1851, in Mayer (ed.), *Marx, Engels and Australia*, p. 104.

[33] Engels to Marx, 21 August 1852, Ibid., p. 105. Engels' strictures on the Australian Emigration were echoed by the latter-day Chartist leader Ernest Jones, 'It is not brave to flee from the work that must naturally devolve upon Englishmen, sooner or later—viz. that of struggling against the oppression of the people'. See the *Peoples Paper*, 28 August 1852.

[34] Samuel Sidney claimed that what saved England from bloody rebellion in 1848, when 'all Europe was convulsed by revolutionary throes', was 'the annual emigration of our discontented spirits.' See *Sidney's Emigrant's Journal and Traveller's Magazine*, no. 5 (1849), pp. 239-40.

6: *Native Affairs 1828-50*

[1] Sydney to Phillip, 25 April 1787, *H.R.A.*, series 1, vol. 1. pp. 13-14. The most recent and detailed work on official British opinion regarding Australian Aboriginals can be found in Reece, *Aborigines and Colonists*, ch. 3. See also the documentary survey by Reynolds (ed.), *Aborigines and Settlers*.

[2] This presumption of pre-eminence was not restricted to British contact with native races, but was symptomatic of a deep-seated cultural chauvinism which led many British settlers, administrators, and statesmen in the pre-Darwinian half of the nineteenth century to disparage all non-British peoples including Boers and French Canadians. Geoffrey Moorhouse has described

how for most Anglo-Saxons during this period, the 'wogs' began at Calais. See *Guardian*, 11 February 1971.

3 Stanley to Gipps, 20 December 1842, CO 202/45. Full descriptive details of the fruitless but reiterated attempts to turn nomadic Aboriginals into peasant farmers can be found in Barry Bridges, 'The Aborigines and the Land Question in New South Wales', *Journal of Royal Australian Historical Society*, vol. 56, pt. 2 (1970), pp. 97-101.

4 Pascoe, *Two Hundred Years of the S.P.G.*, vol. 1, pp. 386-401.

5 Tyerman and Bennet to L.M.S., 12 November 1824. Tyerman and Bennet Deputation 1821-1829, box 1, folio 4, London Missionary Society Records, London.

6 Foxcroft, *Australian Native Policy*, p. 22.

7 *Black Australians*, p. 89.

8 Broughton (N.S.W.) to Campbell (Secretary, S.P.G.), 9 December 1834. 'The question in truth which the people of this nation [i.e. Britain] have to consider is whether they are prepared to lay the foundation of a vast community of infidels . . .' Letters Received—Australia, vol. 1, records of Society for the Propagation of the Gospel. See also Woodcock to Broughton, 8 June 1847, in which an almost identical complaint is made concerning incipient heathenism amongst the settlers of South Australia. South Australia, box 1, 1834-49, records of Society for the Propagation of the Gospel, London.

9 Coates to Glenelg, 17 December 1835, Home Letterbooks, Out CH/L2, records of the Church Missionary Society. See also extracts from missionaries journals reprinted in *Church Missionary Record: Detailing the proceedings of the Church Missionary Society*, 1833, p. 88; ibid., 1839, p. 156.

10 Fingard, *The Anglican Design in Loyalist Nova Scotia 1783-1816*, p. 5.

11 Reece, op. cit., pp. 62-103; Reynolds (ed.), op. cit., pp. 132-50.

12 Printed draft of a report by Sir James Stephen on Australian Legislature, 21 February 1849, Colonial Papers—Australia, Grey Papers.

13 Murray to Arthur, 31 February 1829, CO 408/5.

14 Murray to Stirling, 30 December 1828, CO 397/1.

15 Hasluck, op. cit., p. 171.

16 'The Picture of Australia', *W.R.*, vol. 12, no. 23 (1829), pp. 179-86. Unflattering descriptions of the Aboriginals had been quite common since the report made by William Dampier in 1688, though in this instance the *Review's* critic was referring to Cunningham's, *Two Years in New South Wales*, vol. 2, p. 202.

17 'The Present State of Australia', *Gentleman's Magazine*, vol. 101, pt. 1 (1831), p. 238.

18 Goderich to Stirling, 28 April 1831, CO 397/2.

19 Goderich to Stirling, 30 May 1831, CO 397/2.

20 Crowley, *Australia's Western Third*, p. 30.

21 *Journals of the House of Commons*, vol. 89, session 1834, p. 449.

22 'Van Diemen's Land', *W.R.*, vol. 21, no. 41 (1834), p. 25.

23 'New South Wales', *Q.R.*, vol. 53 (1835), p. 10.

24 Glenelg to Stirling, 23 July 1835, CO 397/2.

25 Glenelg to Bourke, 26 July 1837, CO 202/37.

26 Stirling to Aberdeen, 10 July 1835, CO 18/15. This was a very common view in England and was not restricted to the 'men on the spot' in the colonies. See Kiernan, *The Lords of Human Kind*, p. 280.

27 Gipps to Russell, 7 April, CO 201/309. See also Mellor, *British Imperial Trusteeship 1783-1850*, pp. 307-8; and Bridges, 'The Aborigines and the

Land Question in New South Wales', *Journal of the Royal Australian Historical Society*, vol. 56, pt. 2 (1970), p. 93. The situation in South Australia was identical, see Rowley, *The Destruction of Aboriginal Society*, pp. 126-7.

[28] Memorandum by William Thomas, 6 April 1854; in Bride (ed.), *Letters from Victorian Pioneers*, pp. 404-13. Full details of the formation, administration and history of the native police forces in Australia can be found in Rowley, op. cit., pp. 39-43, passim.

[29] Glenelg to Bourke, 13 April 1836, CO 202/34.

[30] Aborigines Protection Society, *Report of the Parliamentary Select Committee on Aboriginal Tribes (British Settlements): Reprinted with Comments by the Aborigines Protection Society* (London, 1837), p. 12.

[31] Ibid., p. 10.

[32] *Parliamentary Papers*, 1837 (425) VII.

[33] Perhaps Stephen intended to refer to Western Australia rather than Van Diemen's Land in this letter, as there were no Aboriginals left in Van Diemen's Land by 1837.

[34] Stephen to Spearman, 30 August 1837, CO 202/36.

[35] Guistiniani to L.M.S., 26 October 1837, Australia 1833-1844, box 3, folio 2, records of the London Missionary Society.

[36] Gipps to Stanley, 16 May 1842; and enclosure La Trobe to Gipps, 4 March 1842, CO 201/320.

[37] Stanley to Gipps, 20 December 1842, CO 202/45.

[38] Foxcroft, *Australian Native Policy*, p. 78.

[39] Grey to Russell, 13 September, 20 October, 10 November 1841, CO 13/21. See also Hodder, *George Fife Angas*, p. 146.

[40] *Black Australians*, pp. 74-80.

[41] Stanley to Fitzroy, 13 August 1844, CO 202/48.

[42] 'Australian Sketches', *S.C.M.*, vol. 4 (1845), pp. 257-9.

[43] Stanley to Gipps, 2 March 1844, CO 202/48, Grey to Fitzroy, 27 January 1849, CO 202/56.

[44] See [George Groly], 'The Navigation of the Antipodes', *Blackwood's Edinburgh Magazine*, vol. 62, no. 385 (1847), p. 517.

[45] *A Dictionary, Geographical, Statistical and Historical*, vol. 2, p. 230.

[46] 'Cooksland and Phillipsland', *Westminster Review*, vol. 48, no. 94 (1847), p. 240.

[47] *Cooksland in North-Eastern Australia*, pp. 274-6. Similar assertions also appeared in Harris, *Settlers and Convicts*, p. 211; and in Mundy, *Our Antipodes*, vol. 1, p. 232.

[48] [George Groly], 'Colonization', *Blackwood's Edinburgh Magazine*, vol. 64, no. 393 (1848), p. 71.

[49] Stanley to Fitzroy, 13 August 1844, CO 202/48.

[50] [Edward Phillips], 'Colonization of New Countries No Injustice to the Aborigines of those Countries', *Simmonds's Colonial Magazine*, vol. 13 (1848), pp. 19-20.

[51] Grey to Fitzroy, 5 November 1850, CO 202/58.

[52] Bolt, *Victorian Attitudes to Race*, p. 214.

[53] Mason, *Patterns of Dominance*, pp. 31-2.

[54] *The Image of Africa: British Ideas and Action 1780-1850*, p. 370.

[55] Ibid., p. 364.

[56] Davies, *Phrenology, Fad and Science*, p. 11.

[57] Thomas Hodgkin, 'On Inquiries into the Races of Man', *Report of the Eleventh Meeting of the British Association for the Advancement of Science 1841* (London, 1842), p. 333. In 1852 the questionnaire was refined and

developed, though the reliance on phrenology remained. See Thomas
Hodgkin and Richard Cull, 'A Manual of Ethnological Inquiry; being a
Series of Questions concerning the Human Race, prepared by a Sub-
Committee of the British Association for the Advancement of Science,
appointed in 1851 (consisting of Dr. Hodgkin and Richard Cull, Esq.), and
adapted for the Use of Travellers and Others studying the Varieties of Man',
*Report of the Twenty-Second Meeting of the British Association for the
Advancement of Science 1852* (London, 1853), p. 244.

[58] *Our Antipodes*, vol. 1, p. 219.

[59] Nott and Gliddon, *Types of Mankind*, p. 434.

[60] Curtin, op. cit., p. 364. See also Marchant, 'Social Darwinism', *Australian
Journal of Politics and History*, vol. 3, no. 1 (1957), pp. 50-2.

7:   Arcady the Brave

[1] Eddy, *Britain and the Australian Colonies*, p. 126, describes the years between
1819 and 1825 in New South Wales as encompassing 'a pastoral boom
comparable with that of the thirties'.

[2] Figures from Crawford, *Australia*, p. 61; and Burroughs, *Britain and Australia*, appendix 1.

[3] Commissioner J. T. Bigge's report on the state of agriculture and trade in
New South Wales in 1823 had clearly stressed the rising importance of wool;
and this opinion was endorsed the following year by Sir Thomas Brisbane
the governor of New South Wales. See Eddy, op. cit., pp. 213-15. Some of the
more perceptive British commentators were also aware that agriculture was
unsuited to provide an export staple for Australia; see [Sydney Smith], 'New
South Wales', *Edinburgh Review*, vol. 47, no. 93 (1828), p. 97; and 'New
South Wales', *Quarterly Review*, vol. 37 (1828), p. 3.

[4] *Gentleman's Magazine*, vol. 99, pt. 1 (1829), p. 73.

[5] 'New Colony on Swan River', *Quarterly Review*, vol. 39 (1829), pp. 316-40.

[6] Vol. 25 (1829), p. 501.

[7] Aileen Ward, *John Keats: The Making of a Poet* (New York, 1963), p. 189.

[8] 'And did those feet in ancient time', in F. W. Bateson, *Selected Poems of
William Blake* (London, 1961), p. 71. Blake's poems are difficult to understand, but there is little doubt that in this instance he was referring directly
to factories and industrial machinery. See Erdman, *Blake Prophet Against
Empire*, pp. 367-8.

[9] 'Jerusalem', ch. 3, sec. 65, in D. J. Sloss and J. P. R. Wallis, *The Prophetic
Writings of William Blake* 2 vols. (Oxford, 1964), vol. 1, p. 567. I am indebted
to Coral Lansbury for some of the ideas in this chapter. She develops the
theme of a British pursuit of a colonial arcady in the Australian colonies at
some length. See Lansbury, *Arcady in Australia*, passim.

[10] Brinton, *The Political Ideas of the English Romanticists*, p. 50. See also
Fairchild, *The Romantic Quest*, p. 12.

[11] Lansbury, op. cit., p. 37.

[12] Mack, *Public Schools and British Opinion 1780 to 1860*, pp. 95-6.

[13] William Cobbett, *Rural Rides* (London, 1830). Benjamin Disraeli, *Con-
ingsby, or the New Generation* (London, 1844), and *Sybil or the Two Nations*
(London, 1845). See also the Chartist leader, Feargus O'Connor's commitment to a return to the land, in Rosenblatt, *The Chartist Movement*, pp.
108-10.

[14] 'Southey's Colloquies on Society', *Edinburgh Review*, vol. 50, no. 100 (1830),
p. 540.

[15] Broughton to Campbell, 9 December 1834. Copies of letters received—Australia, vol. 1, S.P.G. Records.

[16] *A Letter from Sydney*, p. 22.

[17] Mill, *Principles of Political Economy with Some of their applications to Social Philosophy*, p. 972.

[18] Undated memorandum by Howick on Australian Waste Lands Bill [1842?], Colonial Papers—Australia, Grey Papers.

[19] Notes by Grey on correspondence dealing with the occupation of unsold lands in Australia 1845-46. Colonial Papers—Australia, Grey Papers.

[20] Bloomfield, *Edward Gibbon Wakefield*, pp. 111-14; Burroughs, *Britain and Australia*, p. 190; Pike, *Paradise of Dissent*, p. 52; Mills, *The Colonisation of Australia 1829-42*, p. 140. Wakefield was something of a paradox. In the first place there were elements of utilitarian utopianism in his attempts to create a new society overseas according to his own ideal blueprint; but he seems to fit better into the camp of primitivists and romantics, as the details of his plan for colonial settlement reveal a constant harkening back to a form of hierarchical society—once supposed to have existed in pre-industrial Britain—which might be recreated in the non-industrial colonies of settlement. It is interesting that his most recent biographer should note that Wakefield, although a hard-headed practical man, had a streak of 'agricultural mysticism' in his personality. See Bloomfield, op. cit., pp. 97-8.

[21] *Letter from Sydney*, p. 10.

[22] Ibid., p. 9.

[23] W. H. G. Armytage, 'Owen and America', in Pollard and Salt, *Robert Owen Prophet of the Poor*, pp. 214-38. See also Harrison, *Robert Owen and the Owenites in Britain and America*.

[24] *Letter from Sydney*, p. 22.

[25] Burroughs, *Britain and Australia*, p. 18.

[26] *England and America*, p. 249.

[27] Ibid., p. 246. Detailed descriptions and summaries of Wakefield's theories are available in Mills, *The Colonisation of Australia*, pp. 90-139; Pike, *Paradise of Dissent*, pp. 77-83; and Burroughs, *Britain and Australia*, pp. 16-20. Contemporary comment and summary can be found in Mill, *Principles of Political Economy*, pp. 972-4; and Merivale, *Lectures on Colonization and Colonies*, pp. 387-8.

[28] Bloomfield, *Edward Gibbon Wakefield*, p. 111.

[29] Mills, op. cit., p. 167. Philipp, 'Wakefieldian Influence and New South Wales, 1830-1832', *Historical Studies, Australia and New Zealand*, vol. 9, no. 34 (1960), pp. 173-8; Burroughs, op. cit., pp. 37-42.

[30] Howick's Journal, 26 and 28 March 1833, Grey Papers.

[31] Wakefield to Howick, 5 September 1831. Wakefield, Edward Gibbon File, Correspondence Files, Grey Papers.

[32] Howick to Wakefield, 7 September 1831. Lord Howick's Private Letter Book, January 1831—June 1833, Grey Papers.

[33] The result was *England and America*.

[34] Burroughs, op. cit., p. 40.

[35] Goderich to Darling, 9 January and 14 February 1831, CO 202/25; Goderich to Arthur, 28 January 1831, CO 408/7; Goderich to Stirling, 28 April 1831, CO 397/2. It should be noted that other writers disagree with Burroughs's assessment and see the Ripon Regulations as a significant departure from previous patterns of development and at least partly attributable to Wakefield. See Philipp, *A Great View of Things*, pp. 40-1; 57-66.

[36] Goderich to Arthur, 27 January 1832, CO 408/7.

[37] Aberdeen to Bourke, 25 December 1834, CO 202/32.

[38] Glenelg to Bourke, 13 April 1836, CO 202/34.

[39] Ibid., See also Glenelg to Bourke, 15 February 1837, CO 202/34. In addition to advancing the cause of civilization, concentrated settlement would reduce the cost of colonial administration which was an important consideration in an age of retrenchment.

[40] Eddy, *Britain and the Australian Colonies*, p. 90.

[41] *Times*, 21 February 1831.

[42] Ibid., 28 June 1833.

[43] Burroughs, *Britain and Australia*, p. 33. See also Burroughs, *The Colonial Reformers and Canada 1830-1849*, op. cit., p. 14.

[44] 4 and 5 William IV, c. 95.

[45] 'New South Australian Colony', *Westminster Review*, vol. 21, no. 42 (1834), p. 448.

[46] *Courier*, 1 July 1834. See also similar opposition from *Operative*, 3 February 1839.

[47] *Times*, 2 July 1834; *Courier*, 8 July 1834. The economist Alexander Baring accused the South Australian Association of being a set of 'experimental philosophers', and proposed that they be restricted to an area of 'sixty or a hundred miles square; and he asked, if that was not enough for these gentlemen to play their pranks in'. *Hansard*, 3rd series, vol. XXV, 29 July 1834, cols. 701-2.

[48] *Times*, 3 July 1834.

[49] Ibid., 4 July 1834.

[50] *Courier*, 30 July 1834; *Standard*, 30 July 1834. See also *Edinburgh Evening Courant*, 2 August 1834. Systematic colonization found enthusiastic supporters, however, see *Spectator*, 14 June, 12 and 19 July 1834; *Examiner*, 29 June, 6 and 20 July 1834; *Morning Chronicle*, 9, 28 and 31 July 1834; *Caledonian Mercury*, 5 July 1834.

[51] Wakefield to Gouger, 25 May 1835, cited in Bloomfield, *Edward Gibbon akefield*, p. 138.

[52] For a detailed history of the causes and effects of the early failure of the South Australian colony, see Pike, *Paradise of Dissent*, pp. 169-279.

[53] For a brief account of the Australind settlement see Burroughs, *Britain and Australia*, pp. 349-54.

[54] Wakefield published extensively during these years, but perhaps this most influential work was *England and America*. In addition, he testified at length before two parliamentary committees, the select committee on the disposal of colonial waste lands (1836), and the select committee on transportation (1837-8). For Wakefield's role in the founding of New Zealand, see Sinclair, *A History of New Zealand*, pp. 62-7.

[55] S. H. Roberts has commented that Wakefield and his supporters 'advertised themselves to the point of nausea', and that their dogmatic persistence eventually convinced parliament, the Colonial Office and the public. See *The Squatting Age in Australia, 1835-1847*, p. 201.

[56] 'Comparative Prospects of our New Colonies', *W.R.*, vol. 35, no. 1 (1841), p. 140.

[57] 'The Australian Colonies', *Quarterly Review*, vol. 68 (1841), pp. 90-135.

[58] 'A View of the Art of Colonization', in Prichard (ed.), *The Collected Works of Edward Gibbon Wakefield*, p. 976.

[59] Ibid., pp. 976-7.

[60] Ibid., p. 975.

[61] Vol. 1, (1844), preface.

[62] 'Our Colonies—Which and where are they?', *S.C.M.*, vol. 1 (1844), p. 12.

[63] *Courier*, 16 March 1841; *Globe*, 7 April 1843.

[64] Colin T. Campbell, 'Lord John Russell's Proposition Respecting a Systematic Plan of Colonization', *S.C.M.*, vol. 5 (1845), p. 157.

[65] 'Australian Colonies or Republics', *F.M.*, vol. 37, no. 219 (1848), pp. 371-2.

[66] 'Colonization', *B.E.M.*, vol. 64, no. 393 (1848), p. 66.

[67] 'The Navigation of the Antipodes', *Blackwood's Edinburgh Magazine*, vol. 62, no. 385 (1847), p. 517.

[68] *Operative*, 25 November 1838.

[69] *Hansard*, 3rd series, vol. XLVIII, 25 June 1839, col. 847.

[70] *Operative*, 10 February 1839.

[71] *Sidney's Australian Handbook*, preface.

[72] *The Operative*, no. 66 (1852), p. 343.

[73] *The Three Colonies of Australia*, p. 17.

[74] *Britain and Australia*, p. 248.

[75] 'New South Australian Colony', *Westminster Review*, vol. 21, no. 42 (1834), p. 459.

[76] The first half of the nineteenth century was a time of turmoil and change in British foreign and colonial investments, and numerous overseas transactions during these years were characterized by venality and rash speculation. Of twenty-six foreign loans floated on the British money market between 1823 and 1825, for example, only ten did not default. Moreover, of some 624 joint-stock companies promoted in the same period, only 127 were still in existence by 1827. British banks and financial houses involved in the risky business of overseas investment continued to crash at regular intervals throughout the period under review. See Reid, *Economic History of Great Britain*, pp. 293-6.

[77] The North British Australasian Company was founded in 1839 and its contract of copartnery envisaged annual profits in excess of 40 per cent. See Macmillan, *Scotland and Australia*, p. 338. The Scottish Australian Company was founded in 1840, and its contract of copartnery also made provision for a similar rate of profit. See Macmillan, *The Debtor's War*, pp. 2-3.

[78] Macmillan indicates that the main concern of Scottish shareholders in these companies was that dividend payments be high and often. See Macmillan, *The Debtor's War*, pp. 7-8.

[79] F. M. L. Thompson, *English Landed Society in the Nineteenth Century*, pp. 21-2. See also Douglas Woodruff, 'The Aristocratic Idea', in British Broadcasting Corporation (ed.), *Ideas and Beliefs of the Victorians: An Historic Revaluation of the Victorian Age* (London, 1949), p. 285.

[80] Michael Roe has shown that although squatters may have paid lip-service to the ideal of a conservative, law-abiding and well regulated society their behaviour during the 1840s separated many of them from the ranks of the colonial gentry and showed them to be men 'acting without grace or restraint or care for the public good'. See *Quest for Authority in Eastern Australia*, p. 61.

[81] [Harris], *Settlers and Convicts*, p. 130. See also Lytton, *The Caxtons*, pt. 17, ch. 2; 'There is something in this new soil—in the labour it calls forth, in the hope it inspires, in the sense of property which I take to be the core of social morals—that expedites the work of redemption with marvellous rapidity'. Even the debased convict Abel Magwitch reflects the romantic pantheism of the times when he gives his oaths of revenge more power by going outside to swear them 'under the open heavens' of the Australian bush. Charles Dickens, *Great Expectations* (London, 1860), ch. 39.

[82] Alexander Gray, *The Development of Economic Doctrine: An Introductory Survey* (London, 1934), pp. 98-9.

[83] *The Caxtons*, pt. 17, ch. 2. These sentiments also appeared in Hardy's *Australia*, and the point was often made in Samuel Sidney's publications though less exuberantly than by Lytton.

[84] *Emigration Fields*, pp. 90-1.

[85] Ibid.

[86] *The Caxtons*, pt. 17, ch. 1.

[87] *The Three Colonies of Australia*, p. 323.

[88] George Crawley to George Henry Gibbs, 11 April 1839. Family letters, vol. XVI (1833-40), Gibbs Papers.

[89] Henry H. Gibbs to Georgiana Polson, 28 July 1842. Family letters, vol. XVII (1841-44), Gibbs Papers.

[90] *Economist*, 16 September 1843.

[91] Ibid., 13 April 1844.

[92] Thompson, *English Landed Society*, p. 21.

[93] See chapter 3 above.

[94] The loss of the American colonies in 1783 and the Canadian rebellions in 1837 reinforced such an outlook, so that by 1847 even the conservative W. E. Gladstone had recognized that democracy was a natural outcome of colonial conditions and experiences. See Knaplund, *Gladstone and Britain's Imperial Policy*, pp. 60-1.

[95] During these short years the Church of England in New South Wales became virtually the established church, in that it was vested with one-seventh of all crown-land in the colony and was given charge over the colony's public schools. Thus the church became potentially wealthy, independent, and through its control over education, influential. In 1829, however, the Church and Schools Corporation's charter was suspended. For full details see, Hartwell, 'The Pastoral Ascendancy, 1820-50' in Greenwood (ed.), *Australia*, pp. 58-61.

[96] Roe, op. cit., pp. 15-16, 64.

[97] Ibid., pp. 15-16.

[98] Ibid., pp. 16, 64.

[99] *Journal of Two Expeditions of Discovery in North-West and Western Australia*, vol. 2, p. 184.

[1] Ibid., pp. 184-5.

[2] Hood, *Australia and the East*, p. 310. See also Mundy, *Our Antipodes*, vol. 1, pp. 283-4.

[3] *The Caxtons*, pt. 17, ch. 1.

[4] Hodgkinson, *Australia from Port Macquarie to Moreton Bay*, p. 145.

[5] C. P. Hodgson, *Reminiscences of Australia*, p. 144.

[6] *The Colonist in Australia*, p. 70.

[7] Notes by Grey on correspondence dealing with the occupation of unsold lands in Australia 1845-6. Colonial Papers—Australia, Grey Papers.

[8] Ch. 39.

[9] Ibid.

[10] Garnett, *Edward Gibbon Wakefield*, p. 80; and Burroughs, *Britain and Australia*, pp. 33-4.

8: *El Dorado 1851–55*

[1] I am indebted to the work of Professor Crawford Goodwin for some of the ideas developed in this chapter. See Goodwin, 'British Economists and Australian Gold', *Journal of Economic History*, vol. 30 (1970), pp. 405-26; and

Goodwin, *The Image of Australia: British Perception of the Australian Economy from the Eighteenth to the Twentieth Century* (Durham N. C., 1974).
2 *Economist,* 27 September 1851.
3 *The Operative,* pt. 8, no. 32 (1851), p. 48.
4 *Economist,* 22 May 1852.
5 *Times,* 13 and 21 May 1852.
6 *Times,* 22 May 1852.
7 *Morning Chronicle,* 2 June 1852; *Spectator,* 22 May and 10 July 1852; *Economist,* 22 May 1852.
8 Pakington to La Trobe, 2 June 1852, CO 411/1.
9 *Times,* 25 June 1852. See also James Maclaren, *The Effect of a Small Fall in the Value of Gold upon Money* (London, 1852), p. 30.
10 'Gold—Emigration—Foreign Dependence—Taxation', *Blackwood's Edinburgh Magazine,* vol. 72, no. 442 (1852), p. 209.
11 *Money and Morals,* p. 183.
12 Ibid., p. 182.
13 'The Old World and the New', *Fraser's Magazine for Town and Country,* vol. 50, no. 300 (1854), p. 305.
14 *Punch or the London Charivari,* vol. 22 (1852), p. 185.
15 'Gold Discoveries', *Quarterly Review,* vol. 91 (1852), p. 520.
16 *Morning Chronicle,* 11 June 1852; *Spectator,* 10 July 1852.
17 Serle, *The Golden Age,* p. 42.
18 'Should our Gold Standard of Value be maintained if Gold becomes depreciated in Consequence of Its Discovery in Australia and California?', *Report of the Twenty-Second Meeting of the British Association for the Advancement of Science,* 1852 (London, 1853), p. 117.
19 *Punch or the London Charivari,* vol. 22 (1852), p. 185.
20 Frank Bower and K. A. H. Egerton, *Dictionary of Economic Terms* (London, 1936), p. 83.
21 Sayers, 'The Question of the Standard in the Eighteen-Fifties', *Economic History (A Supplement to the Economic Journal),* vol. 11, no. 8 (1933), p. 585.
22 *Hansard,* 3rd series, vol. CXXIV, 10 March 1853, col. 1385.
23 Edwin Hodder, *The Life and Work of the Seventh Earl of Shaftesbury, K.G.* 2 vols. (London, 1886), vol. 2, p. 371.
24 'Gold Discoveries', *Q.R.,* vol. 91, 1852, p. 540; see also *Times,* 17 April 1852.
25 *Economist,* 24 July 1852.
26 'On New Supplies of Gold', *Report of the Twenty-Third Meeting of the British Association for the Advancement of Science, 1853* (London, 1854).
27 *Reports on the Condition and Progress of the Colony of Victoria since the Discovery of the Gold-Fields* p. 30.
28 La Trobe to Grey, 10 October 1851, CO 309/2. See also letter from the squatter Hugh Jamieson to Bishop Perry which comments that 'Their services have, during the recent scarcity of labour consequent on the gold discoveries of Australia, been to us and other settlers on the Murray and Darling of great value.' Jamieson to Perry, 10 October 1853, in Bride (ed.), *Letters From Victorian Pioneers,* p. 379.
29 Burroughs, *Britain and Australia,* appendix 1.
30 Pakington to La Trobe, 2 June 1852, CO 411/1.
31 *Household Words,* 17 July 1852.
32 Lubbock, *The Colonial Clippers,* pp. 11-12.
33 'The Extent and the Causes of our Prosperity', *Blackwood's Edinburgh Magazine,* vol. 74, no. 455 (1853), pp. 374-5.
34 R. H. Thornton, *British Shipping,* pp. 43-4.

[35] *Times*, 27 October 1852.

[36] Ibid., 4 November 1852.

[37] 'Gold and Emigration', *F.M.*, vol. 46, no. 272 (1852), pp. 127-38.

[38] *The Operative*, no. 69 (1852), p. 390.

[39] See chapter 3 above.

[40] *Morning Chronicle*, 11 and 28 June 1852.

[41] *Spectator*, 6 March 1852.

[42] William Peter to Pakington, 30 August 1852. Cited in E. Daniel and Annette Potts, 'American Republicanism and the Disturbances on the Victorian Goldfields', *Historical Studies*, vol. 13, no. 50 (1968), p. 145.

[43] Burroughs, *Britain and Australia*, appendix 11.

[44] 'Australia Our Home' (c. 1854) in Anderson, *Farewell to Old England*, p. 189.

[45] *Spectator*, 15 and 22 May 1852. Colonel Mundy also disapproved of the advantages enjoyed by labourers on the goldfields and recognized that prospecting and mining alluvial gold undermined traditional British patterns of social decorum 'nothing indeed, can have a more levelling effect on society than the power of digging gold, for it can be done, for a time, at least, without any capital but that of health and strength; and the man inured to toil, however ignorant, is on more than equal terms with the educated and refined in a pursuit involving so much personal hardship.' Mundy, *Our Antipodes*, vol. 3, p. 309.

[46] *The Three Colonies of Australia*, p. 418.

[47] *Economist*, 27 September 1851.

[48] *Reports on the Condition and Progress of the Colony of Victoria*, p. 71.

[49] *The Land of Promise*, p. 11.

[50] Lubbock, *The Colonial Clippers*, p. 9.

[51] Dobie, *Recollections of a Visit to Port Phillip, Australia in 1852-55*, p. 40.

[52] Hussey, *The Australian Colonies*, p. 33.

[53] *Times*, 7 and 12 May 1852.

[54] *Economist*, 10 June 1854.

[55] Ibid., 20 May 1854.

[56] See chapter 1 above.

[57] *Colonial Policy*, vol. 2, p. 56. Most commentators opposed these views and pointed out that continued transportation was an inducement to crime for it constituted a free trip to the goldfields. See chapter 1 above; and *Spectator*, 21 August 1852; *Morning Chronicle*, 28 December 1852.

[58] Serle, *The Golden Age*, pp. 40-1.

[59] Lancellot, *Australia as It is*, p. 301.

[60] *Times*, 7 May 1852.

[61] *The Gold-Finder of Australia: How he Went, How he Fared and How he Made his Fortune*, p. 53.

[62] Serle, op. cit., pp. 35-6.

[63] *A Lady's Visit to the Gold Diggings of Australia 1852-53*, p. 95. See also an undated entry in a contemporary diary, 'Night-time at the diggings: bonfires, gun-explosions, the crashing of bottles, mixed with the noise of hurdie-gurdies and dog-fights.' McCrae (ed.), *Georgiana's Journal: Melbourne 1841-1865*, pp. 217-18.

[64] D'Ewes, *China and Australia and the Pacific Islands in the Years 1855-56*, pp. 38-9.

[65] *Economist*, 1 January 1853.

[66] *Times*, 7 May 1852.

[67] *Economist*, 25 September 1852.

9:   The Land of Contrarieties

¹ For the ancient belief in the existence of monsters living in the southern hemisphere see, R. Wittkower, 'Marvels of the East, A Study in the History of Monsters', *Journal of the Warburg and Courtauld Institutes*, vol. 5 (1942), pp. 159-97. See also Thomson, *History of Ancient Geography*, p. 389.

² Smith, *European Vision and the South Pacific 1768-1850*, p. 34.

³ *The Present State of Australia*, p. 103.

⁴ *A Voyage round the World, including Travels in Africa, Asia, Australasia, America*, vol. 4, p. 473.

⁵ *Leeds Mercury*, 5 May 1832.

⁶ See chapter 1 above.

⁷ *Mirror of Parliament*, vol. IV, 19 May 1840, p. 3122.

⁸ pp. 87-8.

⁹ Smith, op. cit., p. 34 shows that the idea of antipodal inversion was not confined to Australia, and that it had been applied to Australia because Englishmen were already making use of the concept in a satirical form following the voyage of Sir Joseph Banks and Captain James Cook to the South Seas in 1768-9.

¹⁰ *Globe*, 22 October 1853.

¹¹ *The Contrast or Gone to the Diggings.*

¹² See appendix 1 for full text.

¹³ Lancelott, *Australia as It Is*, pp. 3-4, 41.

¹⁴ *A Sketch of Modern and Ancient Geography for the Use of Schools*, p. 74.

¹⁵ *Poetical Works*, vol. 4, pp. 23, 71-4.

¹⁶ Ibid., p. 11.

¹⁷ *Account of an Expedition to the Interior of New Holland*, p. 1, passim.

¹⁸ *Australia*. op. cit.

¹⁹ Smith, *European Vision and the South Pacific*, pp. 180-201.

²⁰ *Caledonian Mercury*, 18 February 1841; *Morning Chronicle*, 12 May 1845; and Hodgson, *A Lecture on Colonization and Emigration*, p. 29.

²¹ Bathurst to Sir George Murray, 11 November 1822, B. M. Loan 57/64. Cited in McLachlan, 'Bathurst at the Colonial Office, 1812-27: A Reconnaissance', *Historical Studies*, vol. 13, no. 52 (1969), p. 485.

²² 'Discoveries in New South Wales', *Edinburgh Review*, vol. 47, no. 93 (1828), pp. 205-6.

²³ Ibid., pp. 207-9.

²⁴ 'Foreign Relations of Great Britain', *E.R.*, vol. 68, no. 138 (1838), p. 524.

²⁵ 'New South Wales', *B.E.M.*, vol. 44, no. 277 (1838), p. 692. See also *Spectator*, 22 November 1845 for a similar differentiation.

²⁶ Ibid.

²⁷ Ibid., p. 690.

²⁸ *A Lecture on Colonization and Emigration*, p. 29.

²⁹ *The Caxtons*, pt. 17, ch. 2.

³⁰ 'The Navigation of the Antipodes', *Blackwood's Edinburgh Magazine*, vol. 62, no. 385 (1847), p. 533.

³¹ 'Colonization', *Blackwood's Edinburgh Magazine*, vol. 64, no. 393 (1848), p. 66.

³² 'Colonization and the Irish Famine', *Edinburgh Review*, vol. 91, no. 183 (1850), pp. 30-61. This chauvinistic stream of national consciousness clearly foreshadows the truculent jingoism of the period leading up to the outbreak of the Crimean War five years later.

³³ Sturgis, *John Bright and the Empire*, pp. 80, 83, 90-6; and MacDonagh, 'The Anti-Imperialism of Free Trade', *Economic History Review*, vol. 14, no. 3

(1962), p. 500. It should be noted, however, that these criticisms were not applied to India. See Sturgis, op. cit., pp. 22, 38; and MacDonagh, op. cit., pp. 496-7.

[34] *Times,* 25 January 1831, see also *Spectator,* 15 April 1843.

[35] Fieldhouse, *The Colonial Empires,* p. 203.

[36] 'Commercial Policy—Ships, Colonies, and Commerce', *Blackwood's Edinburgh Magazine,* vol. 54, no. 335 (1843), p. 409.

[37] Ibid., p. 411.

[38] 'Emigration or Manufactures?', *Westminster Review,* vol. 40, no. 1 (1843), pp. 118-19. See also similar arguments presented by [Aubrey De Vere], 'Colonization and the Irish Famine', *Edinburgh Review,* vol. 91, no. 183 (1850), p. 34. These views were shown to be fundamentally unsound in 1858, when Canada did raise a tariff against British goods.

[39] Roe, *Quest for Authority in Eastern Australia,* pp. 71-2.

[40] John M. Ward, 'Historiography', in McLeod, (ed.), *The Pattern of Australian Culture,* p. 202.

[41] *The Struggle for Mastery in Europe 1848-1918* (Oxford, 1954), pp. 283, 293-303, 363-4.

[42] Read, *Press and People 1790-1850,* p. 20.

[43] Bodelsen, *Studies in Mid-Victorian Imperialism,* pp. 13-22; Schuyler, *The Fall of the Old Colonial System,* p. 70, passim.

[44] J. A. Williamson, *A Short History of British Expansion* (London, 1922); Marriott, *The Evolution of the British Empire and Commonwealth*; Newton, *A Hundred Years of the British Empire*; Carrington, *The British Overseas: Exploits of a Nation of Shopkeepers*; Burt, *The Evolution of the British Empire and Commonwealth.* A revisionist interpretation has also been advanced by historians who do not agree with the concept of mid-Victorian anti-imperialism. See Knorr, *British Colonial Theories 1570-1850*; Gallagher and Robinson, 'The Imperialism of Free Trade', *Economic History Review,* vol. 6, no. 1 (1953); and Burroughs, *British Attitudes Towards Canada.*

[45] This is the traditional interpretation, see F. K. Crowley, 'The Foundation Years, 1788-1821', in Greenwood (ed.), *Australia: A Social and Political History,* p. 5.

[46] Blainey, *The Tyranny of Distance,* pp. 32-3.

[47] Greenwood, *Early American-Australian Relations . . . to 1830,* p. 55.

[48] Michael Roe 'Australia's Place in the Swing to the East', *Historical Studies, Australia and New Zealand,* vol. 8, no. 30 (1958), pp. 202-13.

[49] Barnard, *The Australian Wool Market 1840-1900,* p. 26; Eric M. Sigsworth, *Black Dyke Mills: A History* (Liverpool, 1958), pp. 52-4.

[50] Barnard, op. cit., pp. 27-9.

[51] Himmelfarb, *Victorian Minds,* p. xi. See also Burroughs, *British Attitudes Towards Canada,* p. 149.

[52] *Our Antipodes,* vol. 3, p. 411.

Select Bibliography

A. PRIMARY SOURCES
1. Manuscript Collections

(a) *Colonial Office Records in the Public Record Office, London*
The most valuable series for each colony is that described as Correspondence, which includes dispatches from governors, letters from officials, departments and interested individuals, together with enclosures, minutes, memoranda, reports, and drafts of letters-out. The series of Entry Books contains copies of all outgoing correspondence, though not of enclosures.

Consulted for the period 1828-1855.

New South Wales: CO 201 Original Correspondence; CO 202 Entry Books

Van Diemen's Land: CO 280 Original Correspondence; CO 408 Entry Books

Western Australia: CO 18 Original Correspondence; CO 397 Entry Books

South Australia: CO 13 Original Correspondence; CO 396 Entry Books

Victoria: CO 309 Original Correspondence; CO 411 Entry Books

Emigration: CO 385 Entry Books; CO 386 Entry Books and Correspondence Registers from the South Australian Commissioners and the Land and Emigration Commissioners.

(b) *Missionary Society Papers*
Church Missionary Society Papers, C.H./L 1-3 London.

London Missionary Society Papers, Tyermann and Bennet Deputation and Australian Papers, London.

United Society for the Propagation of the Gospel Papers, Australian
  Papers, London.

(c) *Private Papers*

Fulham Papers, United Society for the Propagation of the Gospel,
  London. Papers of Bishop Howley.
Gibbs Papers, MSS. 11,021/15-19; 11,036; 11,053/4-14; Guildhall
  Library, London. Correspondence and miscellaneous papers of
  Henry Hucks Gibbs.
Grey Papers, University of Durham. Papers of the third Earl Grey.
Monteagle Papers, MSS. 427; 545-53; 555-62; 11,140; 13,365; 13,374;
  13,376; 13,377; 13,382; 13,400; National Library of Ireland, Dublin,
  Eire. Papers of the first Baron Monteagle.
Ripon Papers, B.M. Add. MSS. 40,862; 40,878-80; British Museum,
  London. Papers of Viscount Goderich, first Marquis of Ripon, while
  colonial secretary 1830-3.
Russell Papers, P.R.O. 30/22; Public Record Office, London. Papers of
  Lord John Russell.
Wakefield Papers, B.M. Add. MSS. 35,261; British Museum, London.
  Letters of Edward Gibbon Wakefield, mostly relating to New
  Zealand.

2. PRINTED SOURCES

(a) *Parliamentary*

Great Britain: *Parliamentary Papers* relating to Australia 1828-55.
Great Britain: *Hansard: Parliamentary Debates* relating to Australia
  1828-55. 2nd series to July 1830, and 3rd series thereafter to 1855.
Mirror of Parliament, debates relating to Australia 1828-41.

(b) *Newspapers and Periodicals*

Annual Register, 1828-55.
Asiatic Journal and Monthly Register, 1828-45.
Blackwood's Edinburgh Magazine, 1828-55.
Caledonian Mercury, 1828-55.
Cobbett's Two-Penny Trash; or Politics for the Poor, 1831-32.
Colonial and Asiatic Review, 1852-53.
Colonial Gazette, 1838-47.
Courier, 1828-42.
Economist, 1843-55.
Edinburgh Evening Courant, 1828-55.
Edinburgh Review, 1828-55.
Ethnological Journal, 1848-49.
Evening Packet, 1828-55.
Examiner, 1828-55.

Fraser's Magazine for Town and Country, 1830-55.
General Advertiser, 1828-55.
Gentleman's Magazine, 1828-55.
Globe and Traveller, 1828-55.
Household Words, 1850-55.
Leeds Mercury, 1828-55.
London Review, 1835-36.
Manchester Courier and Lancashire General Advertiser, 1828-55.
Metropolitan Magazine, 1834-37.
Morning Chronicle, 1828-55.
New Monthly Magazine and Humorist, 1828-55.
Operative, 1838-39.
The Operative, 1851-52.
Punch or the London Charivari, 1841-55.
Quarterly Review, 1828-55.
Reports of Meetings, British Association for Advancement of Science, 1831-55.
Sidney's Emigrant's Journal and Traveller's Magazine, 1849-50.
Simmonds's Colonial Magazine and Foreign Miscellany, 1844-52.
Spectator, 1828-55.
Standard, 1828-55.
Times, 1828-55.
Westminster Review, 1828-55.

(c) *Collections of Documents and Works of Reference*

Anderson, H., *Farewell to Old England: A Broadside History of Early Australia*. London, 1964.

Bassett, A. T. (ed.), *Gladstone's Speeches*. London, 1916.

Bell, K. N. and Morrell, W. P., *Select Documents on British Colonial Policy 1830-1860*. Oxford, 1928.

Bride, T. F. (ed.), *Letters from Victorian Pioneers: Being a Series of Papers on the early Occupation of the Colony, etc., addressed by Victorian Pioneers to His Excellency Charles Joseph LaTrobe, Esq., Lieutenant-Governor of the Colony of Victoria*. Melbourne, 1898 and 1969.

Burroughs, p. (ed.), *The Colonial Reformers and Canada 1830-1849: Selections from Documents and Publications of the Times*. Toronto, 1969.

Clark, C. M. H., *Select Documents in Australian History 1788-1850*. Sydney, 1950.

Dictionary of National Biography.

Ferguson, J. A., *Bibliography of Australia*. 6 vols. Sydney, 1941-65.

Fetter, F. W., 'The Economic Articles in the *Westminster Review* and their Authors', *Journal of Political Economy*, vol. 70, no. 6, 1962.

Greenway, J., *Bibliography of the Australian Aborigines and the Native Peoples of Torres Strait to 1959*. Sydney, 1963.

Henderson, W. (ed.), *Victorian Street Ballads: A Selection of Popular Ballads sold in the Street in the Nineteenth Century*. London, 1937.

Hewison, A. (ed.), *The Macquarie Decade: Documents Illustrating the History of New South Wales, 1810-1821*. Melbourne, 1972.

Hope, P. (ed.), *The Voyage of the Africaine: A Collection of Journals, Letters and Extracts from Contemporary Publications*. South Yarra, 1968.

Houghton, W. E. (ed.), *The Wellesley Index to Victorian Periodicals 1824-1900*. Toronto, 1966.

Hill, W., *The Overseas Empire in Fiction: An annotated Bibliography*. London, 1930.

Ingleton, G. C., *True Patriots All: or News from early Australia as told in a Collection of Broadsides*. Sydney, 1952.

Kessing, N. (ed.), *History of the Australian Gold Rushes by Those who were There*. Melbourne, 1971.

Mayer, H. (ed.), *Marx, Engels and Australia*. Melbourne, 1964.

Pike, D. (ed.), *Australian Dictionary of Biography 1788-1850*. 2 vols., Melbourne, 1950.

Pike, E. R. (ed.), *Human Documents of the Victorian Age 1850-1875*. London, 1967.

Spence, S. A., *A Bibliography of selected early Books and Pamphlets relating to Australia 1610-1880, with Supplement and Extension from 1881-1900*. London, 1955.

Watson, F. (ed.), *Historical Records of Australia*, ser. 1, 26 vols. Dispatches to and from England 1788-1848. Sydney, 1914.

Winks, R. W. (ed.), *The Historiography of the British Empire—Commonwealth: Trends, Interpretations and Resources*. Durham, 1966.

Young, G. M. and Handcock, W. D. (eds.), *English Historical Documents 1833-1874*. London, 1956.

(d) *Contemporary Printed Works*

Adderley, C. B., *The Australian Colonies Government Bill Discussed*. London, 1849.

——, *Some Reflections on the Speech of the Right Hon. Lord John Russell on Colonial Policy*. London, 1850.

——, *Transportation not Necessary*. London, 1851.

Anley, Mrs C., *The Prisoners of Australia: A Narrative*. London, 1841.

Arthur, G., *Defence of Transportation in Reply to the Archbishop of Dublin*. London, 1835.

Aspin, J., *Cosmorama: A View of the Costumes and Peculiarities of all Nations*. London, 1826.

Australia a Mistake. New Brunswick for the Emigrant. London, 1855.

Backhouse, J., *A Narrative of a Visit to the Australian Colonies.* London, 1843.

Breton, R. N., *Excursions in New South Wales, Western Australia, and Van Diemen's Land, during the Years 1830, 1831, 1832 and 1833.* London, 1834.

Buller, C., *Responsible Government for Colonies.* London, 1840.

Butler, S., *A Sketch of Modern and Ancient Geography for the Use of Schools.* London, 1849.

Capper, J., *Australia as a Field for Capital, Skill, and Labour.* London, 1854.

Clacy, Mrs C., *A Lady's Visit to the Gold Diggings of Australia 1852-53.* London, 1853.

Cobbett, W., *The Emigrant's Guide in Ten Letters addressed to the Tax-Payers of England.* London, 1830.

The Contrast or Gone to the Diggings. London, 1854.

Cooke, W. B., *Colonial Policy, with Hints upon the Formation of Military Settlements.* London, 1835.

Cozens, C., *Adventures of a Guardsman.* London, 1848.

Cunningham, P., *Two Years in New South Wales; comprising Sketches of the actual State of Society in that Colony; of its perculiar Advantages to Emigrants; of its Topography, Natural History, Etc., Etc.* 2 vols. London, 1827 and Melbourne, 1966.

Curr, E. M., *Recollections of Squatting in Victoria then called the Port Phillip District, 1841-1851.* Melbourne, 1883.

Darwin, C., *Journal of Researches into the Geology and Natural History of the Various Countries visited during the Voyage of H.M.S. Beagle round the World.* London, 1906.

Dawson, R., *The Present State of Australia.* London, 1831.

D'Ewes, J., *China and Australia and the Pacific Islands in the Years 1855-56.* London, 1857.

Dixon, J., *The Condition and Capabilities of Van Diemen's Land as a Place of Emigration.* London, 1839.

Dobie, W. W., *Recollections of a Visit to Port Phillip Australia in 1852-55.* Glasgow, 1856.

Dutton, F., *South Australia and its Mines.* London, 1846.

Fletcher, J., *Letter to the Right Hon. Earl Grey on the Subject of Emigration; with a Short History of the Colony of Port Phillip.* Edinburgh, 1847.

Ford, C. P., *The Emigrant Family.* London, 1851.

——, *The Sunday-School Boy in Australia.* London, 1851.

Fox, Lady M. (ed.), *Account of an Expedition to the Interior of New Holland.* London, 1837.

Franklin, J., *Narrative of some Passages in the History of Van Diemen's Land.* London, 1845.

Gill, A., *Western Australia, containing a Statement of the Condition and Prospects of that Colony, and some Account of the Western Australian Company's Settlement of Australind.* London, 1842.

Grey, G., *Journal of Two Expeditions of Discovery in North-west and Western Australia.* 2 vols. London, 1841.

Grey, Earl, *Speech on Emigration to Australia and Reply on the same Subject to Lord Monteagle.* London, 1848.

——, *The Colonial Policy of Lord John Russell's Administration.* 2 vols. London, 1853.

Griffith, C., *The Present State and Prospects of the Port Phillip District of New South Wales.* Dublin, 1845.

Hardy, H. H., *Australia: A Prize Poem recited at Rugby School.* Rugby, 1843.

[Harris, A.?], *Settlers and Convicts; or Recollections of Sixteen Years Labour in the Australian Backwoods.* London, 1847 and Melbourne, 1954.

Harris, A., *Martin Beck: or the Story of an Australian Settler.* London, 1852.

Hill, R., *Home Colonies: Sketch of a Plan for the gradual Extinction of the Pauperism and for the Diminution of Crime.* London, 1832.

Hodgkinson, C., *Australia from Port Macquarie to Moreton Bay.* London, 1845.

Hodgson, A., *A Lecture on Colonization and Emigration.* London, 1849.

Hodgson, C. P., *Reminiscences of Australia.* London, 1846.

Holman, J., *A Voyage round the World, including Travels in Africa, Asia, Australia, America.* 4 vols. London, 1834.

Hood, J., *Australia and the East.* London, 1843.

Howitt, W., *Colonization and Christianity: A popular History of the Treatment of the Natives by the Europeans in all their Colonies.* London, 1838.

Horton, R. W., *Inquiry into the Causes and Remedies of Pauperism.* London, 1830.

Hussey, H., *The Australian Colonies.* London, 1855.

Irwin, F. C., *The State and Position of Western Australia; commonly called the Swan-River Settlement.* London, 1835.

Kingston, W. H. G., *The British Colonies Described; with Advice to those who cannot obtain Employment at Home.* London, 1851.

K. E. F., *A Letter to Young Female Emigrants proceeding to Australia.* London, 1850.

——, *Parting Words to Emigrant Parents.* London, 1850.

Knight, C., *The Library Cyclopedia of Political and Forensic Knowledge.* London, 1848.

Lalor, J., *Money and Morals: A Book for the Times.* London, 1852.

Lancelott, F., *Australia as It is: Its Settlements, Farms and Gold Fields.* London, 1852.

The Land of Contrarieties. London, c. 1850.

Lang, J. D., *An Historical and Statistical Account of New South Wales, both as a Penal Settlement and as a British Colony.* 3rd edition. 2 vols. London, 1840.

——, *Cooksland in North-Eastern Australia; the future Cotton-Field of Great Britain: its Characteristics and Capabilities for European Colonization with a Disquisition on the Origin, Manners, and Customs of the Aborigines.* London, 1847.

Leakey, C. W., *Lyra Australis; or Attempts to sing in a Strange Land.* London, 1854.

Lee, Mrs R., *Adventures in Australia; or the Wanderings of Captain Spencer in the Bush and the Wilds.* London, 1851.

Lytton, E. B., *The Caxtons.* London, 1849.

McCombie, T., *The Colonist in Australia: or the Adventures of Godfrey Arabin.* London, 1850.

McCrae, H. (ed.), *Georgiana's Journal: Melbourne 1841-1865.* Sydney, 1966.

McCulloch, J. R., *A Dictionary, Geographical, Statistical and Historical.* 2 vols. London, 1847.

——, *A Treatise on the Circumstances which determine the Rate of Wages and the Condition of the Labouring Classes.* London, 1854.

Matthew, P., *Emigration Fields.* Edinburgh, 1839.

Merivale, H., *Lectures on Colonization and Colonies.* London, 1861.

Mill, J. S., *Principles of Political Economy with some of their Applications to Social Philosophy.* London, 1848.

Mitchell, T. L., *The Journal of an Expedition into Tropical Australia in Search of a Route from Sydney to the Gulf of Carpentaria.* London, 1848.

Montgomery, J., *Poetical Works.* 4 vols. Boston, 1828.

Mortimer, Mrs M., *Far Off: or Asia and Australia described, with Anecdotes and numerous Illustrations.* London, 1852.

Mundy, G. C., *Our Antipodes, or Residence and Rambles in the Australasian Colonies, with a Glimpse of the Gold Fields.* 3 vols. London, 1852.

My Secret Life. 11 vols. Amsterdam, 1888 and New York, 1966.

Nott, J. C. and Gliddon, G. R., *Types of Mankind: or Ethnological Researches based upon the Ancient Monuments, Paintings, Sculptures, and Crania of Races, and upon their Natural, Geographical, Philological logical and Biblical History.* London, 1853.

Prichard, M. F. L. (ed.), *The Collected Works of Edward Gibbon Wakefield.* London, 1968.

Pridden, W., *Australia, its History and Present Condition.* London, 1843.

Quennell, P. (ed.), *Mayhew's London.* London, 1959.

Reade, C., *Gold! A Drama in Five Acts.* London, 1853.

Roebuck, J. A., *The Colonies of England: A Plan for the Government of some Portion of our Colonial Possessions.* London, 1849.

Rowcroft, C., *Tales of the Colonies; or the Adventures of an Emigrant.* London, 1845.

——, *The Bushranger of Van Diemen's Land.* London, 1846.

Shaw, W., *Golden Dreams and Waking Realities; being the Adventures of a Gold-Seeker in California and the Pacific Islands.* London, 1851.

——, *The Land of Promise; or my Impressions of Australia.* London, 1854.

Sherer, J. (ed.), *The Gold-Finder of Australia: How he Went, How he Fared and How he made his Fortune.* London, 1853.

Sidney, S., *A Voice from the Far Interior of Australia.* London, 1847.

——, *Sidney's Australian Handbook.* London, 1848.

——, *The Three Colonies of Australia: New South Wales, Victoria, South Australia.* London, 1852.

——, Gallops and Gossips in the Bush of Australia; or Passages in the Life of Alfred Barnard. London, 1854.

Sloss, O. J. and Wallis, J. P. R. (eds.), *The Prophetic Writings of William Blake.* 2 vols. Oxford, 1964.

Southey, T., *Observations addressed to the Wool Growers of Australia and Tasmania.* London, 1831.

Stanley, A. P., *The Life and Correspondence of Thomas Arnold.* London, 1846.

Strachey, L. and Fulford, R. (eds.), *The Greville Memoirs 1814-1860.* 8 vols. London, 1938.

Tennant, C., *Letters forming Part of a Correspondence with Nassau William Senior concerning Systematic Colonization.* London, 1831.

Thring, H., *The Supremacy of Great Britain not inconsistent with Self-Government for the Colonies.* London, 1851.

Torrens, R., *Systematic Colonization: Ireland saved without Cost to the Imperial Treasury.* London, 1847.

——, *The Principles and Practical Operation of Sir Robert Peel's Act of 1844 explained and defended: with additional Chapters on Money, the Gold Discoveries and International Exchange.* London, 1857.

Vattel, de E., *The Law of Nations or the Principles of Natural Law applied to the Conduct and to the Affairs of Nations and of Sovereigns.* Charles Fenwick (tr.), Neuchatel, 1758 and Washington, 1916.

Wakefield, E. G., *A Letter from Sydney, the Principal Town of Australasia.* London, 1829.

——, *Facts relating to the Punishment of Death in the Metropolis.* London, 1831.

——, *England and America: the Social and Political State of both Nations.* 2 vols. London, 1833.

——, *Outline of a Plan for a proposed Colony in South Australia.* London, 1834.

——, *A View of the Art of Colonization, Letters between a Statesman and a Colonist.* London, 1849.

Westgarth, W., *Reports on the Condition and Progress of the Colony of Victoria since the Discovery of the Gold-Fields.* Edinburgh, 1853.

Whately, R., *Thoughts on Secondary Punishments in a Letter to Earl Grey.* London, 1832.

Wilkinson, G. B., *A Letter to the Right Hon. Lord Ashley, on the Necessity of an Extended Government Plan of Emigration to the Australian Colonies.* London, 1848.

——, *The Working Man's Handbook to South Australia.* London, 1849.

Wilson, T. B., *Narrative of a Voyage round the World.* London, 1835.

The Young Emigrants, or a Voyage to Australia. London, 1850.

B. SECONDARY SOURCES

Abbott, G. J., 'The Emigration to Valparaiso in 1843', *Labour History*, no. 19 (1970), pp. 1-16.

Allen, W. O. B. and McClure, E., *Two Hundred Years: The History of the Society for Promoting Christian Knowledge 1698-1898.* New York, 1898.

Barnard, A., *The Australian Wool Market 1840-1900.* Melbourne, 1958.

Barron, T. and Cable, K. J., 'The Diary of James Stephen 1846', *Historical Studies*, vol. 13, no. 52 (1969), pp. 503-10.

Bassett, M., *The Hentys: An Australian Colonial Tapestry.* Melbourne, 1962.

Battye, J. S., *Western Australia: A History from its Discovery to the Inauguration of the Commonwealth.* Oxford, 1924.

Baugh, A. C. (ed.), *A Literary History of England.* New York, 1948.

Beaglehole, J. C., 'The Colonial Office 1782-1854', *Historical Studies, Australia and New Zealand*, vol. 1, no. 3 (1941), pp. 170-89.

Bergman, G. F. J., and Levi, J. S., *Australian Genesis: Jewish Convicts and Settlers 1788-1850.* Sydney, 1974.

Birch, A. H., *Representative and Responsible Government: An Essay on the British Constitution.* London, 1965.

Blainey, G., *The Tyranny of Distance: How Distance shaped Australia's History.* Melbourne, 1966.

Bloomfield, P., *Edward Gibbon Wakefield, Builder of the British Commonwealth.* London, 1961.

Bodelsen, C. A., *Studies in Mid-Victorian Imperialism.* Copenhagen, 1924 and London, 1960.

Bolt, C., *Victorian Attitudes to Race.* London, 1971.

Bolton, G. C., 'The Idea of a Colonial Gentry', *Historical Studies,* vol. 13, no. 51 (1968), pp. 307-28.

Bolton, G., *Britain's Legacy Overseas.* Oxford, 1973.

Bonner, W. H., *Captain William Dampier, Buccaneer-Author.* Stanford, 1934.

Borrow, T., *Lieutenant-Colonel George Gawler K.H. Governor and Commander-in-Chief of South Australia 1838-1841: With a Bibliography designed to show the Means by which the Introduction into Australia of the Wakefield System of Free Colonization was successfully retarded.* Adelaide, 1955.

Bridges, B., 'The Aborigines and the Land Question in New South Wales', *Journal of the Royal Australian Historical Society,* vol. 56 (1970), pp. 92-110.

Briggs, A. and Savill, J. (eds.), *Essays in Labour History.* London, 1960.

Brinton, C., *The Political Ideas of the English Romanticists.* New York, 1962.

British Broadcasting Corporation (ed.), *Ideas and Beliefs of the Victorians: An Historic Revaluation of the Victorian Age.* London, 1949.

Burroughs, P., *Britain and Australia 1831-1855: A Study in Imperial Relations and Crown Lands Administration.* Oxford, 1967.

——, *British Attitudes towards Canada 1822-1849.* Scarborough, 1971.

——, *The Canadian Crisis and British Colonial Policy.* London, 1972.

Burt, A. L., *The Evolution of the British Empire and Commonwealth.* New York, 1956.

Butlin, S. J., *Foundations of the Australian Monetary System 1788-1851.* Melbourne, 1953.

——, *Australia and New Zealand Bank: The Bank of Australasia and the Union Bank of Australia Limited 1828-1951.* Croydon, 1961.

Carrington, C. E., *The British Overseas: Exploits of a Nation of Shopkeepers.* pt. 1. Cambridge, 1950.

Carrothers, W. A., *Emigration from the British Isles.* London, 1929.

Castles, A. C., *An Introduction to Australia Legal History.* Sydney, 1971.

Cell, J. W., 'The Colonial Office in the 1850's', Historical Studies, vol. 12, no. 45 (1965), pp. 43-56.

——, *British Colonial Administration in the Mid-Nineteenth Century: The Policy-Making Process.* New Haven, 1970.

Clark, C. M. H., *A Short History of Australia.* New York, 1963.

——, *A History of Australia*. 3 vols. Melbourne, 1962, 1968, and 1973.

Clark, G. S. R. K., *An Expanding Society: Britain 1830-1900*. Cambridge, 1967.

Clarke, M. L., *George Grote: A Biography*. London 1962.

Conacher, J. B., *The Aberdeen Coalition 1852-1855: A Study in Mid-Nineteenth Century Party Politics*. Cambridge, 1968.

Crook, D. P., *American Democracy in English Politics 1815-1850*. Oxford, 1965.

Coughlan, N., 'The Coming of the Irish to Victoria', *Historical Studies*, vol. 12, no. 45 (1965), pp. 68-85.

Crawford, R. M., *Australia*. London, 1961.

Crewe, Q., *Frontiers of Privilege: A Century of Social Conflict as reflected in 'The Queen'*. London, 1961.

Crowley, F. K., *Australia's Western Third: A History of Western Australia from the First Settlements to Modern Times*. London, 1960.

——, *A Short History of Western Australia*. Melbourne, 1961.

Crowley, F. (ed.), *A New History of Australia*. Melbourne, 1974.

Cumpston, J. H. L., *Thomas Mitchell: Surveyor General and Explorer*. Oxford, 1955.

Curtin, P. D., *The Image of Africa: British Ideas and Action 1780-1850*. London, 1965.

Davies, J. D., *Phrenology, Fad and Science: A Nineteenth Century American Crusade*. New Haven, 1955.

Davis, J. C., 'Utopia and History', *Historical Studies*, vol. 13, no. 50 (1967), pp. 165-76.

Denholm, D., 'Port Arthur: The Men and the Myth', *Historical Studies*, vol. 14, no. 55 (1970), pp. 406-23.

Donaldson, G., *The Scots Overseas*. London, 1966.

Eddy, J. J., *Britain and the Australian Colonies 1818-1831: The Technique of Government*. Oxford, 1969.

Eisenstadt, S. N., *The Decline of Empires*. Englewood Cliffs, 1967.

Ellegard, A., 'The Readership of the Periodical Press in Mid-Victorian Britain', *Goteborgs Universitets Arsskrift*, vol. 63 (1957), pp. 3-38.

Ellis, M. H., *Lachlan Macquarie: His Life, Adventures and Times*. Sydney, 1952.

Erdman, D., *Blake, Prophet against Empire: A Poet's Interpretation of the History of his own Times*. Princeton, 1954.

Fairchild, H. N., *The Romantic Quest*. Philadelphia, 1931.

Fetter, F. W., *Development of British Monetary Orthodoxy 1797-1875*. Cambridge, 1965.

Fieldhouse, D. K., *The Colonial Empires: A Comparative Survey from the Eighteenth Century*. London, 1966.

Fingard, J., *The Anglican Design in Loyalist Nova Scotia 1783-1816*. London, 1972.

Finniss, B. T., *The Constitutional History of South Australia.* Adelaide, 1886.

Fitzpatrick, B., *The British Empire in Australia: An Economic History 1834-1939.* Melbourne, 1949.

Fitzpatrick, K., *Sir John Franklin in Tasmania 1837-1843.* Melbourne, 1949.

Flett, J., *The History of Gold Discovery in Victoria.* Melbourne, 1970.

Forsyth, W. D., *Governor Arthur's Convict System: Van Diemen's Land 1824-36.* Sydney, 1970.

Foxcroft, E. J. B., *Australian Native Policy.* Melbourne, 1941.

Friederich, W. P., *Australia in Western Imaginative Prose Writings.* Chapel Hill, 1967.

Galbraith, J. S., 'Myths of the "Little England" Era', *American Historical Review,* vol. 67 (1961), pp. 34-48.

Gallagher, J. and Robinson, R., 'The Imperialism of Free Trade', *Economic History Review,* vol. 6, no. 1 (1953), pp. 1-15.

Garnett, R., *Edward Gibbon Wakefield: The Colonization of South Australia and New Zealand.* London, 1898.

Gollan, R., 'Nationalism and Politics in Australia before 1855', *Australian Journal of Politics and History,* vol. 1, no. 1 (1955), pp. 38-49.

Goodwin, C., 'British Economists and Australian Gold', *Journal of Economic History,* vol. 30 (1970), pp. 405-26.

Graham, G. S., *The Politics of Naval Supremacy: Studies in British Maritime Ascendancy.* Cambridge, 1965.

Greenwood, G., *Early American-Australian Relations from the Arrival of the Spaniards in America to the Close of 1830.* Melbourne, 1944.

Greenwood, G. (ed.), *Australia: A Social and Political History.* Sydney, 1955.

Gross, J., *The Rise and Fall of the Man of Letters: English Literary Life since 1800.* Harmondsworth, 1973.

Hamburger, J., *Intellectuals in Politics: John Stuart Mill and the Philosophic Radicals.* New Haven, 1965.

Harrison, J. F. C., *Robert Owen and the Owenites in Britain and America: The Quest for the New Moral World.* London, 1969.

——, *The Early Victorians 1832-1851.* London, 1971.

Hasluck, P., *Black Australians: A Survey of Native Policy in Western Australia 1829-1897.* Melbourne, 1942.

Hattersley, A. F., *The Convict Crisis and the Growth of Unity: Resistance to Transportation in South Africa and Australia 1848-1853.* Cape Town, 1965.

Helm, P. J., *Modern British History: Part One 1815-1914.* London, 1965.

Higham, C. S. S., 'Sir Henry Taylor and the Establishment of Crown

Colony Government in the West Indies', *Scottish Historical Review*, vol. 23, no. 89 (1926), pp. 92-6.

Higham, C. S. S., 'The General Assembly of the Leeward Islands, Pt. 2', *English Historical Review*, vol. 41, no. 163 (1926), pp. 366-88.

Himmelfarb, G., *Victorian Minds*. New York, 1968.

Hoare, M., *Norfolk Island: An Outline of its History 1774-1968*. St. Lucia, 1969.

Hobsbawm, E. J., *Industry and Empire: An Economic History of Britain since 1750*. London, 1969.

Hodder, E., *George Fife Angas: Father and Founder of South Australia*. London, 1891.

Holthouse, H., *Up Rode the Squatter*. Sydney, 1970.

Houghton, W. E., *The Victorian Frame of Mind 1830-1870*. New Haven, 1957.

Howe, S., *Novels of Empire*. New York, 1949.

Hurwitz, E. F., *Politics and the Public Conscience: Slave Emancipation and the Abolitionist Movement in Britain*. London, 1973.

Ingham, S. M., 'A Footnote to Transportation to N.S.W. James Ingham 1824-1848', *Historical Studies, Australia and New Zealand*, vol. 12, no. 48 (1967), pp. 522-40.

Inglis, K. S., *The Australian Colonists: An Exploration of Social History 1788-1870*. Melbourne, 1974.

Jeans, D. N., 'Crown Land Sales and the Accommodation of the small Settler in N.S.W. 1825-1842', *Historical Studies, Australia and New Zealand*, vol. 12, no. 46 (1966), pp. 205-12.

Johnston, H. J. M., *British Emigration Policy 1815-1830: 'Shovelling out Paupers'*. Oxford, 1972.

Jones, W. D., *Prosperity Robinson: The Life of Viscount Goderich 1782-1859*. London, 1967.

Keith, A. B. (ed.), *Speeches and Documents on British Colonial Policy 1763-1917*. London, 1966.

Kiddle, M., 'Caroline Chisholm and Charles Dickens', *Historical Studies, Australia and New Zealand*, vol. 3, no. 10 (1945), pp. 77-94.

Kiernan, V. G., *The Lords of Human Kind: European Attitudes to the Outside World in the Imperial Age*. Harmondsworth, 1972.

Knaplund, P., *Gladstone and Britain's Imperial Policy*. London, 1927 and 1966.

Knight, R., *Illiberal Liberal: Robert Lowe in New South Wales 1842-1850*. Melbourne, 1966.

Knorr, K. E., *British Colonial Theories 1570-1850*. Toronto, 1944.

Knox, B. A., 'Moreton Bay Separation: A Problem of Imperial Government 1825-1856', *Historical Studies*, vol. 14, no. 56 (1971), pp. 561-78.

Knox, B. A., 'The Rise of Colonial Federation as an Object of British

Policy 1850-1870', *Journal of British Studies*, vol. 11, no. 1 (1971), pp. 92-112.

Labilliere, F. P., *Early History of the Colony of Victoria from its Discovery to its Establishment as a Self-Governing Province of the British Empire*. 2 vols. London, 1878.

La Nauze, J. A., 'The Gold Rushes and Australian Politics', *Australian Journal of Politics and History*, vol. 13, no. 1 (1967), pp. 90-4.

Lansbury, C., *Arcady in Australia: The Evocation of Australia in Nineteenth Century English Literature*. Melbourne, 1970.

Laver, J., *The Age of Optimism: Manners and Morals 1848-1914*. London, 1966.

Levy, M. C. I., *Governor George Arthur: A Colonial Benevolent Despot*. Melbourne, 1953.

Lubbock, B., *The Colonial Clippers*. Glasgow, 1921.

McCulloch, S. C., 'Unguarded Comments on the Administration of New South Wales 1839-46: The Gipps-La Trobe Private Correspondence', *Historical Studies, Australia and New Zealand*, vol. 9, no. 33 (1959), pp. 30-45.

MacDonagh, O., *A Pattern of Government Growth 1800-60: The Passenger Acts and their Enforcement*. London, 1961.

——, 'The Anti-Imperialism of Free Trade', *Economic History Review*, vol. 14, no. 3 (1962), pp. 489-501.

McIntyre, W. D., *The Imperial Frontier in the Tropics 1865-75: A Study of British Colonial Policy in West Africa, Malaya and the South Pacific in the Age of Gladstone and Disraeli*. London, 1967.

Mack, E. C., *Public Schools and British Opinion 1780 to 1860: An Examination of the Relationship between Contemporary Ideas and the Evolution of an English Institution*. London, 1938.

Mack, E. C. and Armytage, W. H. G., *Thomas Hughes*. London, 1952.

Mackerness, E. D., *A Social History of English Music*. London, 1964.

McLachlan, N. D., 'Bathurst at the Colonial Office 1812-27: a Reconnaissance', *Historical Studies, Australia and New Zealand*, vol. 13, no. 52 (1969), pp. 477-502.

McLeod, A. L. (ed.), *The Pattern of Australian Culture*. New York, 1963.

Macmillan, D. S., *The Debtor's War: Scottish Capitalists and the Economic Crisis in Australia 1841-1846*. Melbourne, 1960.

——, *Scotland and Australia 1788-1850: Emigration, Commerce and Investment*. Oxford, 1967.

Madgwick, R. B., *Immigration into Eastern Australia 1788-1851*. London, 1937.

Manning, H. T., 'Who ran the British Empire 1830-1850?', *Journal of British Studies*, vol. 5, no. 1 (1965), pp. 88-121.

Mansergh, N., *The Commonwealth Experience*. London, 1969.

Marchant, P. D., 'Social Darwinism', *Australian Journal of Politics and History*, vol. 3, no. 1 (1957), pp. 46-59.

Marcus, S., *The Other Victorians: A Study of Sexuality and Pornography in Mid-Nineteenth-Century England*. New York, 1966.

Marriott, J. A. R., *The Evolution of the British Empire and Commonwealth*. London, 1939.

Martin, G., *The Durham Report and British Policy: A Critical Essay*. Cambridge, 1972.

Mason, P., *Patterns of Dominance*. London, 1970.

Melbourne, A. C. V., *Early Constitutional Development in Australia: New South Wales 1780-1856; Queensland 1859-1922*. 2nd ed. Melbourne, 1963.

Mellor, G. R., *British Imperial Trusteeship 1783-1850*. London, 1951.

Mills, R. C., *The Colonisation of Australia 1829-1842: The Wakefield Experiment in Empire Building*. London, 1915 and 1968.

Molony, J. N., *An Architect of Freedom: John Hubert Plunkett in New South Wales 1832-1869*. Canberra, 1973.

Morrell, W. P., *British Colonial Policy in the Age of Peel and Russell*. Oxford, 1930.

Mulvaney, D. J., 'The Australian Aborigines 1606-1929. Opinion and Fieldwork, Pt. 1: 1606-1859', *Historical Studies, Australia and New Zealand*, vol. 8, no. 30 (1958), pp. 131-51.

Nadel, G., *Australia's Colonial Culture: Ideas, Men and Institutions in Mid-Nineteenth Century Eastern Australia*. Melbourne, 1957.

Neale, R. S., 'Roebuck's Constitution and the Durham Proposals', *Historical Studies*, vol. 14, no. 56 (1971), pp. 579-90.

Nelson, H. N., 'The Missionaries and the Aborigines in the Port Phillip District', *Historical Studies, Australia and New Zealand*, vol. 12, no. 45 (1965), pp. 57-67.

Newton, A. P., *A Hundred Years of the British Empire*. London, 1940.

Niebuhr, R., *The Structure of Nations and Empires*. New York, 1959.

Norman, J., *Edward Gibbon Wakefield: A Political Reappraisal*. Fairfield, 1963.

Onslow, S. M. (ed.), *Some Early Records of the Macarthurs of Camden*. Sydney, 1973.

Pascoe, C. F., *Two Hundred Years of the S.P.G.: An Historical Account of the Society for the Propagation of the Gospel in Foreign Parts 1701-1900*. 2 vols. London, 1901.

Peckham, M., *Victorian Revolutionaries: Speculations on Some Heroes of a Culture Crisis*. New York, 1970.

Pelling, H., *A History of British Trade Unionism*. London, 1963.

Philipp J., 'Wakefieldian Influence and New South Wales 1830-1832', *Historical Studies, Australia and New Zealand*, vol. 9, no. 34 (1960), pp. 173-8.

——, *A Great View of Things: Edward Gibbon Wakefield.* Melbourne, 1971.

Pike, D., *Paradise of Dissent: South Australia 1829-1857.* Adelaide, 1957.

——, *Australia: The Quiet Continent.* Cambridge, 1966.

Pollard, S. and Salt, J. (eds.), *Robert Owen Prophet of the Poor: Essays in Honour of the Two-Hundredth Anniversary of his Birth.* London, 1971.

Price, A. G., *The Foundation and Settlement of South Australia 1829-1845: A Study of the Colonization Movement.* Adelaide, 1924.

Price, C. A., *The Great White Walls are Built: Restrictive Immigration to North America and Australasia 1836-1888.* Canberra, 1974.

Quaife, G. R., 'The Diggers: Democratic Sentiment and Political Apathy', *Australian Journal of Politics and History,* vol. 13, no. 2 (1967), pp. 221-30.

Raskin, J., *The Mythology of Imperialism.* Kingsport, 1971.

Read, D., *Press and People 1790-1850.* London, 1961.

Reece, R. H. W., *Aborigines and Colonists: Aborigines and Colonial Society in New South Wales in the 1830s and 1840s.* Sydney, 1974.

Reid, W. S., *Economic History of Great Britain.* New York, 1954.

Reynolds, H. (ed.), *Aborigines and Settlers: The Australian Experience 1788-1939.* North Melbourne, 1972.

Roberts, S. H., *History of Australian Land Settlement 1788-1920.* Melbourne, 1924.

——, *The Squatting Age in Australia 1835-1847.* Melbourne, 1935 and 1966.

Robson, L. L., *The Convict Settlers of Australia: An Enquiry into the Origin and Character of the Convicts transported to New South Wales and Van Diemen's Land 1787-1852.* Melbourne, 1965.

Robson, R. (ed.), *Ideas and Institutions of Victorian Britain: Essays in Honour of George Kitson Clark.* London, 1967.

Roe, M., *Quest for Authority in Eastern Australia 1835-1851.* Melbourne, 1965.

Rosenblatt, F. F., *The Chartist Movement in its Social and Economic Aspects.* London, 1967.

Rostow, W. W., *British Economy of the Nineteenth Century.* Oxford, 1948.

——, *The Stages of Economic Growth.* Cambridge, 1960.

Rowley, C. D., *The Destruction of Aboriginal Society.* Melbourne, 1972.

Sampson, G., *The Concise Cambridge History of English Literature.* Cambridge, 1970.

Sandison, A. G., 'The Imperial Idea and English Fiction', *The Theory of Imperialism and the European Partition of Africa: Proceedings of* a Seminar held in the Centre of African Studies, University of Edinburgh, 3 and 4 November 1967. Edinburgh, 1967.

Sayers, R. S., 'The Question of the Standard in the Eighteen-Fifties', *Economic History (A Supplement to the Economic Journal)*, vol. 11, no. 8 (1933), p. 585.

Schuyler, R. L., *The Fall of the Old Colonial System: A Study in British Free Trade 1770-1870*. New York, 1945 and Hamden, 1966.

Semmel, B., 'The Philosophic Radicals and Colonialism', *Journal of Economic History*, vol. 21 (1961), pp. 513-24.

Serle, G., *The Golden Age: A History of the Colony of Victoria 1851-1861*. Melbourne, 1963.

Shaw, A. G. L., *The Story of Australia*. London, 1955.

——, 'A Revision of the Meaning of Imperialism', *Australian Journal of Politics and History*, vol. 7, no. 1 (1961), pp. 198-213.

——, *Convicts and the Colonies: A Study of Penal Transportation from Great Britain and Ireland to Australia and other Parts of the British Empire*. London, 1966.

——, 'British Attitudes to the Colonies, c. 1820-1850', *Journal of British Studies*, vol. 9, no. 1 (1969), pp. 71-95.

——, (ed.), *Great Britain and the Colonies 1815-1865*. London, 1970.

Sinclair, K., *A History of New Zealand*. London, 1960.

Smith, B., *European Vision and the South Pacific 1768-1850: A Study in the History of Art and Idears*. Oxford, 1960.

Spillett, P. G., *Forsaken Settlement: An Illustrated History of the Settlement of Victoria, Port Essington North Australia 1838-1849*. Melbourne, 1972.

Stock, E., *The History of the Church Missionary Society, its Environment, its Ien and its Work*. 4 vols. London, 1899 and 1916.

Sturgis, J. L., *John Bright and the Empire*. London, 1969.

Sweetman, E., *Australian Constitutional Development*. Melbourne, 1925.

Taylor, N. M. (ed.), *The Journal of Ensign Best 1837-1843*. Wellington, 1966.

Taylor, P. A.M. (ed.), *The Industrial Revolution in Britain: Triumph or Disaster?* Boston, 1966.

Thomson, J. O., *History of Ancient Geography*. Cambridge, 1948.

Thomson, P., *The Victorian Heroine: A Changing Ideal 1837-1873*. London, 1956.

Thompson, F. M. L., *English Landed Society in the Nineteenth Century*. London, 1963.

Thornton, A. P., The Imperial Idea and its Enemies: A Study in British Power. London, 1959.

——, *Doctrines of Imperialism*. New York, 1965.

Thornton, R. H., *British Shipping.* 2nd revised edition. Cambridge, 1959.

Townsley, W. A., *The Struggle for Self-Government in Tasmania 1842-1856.* Hobart, 1951.

Travers, R., *The Tasmanians: The Story of a Doomed Race.* Melbourne, 1968.

Trevelyan, G. M., *English Social History: A Survey of Six Centuries.* London, 1942.

Tyrrell, A., 'Class Consciousness in Early Victorian Britain: Samuel Smiles, Leeds Politics, and the Self-Help Creed', *Journal of British Studies,* vol. 9, no. 2 (1970), pp. 102-25.

Wagner, G., 'The Novel of Empire', *Essays in Criticism,* vol. 20 (1970), pp. 229-42.

Waldersee, J., *Catholic Society in New South Wales 1788-1860.* Sydney, 1974.

Wannan, B., *Early Colonial Scandals: The Turbulent Times of Samuel Marsden.* Melbourne, 1972.

Warburg, J. (ed.), *The Industrial Muse: The Industrial Revolution in English Poetry.* Oxford, 1958.

Ward, J. M., 'The Third Earl Grey and Federalism', *Australian Journal of Politics and History,* vol. 3, no. 1 (1957), pp. 18-32.

——, *Earl Grey and the Australian Colonies 1846-1857: A Study of Self-Government and Self-Interest.* Melbourne, 1958.

——, 'A Note: Colonial Policies of the Third Earl Grey', *Australian Journal of Politics and History,* vol. 5, no. 1 (1959), pp. 269-72.

——, *Empire in the Antipodes: The British in Australasia: 1840-1860.* London, 1966.

Ward, R., *The Australian Legend.* Melbourne, 1958.

Webb, R. K., *The British Working Class Reader 1790-1848.* London, 1955.

Webb, S. and B., *The History of Trade Unionism 1666-1920.* London, 1919.

Wesson, R. G., *The Imperial Order.* Berkeley, 1967.

Whitfeld, L. A., *Founders of the Law in Australia.* Canberra, 1971.

Willard, M., *History of the White Australia Policy to 1920.* London, 1967.

Williams, E., *Capitalism and Slavery.* London, 1964.

Wilson, D. A., *Carlyle at his Zenith 1848-53.* London, 1927.

Winch, D. N., 'Classical Economics and the Case for Colonization', *Economica,* vol. 30 (1963), pp. 387-99.

——, *Classical Political Economy and Colonies.* London, 1965.

Young, J. D., 'South Australian Historians and Wakefields "Scheme" ', *Historical Studies,* vol. 14, no. 53 (1969), pp. 32-53.

Index